JACKSON YEARS

OTHER BOOKS BY THE AUTHOR

The March of the Teutons
America and the War of 1812
Opening of the Civil War
America and the Monroe Years

Jackson Years

Eugene Wait

Nova Science Publishers, Inc.
Huntington, New York

Editorial Production:	Susan Boriotti
Office Manager:	Annette Hellinger
Graphics:	Frank Grucci and Jennifer Lucas
Information Editor:	Tatiana Shohov
Book Production:	Donna Dennis, Patrick Davin, Cathy DeGregory, and Lynette Van Helden
Circulation:	Latoya Clay, Anna Cruz, and Lisa DiGangi

Library of Congress Cataloging-in-Publication Data
Jackson Years / Eugene Wait
            p.   cm.
    Includes bibliographical references.
    ISBN 1-56072-831-0
1. Jackson, Andrew, 1767-1845. 2. United States--Politics and government--1829-1837. 3. United States--History--1815-1861. I. Title.
    E381.W27   2000
    973.5'6--dc21   00-042384

Copyright 2000 by Nova Science Publishers, Inc.
    227 Main Street, Suite 100
    Huntington, New York 11743
    Tele. 631-424-6682   Fax 631-424-4666
    e-mail: Novascience@earthlink.net
    e-mail: Novascil@aol.com
    Web Site: http://www.nexusworld.com/nova

DEDICATION

TO MY PARENTS

Eugene Wait
Virginia Rice Wait

CONTENTS

PREFACE

This volume is the fourth in my Age of Lincoln series, covering the years from 1809 to 1865. This book contains the stories of 1829, 1830, and 1831 of which there are 18 or so altogether, and I am working on number 14. I try to include all that is important and also that which is less important but still interesting. I have written on other historical topics ranging from the caveman to Truman and before this book I have four books published out of 40 or so. Before this book there was *March of the Teutons* in 1972 and *America and the War of 1812* and *Opening of the Civil War*. The titles of the others that will probably be out by the time this is published are *America and the Monroe Years* and two volumes of "Zenith of Imperialism, 1896-1906," and "Adams vs. Jackson."

For most of the past 38 years, I have been extensively researching the topics in these books and I have a number of people to thank. First come my parents to whom this book and all of my other books are dedicated because they made it all possible and their support was essential.

I also appreciate the people who took part in these narrative events with empathy, if not always approval. My negative and positive views of Jackson are presented as a case proven by the events. The authors whose works I used also deserve to be thanked. Every historian owes a debt of gratitude to his sources and the long hours they put in on their work, including Niles the editor, whose contributions are clear in this volume.

Every historian owes a debt of thanks to the librarians who helped him. The librarians of Kerrville's Butt-Holdsworth Memorial Library are appreciated. The chief librarians were Evelyn Jaegli, Victoria Mosty Wilson, and Antonio Martinez. Of great importance for the actual work was Willeen Gray whose staffing of the inter-library loan department over several decades made the research possible. Being a poor scholar, I was unable to travel in order to conduct research and the inter-library loan system made the impossible possible. Her supervisor and reference librarian Mary Myers, has helped since 1982, and played a major role in the later period.

I wish to thank the inter-library loan staff including Carla Ashton, Diane Latham, Jan Anderson, and former staff member, Dorothy Glenn Schneider. Those who did double duty in library loan and circulation, Christina Weinzierl and John Patton, are also thanked, as is Debbie Draffkorn. Those who helped in reference were Herb Peterson, Pam Roberts, and Sherry Hiller. Martinez served some hours each week as a reference librarian. Some years ago, Mildred Daniels and Virginia Klingleman did helpful work on my behalf in the library and made life cheerful. There are many others who did yeoman service of great use to my books.

Of family members I thank my brother H. Joe Wait who gave me a printer and my cousin Marie Wait Featherston and her husband Harry Featherston for a grant used in paying inter-library loan return postage for books used.

I also wish to thank the employers who gave and took jobs from me over the decades. Long periods of unemployment (put to good use in writing, caring for parents, and civil contributions) made their contributions especially appreciated. The important poet Sarah Patton will always be remembered for her encouragement and praise for my second book *America and the War of 1812*, which she read with such great joy. She is one of the best poets of her decade and has another book of poems prepared. I also laud editor-publisher Frank Columbus.

I wish to thank some of my teachers, including Mrs. Swayze, Mrs. Jessie Wilson, and notably Zelma Hardy, the wife of George, who insisted that I do not pad my works, so that readers do not have to go through a mass of dross to locate the abundant gold and silver if our history. Thank you for reading the works of,

Eugene Meredith Wait
Kerrville, Texas
June 3, 2000

ABOUT THE AUTHOR

Wait was born in Longview on July 13, 1936, and lived all over Texas before seeing Kerrville for the first time in 1945. In that year, he started earning money by selling magazine subscriptions door to door as well as greeting cards by the box. This started in Port Isabel. A graduate of Tivy High School, Schreiner College, and the University of Texas, he served in the military. He obtained most of a doctorate in history before an illness interrupted that. Most of his time since then has been put to good use researching and writing. This makes his fifth published work with 35 more to go, that have already been written.

Chapter 1

ANDREW JACKSON

The correspondent of Noah's New York *Enquirer* wrote from Washington about the social life of Washington DC. Fashion's tide was "rolling onward with splendor. Music, cards, dancing, visiting and hearing sermons occupy the whole time of the gay world." Secretary Barbour's Saturday nights had been "ravishing. Only transport yourself to his hospitable mansion and gaze around upon the brilliance and beauty that attracts you. Or, if you please, imagine Secretary Clay's Wednesday nights which are more ravishing still." Many styles of women's dresses were present.

He continued to say that such gaiety was "mixed with listlessness and the brightest beauty with the greatest pieces of homeliness. Here is one counting the lustres, there is one comparing the candles; and a little way off, a group criticizing the dancers. In another, a member of Congress saunters about picking out all the long noses he can find and comparing their sizes and complexions with the precision of a Tycho Brake. Here is a dandy from Baltimore trying to match eyes and measure heights and distances; and there is a girl from the West endeavoring to appear with most rueful ease, in a *Cantelo* tightened to suffocation. Some run after waiters and others run from them; the politicians chat, the office-seekers cringe, the foreign diplomats look fierce, and the ladies look sad, gay and exhausted by turns." This was the social scene that Jackson was inheriting. [1]

Mrs. Samuel Smith included the latest news of Washington in her January letter to Mrs. Kirkpatrick. She wrote that that night "General Eaton, the bosom friend and almost adopted son of General Jackson, is to be married to a lady whose reputation, because of her previous connection with him both before and after her husband's death, has been totally destroyed. She is the daughter of O'Neal who kept a large tavern and boarding house whom Littleton knew. She has never been admitted into good society, is very handsome and of not an inspiring character and violent temper. She is, it is said, irresistible and carries whatever point she sets her mind on. The General's personal and political friends are very much disturbed about it; his enemies laugh and divert themselves with the idea of what a suitable lady in waiting Mrs. Eaton will make to Mrs.

Jackson and repeat the old adage, 'birds of a feather will flock together.' Dr. Simm and Colonel Bomford's families are asked. The ladies declare they will not go to the wedding, and if they can help it will not let their husbands go."

The night of the wedding, it snowed heavily. Mrs. Smith wrote the next morning, which was a Friday: "A right down snow storm! The first one we have had this season--it was very complaisant to wait until the gaieties of the holidays were over. Last night the incessant rolling of carriages sounded like continual peals of thunder or roaring of the wind, and every carriage having lights, the appearance was very singular. The night was dark and the lights darting and flying about in every direction (for nothing but lamps were visible) appeared like brilliant meteors in the air. Mr. Smith called me to the door to look at them. The pavement, indeed street, in front of the English Minister's house was light as noonday, a line of torches being placed along the pavement. The street was full of carriages, about 400 it is said, all with lights and motion. His ball was given, it is said, to the President's family and was more brilliant than any former. We kept our resolution and would not go or go to the ball in Georgetown to which we were asked. Senator Eaton's wedding likewise took place last night, so that the streets were as light and as full as in the morning." [2]

So, on the first day of 1829, the love-struck J.H. Eaton married his Peggy with the approval of the president. This action caused trouble in Washington. His Peggy was Margaret O'Neal, the pretty and intellectual daughter of the innkeeper of O'Neal's. The accounts of her beauty and brains were commendatory, but her reputation was dependent upon her job as barmaid and her love for Eaton fully as much as the former. She had been married to a purser of the navy until his death. While the purser was still alive, she and Eaton were in love with each other. Soon Eaton was appointed secretary of war despite Senator John Branch's comment to the president that because of the social complication, Eaton's appointment would be "unpopular and unfortunate." Jackson had more important things on his mind instead of rumors and feminine wiles.

The women of cabinet ministers snubbed Peggy and would not invite her to their parties. Their sense of propriety caused them to uphold the social life even if it endangered their husband's and father's careers. Secretary of State Martin Van Buren was a widower and often served as an escort for Mrs. Eaton. The abuse caused Jackson to turn against all cabinet officials except Van Buren. This opened the way for Van Buren who benefited enormously. It has been noted that this action propelled Van Buren into the presidency when Jackson had finished his career. [3]

On January 17, 1829, the day before Jackson left the Hermitage out of Nashville for Washington and his inauguration, Daniel Webster wrote that no one knew what to expect of the new president but he thought Jackson "will bring a breeze with him." Webster was not as troubled as some such as the outgoing president Adams. Webster had observed Jackson in the Senate in 1823-1825 and found him grave, mild, and reserved. This is the impression Jackson had wanted to leave, to counteract what had earlier been written about him.

In 1824, Jackson's concern over how others viewed him was seen in what he wrote to John Coffee: "Great pains had been taken to represent me as a savage disposition; who always carried a scalping knife in one hand, and a tomahawk in the other, always ready to knock down, and scalp any and every person who differed with me in opinion." Both John Q. Adams and Henry Clay thought Jackson ignorant, and indeed the general did not have some of the advantages of an Adams or even a Clay. For that, they thought him common. Well so did the people and this is why they elected him the previous year. Jackson was not common - he was a self-made aristocrat. He was still fiery, but had calmed down as he had matured. The image he wanted known was different from who he really was, but was not far from his real self. He was hot headed, it is true, but Jackson was in control of himself. He was no more bloodthirsty than the average man of war. As a warrior leader, he used his anger to control his men better. If they feared him more than the enemy, they fought better under fire, as is what happened in at least one occasion. [4]

While Andrew Jackson was diplomatically turning down several invitations to visit various American cities, attending his wife's funeral, and preparing to go to Washington, Americans were reading of the events around the world. In the war between Turkey and Russia, it was reported that the Russians were retreating from before Silistria back to Jersey in the dead of winter. Their cattle perished and the Russians left their artillery behind them. On their way back, they were attacked by Turks. The Russians were prepared to retire for the winter, but the Turks would not let them. Under an able military leader, the Turks seemed determined to drive the Russians from their lands and were not interested in peace.

The British were blockading Tangiers to secure indemnity of one thousand dollars for having illegally detained two merchant vessels. In Ireland, the Irish under Daniel O'Connell, a Catholic Irish lawyer recently elected to Parliament, were pressing for an emancipation and allowing Roman Catholics to sit in Parliament. There was a great deal of excitement in Ireland over the matter. It was reported in Niles' paper that a "grandee and peer of Spain has latterly been breaking stones on a high road in the neighborhood of London, at the rate of 1 shilling a day, to support his wife and three children."

Good news came from Greece. The Turks had been driven out of Morea by the French and as soon as the Greeks had a force powerful enough to hold that large territory, the French would probably withdraw. Greeks were returning to the towns of Morea. The poor were down from the mountain hideouts and the rich were coming back from the islands. [5]

In the winter of 1828-1829, John Ross, chief of the Cherokees, led a delegation to Washington where they were pressed by Major John Eaton to emigrate to the west. Eaton was a close friend of Andrew Jackson and was to be secretary of war, as we have seen. Still, in spite of federal pressure, the Cherokees hoped the Jackson administration would change directions, and because of Jacksonian interest in emigration, Major Ridge made his rounds to preach throughout the Cherokee nation against removal. The Indian wished to strengthen Cherokee spirit and resistance against removal.

On February 9, 1829, The Ridge, as he was called, made one of many eloquent speeches at a meeting in Turkey Town. Ten local citizens there signed a sense of the company drawn up by his educated son John Ridge. They believed that the pressure of expulsion was because the Cherokee "have unexpectedly become civilized, and because we have formed and organized a constituted government. It is too much for us to be honest, virtuous, and industrious rather than aspiring to the rank of Christians and politicians, because it renders our attachment to the soil more strong, and therefore more difficult to defraud us of the possession. Disappointment inflicts on the mind of the avaricious white men, with the mortification of delay or the probability of the intended victim's escape from the snares laid for its destruction. It remains for us, in this situation, to act as free agents in choosing for ourselves to walk in the straight-forward path" of previous presidents and have individuals set their faces to the rising sun and to turn their backs to the sun's setting. They did not wish to budge from the desirable country and did not want to live in the wilderness of the trans-Mississippi west.

Despite the campaigning of The Ridge, the Cherokees were divided. In countering this a law was passed decreeing the death penalty for selling lands in a treaty, without the nation's authority. More trouble loomed on the horizon. Gold was discovered on Cherokee land and prospectors poured in. The legislators of Georgia pressed all the more for Indian lands because of their increased value. [6]

On March 3, 1829, the Cherokees petitioned Congress about the state of Georgia, which annexed Indian lands to the state domain and annulled all Indian lands on that land. The Indians had no protection in a court of law. "No Indian, or descendent of an Indian, could be a competent witness, or a party to any suit to which a white man was a party." This denied them protection of the law as long as they remained in Georgia or had an action of law pending in Georgia. The national congress should take an interest in the matter. "This act involves a question of great magnitude and of serious importance, and which calls for the deliberation and decision of congress. It is a question upon which the salvation and happiness or the misery and destruction of a *nation* depends, therefore it sould not be trifled with." In a state proud of its liberty and rights of man, this was an invasion "of the most sacred rights and privileges of a weak, defenseless, and innocent nation of people, who are in perfect peace with the United States, and to whom the faith of the United States is solemnly pledged to protect and defend them against the encroachments of their citizens."

The petitioners protested that "the right of regulating our own internal affairs, is a right which we have inherited from the author of our existence, which we have always exercised and never surrendered." It is a matter for the national government and the state to decide upon since the Cherokees had no voice in the Constitution. For, "on no principle of justice can an innocent people, who were in no way a party to that compact, be held responsible for its fulfillment; consequently they should not be oppressed, in directly violating the solemn obligation pledged by treaties for their protection."

They were feeling somewhat pessimistic. If the vision could not be achieved for an Indian civilization in the southeast with its abundant resources, than it could not be gained in the lands beyond the Mississippi, or any other location in the United States. If the same zeal that is being used to effect the removal of the Civilized Tribes could be used in solving this problem between Washington and Georgia for the country's honor, it would achieve "the peace, happiness, and preservation of a people. Georgia had no control over Cherokee country, nor would the Cherokee submit. [7]

On the twelfth of February in 1829 in Boston, state legislators met in the New Court House to strengthen the Republican Party in Massachusetts in the interests of Governor Levi Lincoln. This was to be the foundation of the National Republican party. Robert Rantoul was chairman. They decided upon a state-wide political organization on "liberal and national principles, which should not go to the exclusion of plain straight-forward republicans of any denomination." The founders formed a central committee of nine men. Centralized organization was important to them, but a legislative caucus was to decide candidates. This party became the Whig party. [8]

Alcott, then a schoolteacher whose reputation was beginning to grow at age 29, was greatly impressed by Dr. Channing. This divine was pre-eminent "both in originality of thought and felicity of expression." The educator confided in his journal that the Channing mind was remarkable, which "leaves the region of material vision and seeks affinity with the objects and essences of spiritual forms." Looking far into the future and into reality, the Channing mind cast "a penetrating and extensive look over the whole range of the moral kingdom, and defines the Christian principles long enclosed in darkness, revealing "to the plainest understanding its beauty, its accordance with the wants of our nature, its power in elevating that nature to the heights of virtue and happiness, and its influence upon the mind in the investigation of truth as the great end of its action." [9]

[1]Carlson, Oliver, *The Man Who Made News: James Gordon Bennett*, New York: Duell, Sloan and Pearce, 1942, pp. 84-88.

[2]Smith, Margaret Bayard, *The First Forty Years of Washington Society*, Hunt, Gaillard ed., New York: Charles Sribner's Sons, 1906, pp. 252-255. Quotes on pp. 252-255.

[3]Bowers, Claude, *Party* Struggles, 1922, pp. 117-119. Quote on p. 119.

[4]White, Leonard D., *The Jacksonians: A Study in Administrative History, 1829-1861*, New York: Macmillan, 1954, pp. 1-2; Wait, Eugene M., *America and the War of 1812*, Commack, NY: Kroshka Books, 1999, p. 204.

[5]*Niles Weekly Register*, January 31, 1829, p. 364; *Encyclopedia Britannica*, 1911, VII, 476.

[6]Wilkins, T., 1986, pp. 206-209. Quote on p. 207.

[7]*Niles Weekly Register*, August 7, 1830, pp. 423-424. Quotes on pp. 423, 424.

[8]McCormack, *American Party System*, 1966, pp. 43-44.

[9]Alcott, *Journals*, pp. 18-19. Quotes on pp. 18, 19.

Chapter 2

CHOOSING THE CABINET

On February 14, 1829, Jackson met with Amos Kendall privately and assured him that Kendall could count upon a principal clerkship of $2,000 per year or an auditorship with a salary of $3,000, a fine sum for the time with a very good standard of living. He said that he would not hesitate to make him an auditor except that he did not yet know which offices might be abolished. After expressing his regard for Kendall and his disposition to serve him, Jackson terminated the meeting. At another meeting with Kendall, they had a long conversation and Jackson flattered Kendall, speaking well of his capacity and character. Jackson said one of his friends had told him that Amos was capable of a departmental office. He would place him as near to that position as he could. One month later Kendall was awarded with a commission as fourth auditor.

Kendall excelled as a western newspaper editor and publisher and proved himself able and influential in the conduct of his business and in politics. He and Jackson laid the grounds for a wide agreement in politics and economics, being Jeffersonian Republicans and forming and forging a renewed party, to be commonly known as the Democratic party. With a farmer for a father, Amos was born in rural New England on a Sunday, August 16, 1789, sometime after George Washington began his duties as president. Growing up as a farm boy, Amos received what education he could during limited hours of education. His father believed in education and helped him along the way in encouragement, opportunities, and money. Kendall taught and gained his way by his own efforts also. Going to Dartmouth College, he did well in college and was prepared for a good life, but was without any decision about what he wanted to be.

Deciding to study law, Kendall thought it a good expedient to teach in order to finance his study. Lawyer William Merchant Richard advised him to learn law immediately since to teach, as a temporary expedient, would be a loss of time, and promised to let Amos study law in his law office. Soon afterwards, the United States entered the war against England. Kendall supported President James Madison during the war, although he did not take part in the war. He did gain an antipathy towards Federalist ministers who opposed the war and Madison. The wartime depression prompted Kendall to go either west or south. His parents and all of their children dined together for the last time and Amos started on his journey to Washington DC where he secured a job promise in Lexington, Kentucky as a tutor. He went there but the job did not pan out. He turned out to tutor Henry Clay's children. Later, he went on to study law and began to practice law in the town. Then perchance, he came to publish and edit newspapers at Lexington and at near-by Georgetown. He was also postmaster at Georgetown.

In September 1816, Kendall went to Frankfort, Kentucky, on business. He dealt with William Gerard, one of the editors of *Argus of Western America*, a state newspaper. Recognizing a good possibility when he saw it, Gerard proposed that Amos buy out Gerard's partner and become an editor of this western journal, and told Kendall that he would arrange the financing of the said newspaper. Because Kendall did not enjoy the practice of law and his friends advised him to undertake the job, Kendall agreed. He got a good start and was soon involved in the major and minor controversies of Frankfort, the state capital.

At this time, a grave national matter reached the ears of the public. Because of the financial problems of the nation and banks, the charter of the Bank of the United States, a semi-governmental institution, was re-establish, and met the hostility of those such as Amos Kendall. Meanwhile, the Bank of Kentucky tried to deal honestly with the problems at hand and resumed the payment of gold and silver upon demand in the spring of 1817. In 1818, Kendall began his opposition to the Bank of the United States, concerned as he was with its unconstitutionality.

In a series in the *Argus*, Kendall stressed his views about the Bank, attacking it most wholeheartedly. His views differed with those of the Supreme Court which had supported the institution's constitutionality with the fact that the Bank had originally been founded in the government and had been recognized by the legislatures and judge of that court. Kendall denied this argument's viability since he felt that public opinion was paramount. Denying the Supreme Court's view that the Constitution derived its authority from the people, he wrote that the constitution was adopted by each state or people of each state and not from the people as a whole. This states' rights stand was an important point in the Democratic party's platform and was used regularly by those Democrats in other issues.

Once he was personally assured by Jackson of getting a high job, Kendall began to look around for a house for his family. He preferred nearby Georgetown because rent was low there, living more reasonable, and the people more agreeable. The town was close enough so as to be walk to work and good exercise was important. In a letter to Jane, his wife, Kendall wrote about a later long conversation he had with Jackson. After a talk Jackson flattered Kendall to his face. Kendall was capable and had good character, etc. The general said, "I told one of my friends that you were fit for the head of a department, and I shall put you as near the head as possible." This braced him up to withstand the great cold of almost two weeks.

He also wrote that the Potomac was frozen and wood was scarce in the city. Available wood was selling for the high price of from eight to twelve dollars per cord. Poor people were hard pressed. Congress gave some firewood out of their stock. Adam's Treasury Department gave an equal amount. Kendall was soon able to write that he had received his commission as fourth auditor of the Treasury Department and to describe the family with whom he boarded; a preacher named O.B, Brown, a clerk in the General Post Office and a Baptist and his charity minded wife.

Kendall described his duties in his first two weeks in the capital as light labor taking up from one to six hours per week. When he came to learn the laws under which he acted, it would require only a looking at accounts and a signature. His first tasks were to find out "some of the villainous transactions of my predecessor" and others. He hoped to recover large sums illegally paid by those who had been in the Treasury before the Jackson administration. Within weeks, Jackson sent out instructions for the arrest of Kendall's predecessor for frauds. Adding to his previous letter, Kendall was working more hours at Treasury work and at his writing for the press. It required eight hours of more a day. He spent most of the free time walking.

In June of 1829, the grand jury was still hearing evidence against Adams' fourth auditor Watkins and Kendall thought he found a good house to rent, so that his wife and many children might come to Washington DC. He wrote her that he could not get boarding for his "army" at much less than $1,200 so he was determined to rent a house in Georgetown for $175 unfurnished and might rent furniture to fill the house adequately. He told his wife she could set her thoughts towards this idea to be away from the parties of the capital, and for comfort and economy. Not only was the society in Georgetown plainer but it was more agreeable. He told her about the neighborhood and said that perhaps her father knew about the area. The ladies he knew from the city were all against it while those of Georgetown favored the action. She would soon see that his acquaintanceship with the ladies was extensive.

Then he turned more to business. He had found his office to be riddled with corruption under Watkins, with deplorable affairs. There had been negligence and fraud in the accounting office. Watkins had used public money for his own self and his favorites. The money came from extravagant claims. Public money was lent out and never repaid. The previous auditor had benefited. Fraud was even worst where money was paid out for false claims. Watkins appropriated for himself $80,000 more at the end of his term, but this was stopped. Kendall found a difference of $120,000 that had gone into private pockets, which was a very large sum for the day and time.

Kendall thought that the government was not truly representative or democratic. For him, there was no popular government in effect. He was a Jeffersonian, believing that the constitution was made up of enumerated powers and that the Bank was not one of them, despite the inconsistency of the court in its contention that this bank was constitutional. There was no power rendering this bank constitutional. There was no power to establish a bank or cooperation. Further the Constitutional plan which established the powers of the federal government was definite and concrete. The implied powers did not allow for imaginative government. This was the strict Jeffersonian idea that would have made the Louisiana Purchase illegal under the Constitution.

Jefferson had wisely realized the value of the purchase and ignored his principles, but the Jacksonians were more hide-bound and unbending than the third president. Government could not be expanded to include public benefits outside the exact powers. Besides the Jacksonians did not consider the Bank to be a benefit. Kendall had used his newspaper to promote these ideas which Jackson loved so well. No wonder Jackson flattered the fourth auditor and was to include him in his Kitchen Cabinet which was his group of informal advisers. These advisers had more clout than the carefully selected regular and official cabinet. Jacksonian opponents were to use this arrangement against the new president in propaganda.

Kendall considered himself right but allowed for others to have different opinions. In his view the judiciary had exceeded its bounds. Government was too big and expensive. These views, expressive of 1829, were expressed in 1821. Kendall had not changed and Jackson knew that Kendall was a true follower of his. No wonder he flattered Kendall; he was praising himself too. Both had the same ideas, which started with Jefferson and were developed by the Southerners and various Northerners and Westerners. [1]

Jackson chose men for his cabinet whom he could control. First, he selected Senator John H. Eaton to serve as his secretary of war. Van Buren was chosen as secretary of state for his work at switching Crawford supporters to his election. Samuel Ingham was paid off for his election support also. He fitted into the Jacksonian mode as a moderate on the tariff question. Jackson was looking forward to the compromises that were a part of American government, and the tariff issue was one, subject to moderation.

With the above three posts filled with northern and western men, the incoming president looked to the South for the attorney general and the secretary of the navy. The wealthy slaveholder who had ingratiated himself with candidate Jackson in the campaign, John Branch of North Carolina, was nominated to be secretary of the navy. Another slaveholder was John McPherson Berrien, a man high in legal abilities, very suitable for the office offered him by the new president. Like Branch, Berrien was a state rights man. To Jackson's delight, Branch was very critical of the banks and internal improvements. To finish the cabinet, Jackson chose John McLean of Ohio, but he refused to make certain appointments and removals. McLean was replaced by the Kentucky lawyer and professor, William T. Barry for the position of postmaster general of the United States.[2]

In mourning, Jackson reached the capital where he entered without being seen. He forbade any parade or great celebration because of the recent death of his wife and the thousands who had come to Washington to celebrate had only regular entertainment and pastimes to enliven their stays. The outgoing administration had stopped going to parties and members were still suffering from the recent illnesses that had inflicted the capital. Jackson and his family did not attend any parties. Taking after the incoming president's feelings what parties there were were somber and quiet. Social life was at a long time low in the city of joy and festivities. [3]

[1]Kendall, Amos, *Autobiography of Amos Kendall*, ed. Stickney, William, 1872, Rep. New York: Peter Smith, 1949, pp. 1-5, 11-16, 18-20, 26, 30-76, 86, 91-169, 179-201, 206-208, 245-257, 283, 291-293, 300.

[2]Latner, Richard B., "The Eaton Affair Reconsidered," *Tennessee Historical Quarterly*, (Fall 1977), 334-337; *Niles Weekly Register*, February 28, 1829, p. 1.

[3]Smith, *Forty Years*, p. 281.

Chapter 3

JACKSON'S INAUGURAL

In 1927, John McLean, an ambitious executive, with a record of effective operation of the post office, wanted the standing of his federal office to be higher and so he managed to get his salary raised to six thousand dollars, the same salary cabinet officers received. Because the duties of his office were equal to that of the secretaries, the compensation should be the same. Congress made the change at the urgings of McLean. According to Clay, McLean used his office to help Jackson obtain the presidency in 1828. Adams expected this to be so and Jackson believed that such was true. His influence and patronage was used, according to information reaching the president-elect, against the Adams' administration, and Andrew wanted to reward McLean with the position he already held under previous administrations. John privately denied this to Governor Trimble, without harm to his standing. He had not done anything to injure anyone. He claimed to be neutral, meaning he did not help either his boss Adams or the opponent Jackson.

McLean wanted the position of secretary of the treasury, but there were many applicants for the jobs of the cabinet and Samuel D. Ingham was selected. McLean was to be picked for the war department. Complications arose because Jackson wanted his old friend Major John Eaton at his side and decided upon the secretaryship of war for the major. James A. Hamilton proposed to Judge White, a friend of both Jackson and McLean, that he explain the situation and asked John if he would stay as postmaster general if it were elevated to cabinet rank. When John agreed, the list of appointments was published in the official paper. When he received the suggestion that he should use the office for the removal of presidential enemies, McLean said that he would have to be impartial, firing Andrew's friends along with those of his opponent. So, after thought, Jackson asked McLean if he would accept a seat in the Supreme Court. The Kentuckian to whom Jackson promised the office had to settle for an ambassadorship to Columbia to replace William Henry Harrison, a short time in Columbia. This Harrison, later president, went over to the opposition. [1]

The incoming president, Jackson, had promised William T. Barry a judgeship in the Supreme Court. Jackson tried hard to get this cleared with Democrats in Kentucky. Some party members in that state were not easily persuaded. However, the position was switched when the general needed to give the position to John McLean, because he would not be a spoils man. Jackson had asked Berry to join the cabinet in his administration and the president had to arrange the placation of Thomas P. Moore, who hoped to gain the post, when the announcement was made. Jackson had placed Barry into the required position, and Barry was the first cabinet level postmaster general in the history of the United States.

A certain vindication was his and a certain reward also, because of the hard work of a campaign in which Barry won Kentucky for Jackson, although he lost the governorship by seven hundred votes. Now he had a higher position in the highest counsels of the government. Barry was a politician and turned the post office department into a reward system for local party workers to a large, but not definitive degree. Reform to Jackson meant overturning the personnel of what he considered a corrupt government and the department had the jobs to be given to the many political workers who wanted postmasterships. It was compared to the Jefferson turn in 1801, but there were many keeping their jobs and Jackson was not the founder of the so-called spoils system in the American government, nor was it absolute. Later presidents were to perfect the spoils work that Jefferson or Jackson helped develop.

Barry was the man for changing personnel because he believed it was "right and polite to encourage and reward friends." He took the democratic view of "rotation in office" believing in a natural change, keeping the bureaucrats fresh and ever-changing." For, he wrote, that "if the great body of public officers are to be retained, why change the head of the nation. Those who prefer the calmness of perpetuity in office, would certainly be better pleased that the executive head be made permanent. This would not suit a republic." Even still, only one in sixteen postmasters were changed and more than that in clerks, not a great turnover. Most of the changes were made in New England, anti-Jackson country, and in New York, home of Martin Van Buren and Isaac Hill, who was the chief mover of postmasterships in the administration with the help of Amos Kendall. The numbers applied to the first three years of Jackson's presidency. [2]

The selection of the secretary of the treasury involved Jackson in a discordant fight. The president-elect had already made his choice. He wanted Ingram in that post, but the man's tariff views infuriated the Carolinians. It was suggested by a mission of Carolinians that Langdon Cheves, a brilliant young man from South Carolina would be better. This was turned down. McLean was turned down and the Carolinians left Gadsby in a rage. [3]

When Martin Van Buren reached Washington to serve as secretary of state, he learned that Jackson had already promised the ministerial posts in England, France, and Columbia. Senator Littleton Tazewell of Virginia was asked to be envoy to England. He had some background in foreign relations. A Norfolk lawyer, Tazewell had a long congressional career and was now chairman of the Foreign Relations Committee. Born into established family on December 17, 1774, his mother died before he was three and his father was busy with public employments. His maternal grandfather, Judge Benjamin Waller, directed his early life until he died when Littleton Waller Tazewell was in his twelfth year. Later, Littleton attributed the best of his character to the judge. For three years, he was under the personal instruction of Chancellor George Wythe. Next, he went to William and Mary College, where he got his bachelor's degree in 1791. Tazewell completed his legal studies in the office of John Wickham in Richard and obtained his license in May of 1796. A handsome and brilliant man, he took a delight in manly sports. [4]

A member of the Virginia state legislature for two years and of Congress for one session, he moved to Norfolk in 1802. There, he married Anne Stratton Nivison, daughter of a leading lawyer. He practiced there in civil, criminal, admiralty, and international law cases and served in the General Assembly occasionally and in 1807 was spokesman for Norfolk when the British *Leopold* attacked the American *Chesapeake*. In politics, he was an independent choosing on a personal basis what he could support. He thought the time had passed for action when the War of 1812 was proclaimed, but he supported the war action when it came. He was elected to the U.S. Senate in 1824 and became one of the leaders of the opposition to John Quincy Adams and drafted the report against the Panama mission. Having supported Jackson, he was offered the position of secretary of war as well as minister to Great Britain, but he declined both. He later served for two years as governor of Virginia. [5]

For France, Jackson wanted his old friend Senator Edward Livingston, who was a distinguished expert on the law and could speak fluent French. He was New York born, and the youngest son of Robert R. Livingston the elder and his wife Margaret Beckman. Born at "Clermont" in May 28, 1764. Edward was sent to school at Albany, and then Kingston where his father died in 1775 at the beginning of the Revolutionary War. He was prepared for the College of New Jersey, later called Princeton, and entered the junior class in 1779. An indifferent scholar, he learned what was necessary for a degree in 1781. Afterwards, he returned to "Clermont" to study French and German and then to Albany to study law in the office of John Lansing. His fellow students were Alexander Hamilton, Aaron Burr, and James Kent in 1782. When the British left New York City in November of 1783, Livingston returned there to complete his law studies. [6]

At age thirty, in 1794, Edward Livingston was elected to Congress. He and his friends were overlooked when it came to patronage and so they went over to the Clintonians and the Jefferson party. His pet measures to revise the penal code were defeated, but in March of 1796, he did secure a measure to provide "for the relief of American seamen who were impressed or abandoned destitute on foreign shores." He was reelected twice, but retired from the House in 1801, having consistently supported Jefferson. Concurrently, he served as U.S. Attorney and mayor of New York City, but fell victim to the yellow fever spending of 1803 and to the malfeasance of an agent. He resigned his offices and undertook to pay the debts caused by his agent. He started all over again in New Orleans, where he practiced law and took many of his fees in land.

In New Orleans, on June 3, 1805, Livingston married Madame Louise Moreau de Lassy, widow of a French officer and daughter of a rich planter of Santo Domingo who fled the island because of the black insurrections. The years passed until Livingston's paths crossed with those of Andrew Jackson for the second time. He had known Andrew when both were in Congress together and Jackson was to come to New Orleans to fight the British. Jackson turned down Edward's request to be his aide-de-camp but asked him for information about the countryside useful for defense. Livingston organized the people of Louisiana to resist the British. Later, he rewrote the penal code of Louisiana, which was not adopted. Livingston served in Congress once more, voted for Jackson in 1824 and 1828, and worked for his election in 1828. His private affairs prevented him from accepting the Jackson offer of the mission to France in 1829, [7]

Jackson wanted Thomas Patrick Moore from Kentucky to be minister to Columbia and the loyal Jacksonian in Congress for six years agreed. He was a youthful well-connected westerner. Born in about 1796 in Charlotte County, Virginia, but living in Kentucky most of his life, Moore enlisted in the 1st Regiment of Kentucky Light Dragoons during the War of 1812. Afterwards Thomas attended Transylvania University and studied law under Judge John Green. First, Moore served in the state house of Kentucky, and next, served in Congress from March of 1823 to March of 1829. While there he was on the committee on manufactures and served Jackson most faithfully. For this loyalty, he was rewarded with the post of minister to Bolivar's Columbia, which he accepted. In Columbia, Moore became a friend of Simon Bolivar and in return received important commercial concessions within the first few weeks of his ministry. [8]

Tazewell turned down his offer of London. Van Buren could live with the Moore appointment because they were friends, but he was uncomfortable with the close call of Tazewell and Livingston, although both were able men. Maybe, it was because they were not Van Buren men also. Later, Van Buren and Jackson talked and the president admitted a great mistake in making the appointments. Should Van Buren have made suggestions of men for diplomatic posts, it was more than probable that he would accept them. All of this was easier said than done and Van Buren made several ill-fated attempts later. It was hard to find suitable men to serve as ministers to foreign countries. [9]

Regency Democrat Churchill C. Cambreleng wrote of the incoming secretary of state, Martin Van Buren, his particular leader, that it was "most fortunate for our party that we start with an opposition--it unites the main body of the old republican army and relieves us at once of a parcel of mere hangers on." They knew their "enemies and our motto should be those who are not for us are against us. We shall now have a party administration governed by party principles." Cambreleng was a former merchant who was then congressmen from New York since 1821. He was to serve as House leader for Jackson and later Van Buren. [10]

Plans were made for having a great celebration of the newly-elected president's entry into the city. Common people were everywhere awaiting Jackson's arrival. Webster wrote to his brother that he had "never seen such a crowd before. People have come five hundred miles to see General Jackson and they really seem to think that the country has been rescued from some dreadful danger." A modern historian has observed that what the people thought was that they had come into their own and would witness the inauguration of their president. Many hoped they would receive part of their reward.

Jackson came into town quietly, four hours earlier than expected, and took up residence at Gadsby's. Soon news of his arrival was everywhere and the celebration began with cannon firing and drums beating. People were cheering in the streets. They converged upon the Gadsby hotel and pressed their ideas, hopes, and dreams upon Jackson. He listened to the most common and obscure in those days before the inaugural, not giving away his own plans. Jackson joked from time to time, but his jokes were somewhat cruel, Isaac Hill was to write. No aspirant to the presidency should be given cabinet level office. Jackson had decided upon that early. He had watched aspirants in Monroe's cabinet and seen the demoralizing effect that had on public policy. [11]

The vice-president-elect had presided over the Senate since eleven and had taken his oath. Next Calhoun gave the oath for the new senators, fourteen in number. The senators adjourned until the next day and were soon to see Jackson enter the portals of the larger chambers promptly occupied by the senators. Margaret Smith was to write that there had been no vacant lodgings so that many people had to go to Georgetown or Alexandria to stay for the night. A national salute had been fired in the morning, but by ten the area around the capitol was crowded by carriages, wagons, and carts. There were men, women, and children of all classes and dress from finery to rags. There was a living stream and the area was filled early with people.

Jackson's day, his inaugural day, was a great celebration for the people and they swarmed into the capital. That morning was balm and mild. It was almost spring weather. Someone estimated the crowd to be 15-20,000 people in front of the capital's south portico. They looked like a sea of humanity, pushing and shoving, and jumping up and down. Shortly, they spotted their hero. They yelled their hurrahs. General Jackson bowed low in reply. The men took off their hats. Old Hickory sat down between Calhoun and Chief Justice John Marshall. As soon as the noise let up, he got up and gave his address. It was short. He would protect states rights, he said, and extinguish the national debt. Only constitutional internal improvements would be acceptable. His tariff would be acceptable and his reforms would be great and correct. Marshall then administered the oath of office.

In order to avoid the mob, Jackson exited through the capitol, walked down the hill and mounted his horse to ride to the White House. Preparations had been made, but no one expected to see the crowd come in to the mansion from the highest and most polished to the most vulgar and gross. Jackson was almost crushed, suffocated, and torn by the eagerness of the mob. He headed out the back or south way. Making the escape once again, he headed for his lodgings at Gadsby's. In the White House, someone got the idea to carry the barrels of punch out to the garden and the people rushed out there. Some men jumped out of the windows on the ground floor to get at the punch. They broke glass and china and muddied damask satin-covered chairs in the mayhem. The hour of the people had arrived in America. [12]

To give more of what he said in his speech, we have the following. Jackson expressed his gratitude for the confidence and acknowledged his responsibility and accountability in his high office. Explaining his position and principles, he promised to keep in mind the limitations as well as the extent of the office in dealing with Congress. He would be economical. The interests of the farmer, merchant, and industrialists should be equally protected. Standing armies were dangerous and he would not enlarge the government establishment. He would be moderate. The militia would be the nation's best defense. The president-elect talked of a liberal Indian policy and reform. There would be fewer and abler public officials. He would follow the example of his predecessors. [13]

Southerners could feel safe with Andrew Jackson as their president, because he was a large slaveholder in Tennessee, typical in his belief in slavery and his, at times, harsh treatment of his slaves. In this and other things, he imposed his will, being in his estimation always right and justified. He, like Jefferson and other slaveholders, feared freed slaves and wanted them exiled to colonies in Indian territory or Africa. In this, he sold Frances Wright land near Memphis to start a colony she called Nashoba. [14]

---

[1] Fowler, Dorothy Ganfield, *The Cabinet Politician: The Postmaster General, 1829-1909*, New York: Columbia University Press, 1943, Rep. AMS Press, 1967, pp. 1-4. See Wait, Eugene M., *America and the War of 1812*, Commack, NY: Kroshka Books, 1999, for the early life of Harrison. When Harrison turned Whig that set up the events of 1840 and ousted Martin Van Buren, the friend of Jackson, as president, in an election.

[2] Fowler, *Cabinet*, pp. 5-11. Quote on p. 8.

[3] Bowers, *Party*, pp. 42-43.

[4] Belohlavek, *Eagle*, p. 28, *Dictionary of American Biography*, IX (2) 355.

[5] *Dictionary of American Biography*, IX(2) 355-356.

[6] Belohlavek, *Eagle*, pp. 28-29; *Dictionary of American Biography*, VI (1), 309.

[7] *Dictionary of American Biography*, VI (1), 309-311.

[8] Belohlavek, *Eagle, pp. 28-29;* Dictionary of American Biography, VII (1), 139.

[9] Belohlavek, *Eagle*, pp. 29, 272 n. 7.

[10] Nathan, p. 30 n. 7; *Dictionary of American Biography*, II (1), 432-433.

[11] Bowers, *Party*, pp. 36-40. Quote p. 37.

[12] Remini, Robert V., *The Jacksonian Era, Arlington Heights Ia: Harlan Davidson, 1989, pp. 20-22; Smith,* Forty Years, *pp. 290-291;* Niles Weekly Register, *March 7, 1829, p. 28.*

[13] *Niles Weekly Register*, March 7, 1929, pp. 28-29.

[14] Meltzer, Miltar, *Andrew Jackson and His America*, New York: Franklin Watts, 1993, pp. 21, 27, 30-31, 37-38, 86-87, 104.

Chapter 4

THE CROWD

The Smiths were unable to get into the White House because of the crowd, so they walked awhile and went home. When they learned that the crowd had lessened at the executive mansion they went there and were aghast at what they found. There was no more peoples' majesty. There was only the rabble, white and black; there had been no policemen on duty and the place was a shambles. Several thousand dollars of china and glassware had been broken and cluttered the floors. It was said there had been twenty thousand people there and the place looked like such was the case. This was an exaggerated number, but there was a multitude. Ladies had fainted and men had received bloody noses. Jackson came close to losing his life by being pressed to death by the people who wanted to shake his hand. The people that had worshipped him almost killed him. Only the protective barrier of his friends saved his life. [1]

A saved Jackson operated as a military-man in his administration of policy. He used his official and unofficial cabinets as lieutenants to arrange the administration of Jackson's policy. He met with his formal cabinet only sixteen times in eight years. First, he never took a vote at the meeting. He would listen and then come to an opinion or decision. Second, Jackson preferred to meet with each assistant separately, mostly about events and policy in each official's department. In some cases, he would talk over issues beyond one's department, but generally would not.

His Kitchen Cabinet met increasingly and was usually composed of a group of trusted westerners. These men were not intellectual heavyweights, but they could be trusted to give Jackson the right advice or support what Jackson wanted. His friend and adviser William B. Lewis was a custodian for the renewal and repair of the White House furniture, but generally his tasks were of a higher level than that. At first they were newspapermen, then cabinet official, and then vice-president. Flawed by an inability to delegate authority, Jackson made the decisions on all levels, even such details as the location of the privies. There was little discretion in judgment for subordinates who were merely executive agents. The federal government was still small. [2]

When President Andrew Jackson was inaugurated on March 4, 1829, he initiated an Indian policy whose keystone was the removal of the Cherokee and Creeks to lands beyond the Mississippi. This policy had been expected by many concerned southerners and westerners in the United States. Jackson believed that the Indians were an obstacle to American expansion and he would remove that obstacle. He would also move them outside of Georgia state's jurisdiction to what he thought to be permanent locations in western lands. However, he would allow a few of the most educated and property-minded mixed bloods to remain on farms. By these means, Jackson would open large sums of lands to white settlement. He also thought of an Indian state in the west that never materialized. It was his argument that the Indians could only have peace and happiness across the great river.

Politicians in Georgia, Alabama, and Mississippi had recently passed laws that would extend state laws to the Indians and disrupt tribal government so much that the Indians would emigrate. A Jacksonian presidency would have only a short period of time to act before these laws would tie federal hands. In order to prevent warfare the administration would have to mediate the dispute by arranging the migration itself. Shortly after the laws were passed, Jackson urged the Cherokee and the Creeks to move outside the limits of the states. He promised them reimbursements for all improvements on their old land and compensation for any lost livestock. Further, he warned them that should they remain where they were they would receive no protection from the federal government.

Jackson sent his old friend William Carroll to the Indians in Georgia to gain sympathy among the Indians for the policy of the administration. He had considerable influence among the southern Indians. Carroll's influence was to no avail. They refused to leave their native soil. Humanitarian groups learned about this effort and rallied together to defend their beleaguered red brothers in the southern states. The American Board of Commissioners for foreign missions, centered in Boston, defended Indian rights to remain upon their lands.

The president assigned Thomas L. McKenney the task of molding public opinion in favor of removal. McKenney had served as superintendent of Indian trade and was head of the Bureau of Indian Affairs. Since he had a non-Jacksonian record, he was interested in gaining Jackson's support for his job and was, in this way, highly motivated to put the Jacksonian policy in effect. He was well informed and known as a humanitarian, so that he could marshal great clout. Also, McKenney believed that removal was in the best interests of the Indians so that he was eager to support Jackson's policy.

First, McKenney appealed to Episcopalian bishop John H. Hobard to publicly endorse Indian removal and establish a religious association that would promote this policy. McKenney told him that the suggested body could pressure Congress to support it and send emissaries to the several tribes. Hobard would take no action. In May, he took an open stand against the board and tried to interest the Dutch Reformed Church in his policy. He warned that soon the state laws would effect them and that they would perish. In this endeavor, he was successful. He convinced Stephen Van Renaaselaer to head his board. It would cooperate with Jackson and his Indian official McKenney in promoting removal. [3]

Jackson's conception of the people he represented cut across class lines, but generally meant the lower and lower middle class. He did not think he was the spokesman for all of the people, just the majority he specified. The merchants and the intelligentsia were excluded. When the president spoke of "the real people," he meant first of all the agricultural class, both planters and farmers. Next, were the mechanics or skilled labor, those who worked in the factories and in the villages. Finally, we have the laborers on farms and in the towns and cities. This preference for labor and agriculturists left out a large number with whom Jackson was never concerned.

Not only was the president the spokesman, but he was the reform minded patron of labor and agriculturists. He worked to preserve and extend their morals, habits, and character against progress that would threaten them. He expected the best out of his people, considering them superior to European people because of their "independent spirit, their love of liberty, their intelligence, and their high tone of moral character." Those who worked the land were favored because of their qualities and because they solved all their needs on the farm.

The one class of laboring men whom Jackson never represented or helped was the lowest of the classes--the slaves. Few people in Jacksonian America fought in words for the welfare of the slaves. The few were the much hatred abolitionists. To Jackson, they were among the capitalists, that is, an impurity in republican America. [4]

The basic motive for Jackson's switch to Van Buren from Calhoun was the greater strength of Van Buren in national politics. Calhoun had provided the extra plus which had brought Jackson so close to the presidency in 1824. Jackson was grateful and drew upon Calhoun for support and the vice-presidency in 1828. When the president found out that Calhoun had once opposed him on his Florida venture, Jackson lost his interest in the southerner and turned to Van Buren, whose organization and support was so crucial in 1828. Jackson never learned to forgive. Van Buren wanted a national union for the new Jacksonian Democracy which would keep that party in power. The Little Magician, as he was called, paid the price to key New York State by opposing the Bank of the United States and to the South by supporting the interests of slavery. He recognized Jackson's appeal to the west as the obvious rallying cry of the Democrats for the future and thus could count on support for his party in most of the states. New England was ignored, but not alienated. [5]

There was a steady struggle for power in the Jackson administration. Several prominent politicians hoped to benefit from the Jackson presidency. Vice-president Calhoun hoped to use his influence to gain a tariff reduction for the tariff. There did not seem much chance for a lower tariff in the spring of 1829. Calhoun had lent his prestige for a lost cause it seemed. His standing had gained conservative support for Jackson, but it was planned that he was to be rejected by Jackson. The price of Crawford's valuable support was the ditching of Calhoun. Jackson had won because of the support of both men and now one was to suffer. Van Buren stood to benefit more than anyone else.

Calhoun had hoped to succeed Jackson as president in 1933, but he soon lost the illusion of that thought.

When the cabinet was announced, Calhoun was disappointed. Eaton, Crawford, and Van Buren were influences upon Jackson and soon held great power in the nation. Calhoun left Washington in mid-March and Van Buren soon arrived in the capital. It was to require some time to purge Calhoun. Nothing could be done then. [6]

Jackson wrote of his criteria for appointments soon after entering office. Believing that merit resided in people of all social status, except slaves, the new president wrote of the road "to office and preferment being accessible to the rich and poor alike, the farmer and printer, honesty, probity, and capability constituting the sole and exclusive test, will, I am persuaded, have the happiest tendency to preserve unimpaired, freedom of political action; change it and let it be known that any class or portion of citizens are and ought to be proscribed and discontent and dissatisfaction will be engendered." [7]

As the white man moved west, the Indian was forced by war and treaty to emigrate to the west beyond the line of settlement. To placate settlers and land speculators, government officials got the treaties they wanted by bribery, deception, and threats. American administrators recognized tribal sovereignty and used the leaders to get what the white men wanted. The chiefs were specially bribed. These treaties did not last long because the frontiersmen were after more land. Even when they civilized the Indians, allowed them to stake out settlements, and sponsored assimilation, they were to force the Indians to move out of lands the whites coveted. They did not allow their high blown ideas to supersede their desire to push the natives out of their long-held lands.

In particular, the Cherokees became more civilized in the hopes of retaining their lands. They even wrote a tribal constitution and proclaimed themselves an independent nation and the right to tribal lands as they existed in 1827. This was not to protect their lands as they were to find out during Jackson's administration. In addition, a dissatisfied Georgia took matters into their own hands when Adams had refused to force the Cherokee off their lands. Not only did Southerners want land but they wanted the end of Indian grants of refuge to escaped slaves. Their new Indian masters were more humane and the slaves did not want to return. Southerners had outraged fear their blacks would join the Indians to attack adjacent white communities. Only at the end of the Adams administration, did the government of Adams come to view the problem like the Southerners did. There was no time for him to act however.

Now his successor was being inaugurated. Jackson had fixed views and a predictable course of action was followed according to the westerner he was. Georgia was satisfied for the present when it saw Jackson nominate John E. Eaton from Tennessee and John M. Berrien of Georgia. Both were advocates of Indian removal and Berrien was a staunch opponent of the tariff. Georgians and other Southerners were placated. Eaton as secretary of war would be in charge of Indian policy legally, but it was already clear that the policy would be one which Georgians and westerners would approve.

Jackson views on the Indian policy and the federal government was based upon American destiny and needs. One of the primary needs of growth was to free up Indian lands for new white settlement. This dated back to his early years when he himself had emigrated westward for new opportunities. Although the federal government arranged treaties, most of the western movement was undertaken by individuals individually and cooperatively. The United States government was suited to remove obstacles and the Indians were obstacles. From his own experience, Jackson had come to look with distaste upon the treaty making process as producing federal obligations.

The new president had a formula that would move the Indians outside the existing states so that there would no longer be tribal government existing within sovereign states. Across the Mississippi, they could receive permanent titles to land in exchange for eastern lands. Only a few of the educated and property minded mixed bloods would receive farms in the east at their request. In his view, the Indians could only find peace and happiness in the west. If they became civilized, they could be concentrated and come into the Union as a separate state. [8]

Riding a tiger as he was, Jackson was forced to act quickly. His support for Indian removal was tied to action, but did not blunt the western and southern hurry for action. He hoped to end the controversy quickly because of the conflict that had heated up. In his inaugural address, he told the partisan crowd that it was his desire to have a just and liberal policy toward the Indians with the habits of the American government and feelings of the American people. This last was the key to the whole policy. There was no time to lose because legislation had been approved in Georgia, Alabama, and Mississippi that would extend state jurisdiction over the Indians. The Jacksonian view on state supremacy was such that he believed the government could not go against state law.

Within a few weeks, Andrew had urged the Creeks and the Cherokees to move west. He promised them generous terms. His government would reimburse them for the improvements they had made in their land and compensate them for any lost livestock. Those willing to stay must live under state law. He would extend a paternal and superintending care to the Indians in the lands they would be moved to in the west. He warned them that they would not find solace in their old lands or protection there, from the federal government. Jackson found opposition from the Indians and their friends, those humanitarians led by the American Board of Commissioners for Foreign Missions. In reply, the president sought support from other church groups to be gained through the effort of Thomas L. McKenney. He was successful in organizing a society to effect removal and develop a propaganda campaign. [9]

---

[1]Smith, *Forty Years*, pp. 295-296.

[2]Belohlavek, *Eagle*, pp. 24-28.

[3]Satz, Ronald N., *American Indian Policy in the Jackson Era*, Lincoln, Neb: University of Nebraska Press, 1975, pp. 8-16.

[4]Meyers, Marvin, *The Jacksonian Persuasion: Politics and Belief*, Stanford: Stanford University Press, 1957, pp. 15ff.

[5]Brown, Richard H., "The Missouri Crisis, Slavery, and the Politics of Jacksonianism," *South Atlantic Quarterly*, LXV (Winter 1966), 55-72.

[6]Wiltse, Charles M., *John C. Calhoun, Nullifier, 1829-1839,* Indianapolis: Bobbs-Merrill, 1949, pp. 15-25.

[7]Aronson, *Status and Kinship*, 1964, p. 14. Quote on p. 14.

[8]Satz, *American*, pp. 1-4, 9-12.

[9]*Ibid.*, pp. 11-16.

Chapter 5

POLICIES

The spoils system under Andrew Jackson was a natural development of politics. President George Washington had wholesale rewards of office to Federalists. There was a two fold objective. First, one filled the high offices with men who would support the government and carry out the ideas and policies of the party. Secondly, one rewarded supporters. For Jackson, the idea was to clean out the administration of corruption as well as the two objectives. There had not been a major sweep since Jefferson came to power. Jackson's partisans were eager to install what they called a "salutary system of reformation into every branch of government." Shortly after assuming office, Jackson sent the Senate 76 names for top jobs in the federal bureaucracy. These were quickly confirmed by the time of congressional adjournment on March 17, 1829, and once secure, Jackson began to replace others. Opposition politicians protested, influencing generations of historians. Pro-Jackson journalists wrote that the removal was in the public interest. Out of 319 nominations, the Senate rejected only six. Some of the replaced clerks and officials were persecuted for appropriating federal funds or property for their own use. [1]

Under Jackson, the American goals in foreign policy were chiefly the settlement of claims against violators of American shipping during the Napoleonic Wars and the encouragement of commerce. Great Britain was mistress of the seas in both periods and was indeed one of the reasons for commercial violations as well as the problems faced in commerce in general. Belohlavek notes that in the smaller countries of Europe such as Portugal, Spain, the Netherlands, and Belgium, "British political influence and commercial domination made the negotiations of treaties difficult, if not impossible." The Americans found the other nations to be stuck in a similar situation. Jackson made these uphill paths of commercial agreements passable. His diplomats achieved spoliation claims treaties with Denmark, France, Portugal, and Spain and new commercial agreements or revisions with Great Britain, France, Russia, and Japan. Exports were to increase by more than 75 percent by 1836 and imports were up 250% in the same seven years. To get this result, Jacksonians "combined the ability to threaten, cajole, and intimidate with patience, flattery, and understanding, depending upon the nation and the circumstance." [2]

At his inaugural, Jackson had stated his intent "to observe toward the Indian tribes within limits a just and liberal policy, and to give them humane and considerate attention to their rights and wants which is consistent with the habits of our government and the feelings of our people." This did not mean a policy of protection for the native, but a just and liberal policy for the white man. That Indian rights were to be ignored was evident when Jackson appointed John H. Eaton as secretary of war and John M. Berrien as attorney general. Both were advocates of Indian removal. The talk that the president gave about Indian rights is understood when we consider that to the whites, a just policy meant that there be Indian lands for the settlers. That policy was consistent with the habits of government and feelings of the people, which meant to the settler in the South, to be a policy consistent with Indian removal. Humane action was to mean protection for the Indians after they were moved to the west. This humane action also signified some form of civilization and good treatment to many Americans.

Events had moved forward so quickly that Jackson was impelled to act immediately. Legislation in Georgia, Alabama, and Mississippi was bound to be effective. This would extend state jurisdiction over the Indians and prevent Jackson's particular policy from being established. Also, Cherokee assertions of native sovereignty were angering Southerners and created a crisis which might mean war on the frontier. [3]

President Jackson sent Colonel Crowell to the Creek Indians with a message addressed to them as friends and brothers. He wrote that he had the permission of the Great Spirit above and the voice of the people below to be president. The warriors had known him for a long time. Jackson loved, he averred, "my white and red children, and always speak with a straight, and not with a forked tongue, that I have always told you the truth. Your bad men have made my heart sicken and bleed, by the murder of one of my white children in Georgia. Our peaceful mother earth has been stained by the blood of the white man, and calls for the punishment of his murderers, whose surrender is now demanded under the solemn obligations of the treaty which your chiefs and warriors in council have agreed to. To prevent the spilling of more blood, you must surrender the murderers, and restore the property they have taken. To preserve peace, you must comply with your own treaty."

Then, he showed his sure intent. Whites and Indians lived too near for peace. Indian game was destroyed and many Creek Indians would not till the ground, so they had to move beyond the Mississippi where some Creek Indians had already gone. There was room enough for all of them in the vastness. Once there, "your white brothers will not trouble you; they will have no claims to the land, and you can live on it, you and all your children, as long as the grass grows or the water runs, with peace and plenty. It will be yours forever." They would be paid for the improvements they had made on the lands and the stock they could not take with them. The presidents would protect them there, feed them, and keep any whites from encroachment. The whites had always claimed the land in Georgia but would never claim the land beyond the Mississippi.

Meanwhile, they must turn over the murderers. They would be punished in accordance with the law. He sent an agent and Crowell to take the murderer back to the white country. They would also discuss the removal and place such Indians as they wished on farm acreage in Alabama. However, they would be subject to Alabama law. If beyond the Mississippi, they could have their own laws and presidential care. The president would treat them with kindness, and the lands would be theirs forever. Jackson signed and dated the message on March 23, 1829.

The Creek had a reply to this message. In the *Cherokee Phoenix* in New Echota, the editor wrote that those of his fellow Indians who were conversant with the migration knew that the Creeks, Choctaws, and Chickasaws who had seen the western lands were not impressed. What they saw bound them further to their homelands in the southeast. The Creeks found the land to be poor and they were in a poor condition. If more Indians moved west, then there would be overcrowding. Those who wanted the Indians to move were misrepresenting things to get the Indians to move out of lands they already inhabited.

D. Bearly counterattacked in the *National Intelligencer* that all of the Indian migrants west of the Mississippi were pleased about their western settlements, but this rang hollow. The delegation of five distinguished Indians had returned to state that they were well pleased with the new lands, but as usual, they were rewarded for their trip and sentiments as they were before they moved. This was a common procedure in Indian history, especially at this time. Those who wanted to move were always a minority, influenced by American money and attention. [4]

The future victor of San Jacinto and president of Texas, General Sam Houston resigned the governorship of Tennessee on April 16, 1829. He was replaced by General William Hall, speaker of the senate of the state, as was required by the constitution of Tennessee. Houston wrote that in ending the political connection, he would express grateful recollections. He had always from youth, worked for the common good and never allowed private interest or private ambition to mingle with higher duties of public trust. Further, the veneration for public opinions, measured during his public life, "has taught me to hold no delegated power which could not be daily renewed by my constituents, and the choices be daily submitted to a sensible expression of their will." However, he was glad to place the office in the hands of one of integrity and worth such as General Hall, who would "pursue the true interest of the state". [5]

The city fathers in Cincinnati, Ohio, had not enforced a provision of Ohio's Black Code, which would force free blacks to post a $500 bond to guarantee their good behavior. This was a very large amount at the time. When census reports became available, it was discovered that from 1826 to 1829, the black population had risen from 4 to 10 percent of the total population. Alarmed whites gave support to the Cincinnati Colonization Society to settle African Americans in Africa. In July of 1829, the trustees of the city declared they would enforce the bond requirement. This was not enough for whites. They gathered and raided the black ghetto of Bucktown. By the end of the year half of the black population had left. Most of those who left were the most sober, honest, industrious, and useful blacks. [6]

By later standards extremely few Americans went to college in the year of Jackson's first inaugural. There was on average one student in college for each 2,000 in New England with Massachusetts leading the way at one in 1,300. For the middle states, there was one for 4,000 with one in 3,400 in New Jersey and 3,700 in New York State. In the western and southern states there was one for every 6,000, with Louisiana having one in 25,000 at the bottom of the heap. One in seven of all college students were in Massachusetts. [7]

Office seekers pursued administration heads all spring and summer to try to obtain jobs for them. They often brought wives and daughters to reinforce their demands for jobs in the social stream of Washington. They pointed out to these dependents as reason for the necessity of having jobs. Cabinet officers found themselves harassed for jobs held by occupants of previous administrations. It was necessary for them to lock their doors to prevent importunity until the late afternoon in order to get their business done.

One man sought the collectorship of New York and wrote to another office seeker: "No damn rascal who made use of an office or it is profits for the purpose of keeping Mr. Adams in and General Jackson out of power is entitled to the least leniency save that of hanging. Whether or not I shall get anything in the general scramble for plunder remains to be seen, but I rather guess I shall. I know Mr. Ingham slightly, and would recommend that you push like the devil if you expect anything from that quarter."

Some one and a half years later, Amos Kendall was able to note that Jackson was "charged with having turned out of office all who were opposed to him, when a majority of the office-holders in Washington are known to be in favor of his rivals. In that city, the removals have been but one seventh of those in office, and most of them for bad conduct and character."

Jackson had found an able hand in Mordecai M. Noah, whom he wanted for the job of surveyor and inspector of the port of New York. In the early part of the century, he had pressed for the use of warships rather than ransom for the pirate captures of Americans in the western Mediterranean. Noah had written a book about his travels. When Jackson ran for the presidency, Noah had given help to the westerner in the elections. The president sent his nomination of Noah to the Senate. The enemies of both voted against him and he was not confirmed. The Senate delighted in his defeat.

Opponents tried also to kill the nomination of Amos Kendall. When it came to the vote, it was a tie broken by Calhoun's vote. Also crucial was the vote of Hendricks of Indiana, supported by Adams, but he was enticed away to vote for Kendall. Without Hendricks, Kendall would have been defeated, but then any voter for him could have changed his vote and defeated him. He was beholden to many.

Jackson was aroused by the defeat of Noah and sent his name again to the Senate for confirmation. This was accomplished, but required the tiebreaker by Calhoun as vice-president. Issac Hill's rejection held, but Hill was elected senator in his native New

Hampshire and walked down the aisle of the U.S. Senate to become a senator among those who had voted on him somewhat before. [8]

Jacksonians had several economic theses to read in the earlier period of the administration in the days in which liberal and radical sentiments were dominant. The Jacksonian Theodore Sedgwick read a book by self-termed Owenite pamphleteer Langton Byllesby who tried the invention of numerous contraptions and wrote poems. In 1823, Byllesby published a newspaper, *The Spirit of Pennsylvania and Pennsylvanians* and promoted the elderly democrat Andrew Gregg for governor. Gregg had opposed Jefferson on Jay's Treaty and on the War of 1812 and lost when he ran many years later with Byllesby as his campaign advisor.

When Gregg lost the election, gone were Byllesby's dreams of lucrative government patronage and public printing. The editor Byllesby went to Philadelphia where he found employment and in 1826 published his *Observations on the Sources and Effects of Unequal Wealth.* The book was a radical denunciation of such materials as methods of inheritance, banking, and mercantile speculations but he predated a nation of associations in which shareholders divided profits, the working man got a wage and the inventor received a reward.

Sedgwick read other books and then produced *Public and Private Economy,* in which he advised depressed and overworked laborers to give up gaudy display and luxuries. The way to gain freedom was to save money to buy farmland out west or to start a business in the old states.

Another Jacksonian era thinker was the fiery anticlerical Reverend Theophilus Fisk. This man opposed the idea of getting beyond one's means in debt. Business rules should prevail when going into debt. New York journalist William Leggett has been cited as a radical, but when it came to labor federations, he stood opposed to a monopoly of labor. Such was his fervor that his statement was that labor organization was a creator of social anarchy and chaotic confusion.

Philadelphia's so called labor leader, the Thomas Brothers, printed the following statement which was anti-labor. The author of it submitted it to Brothers' newspaper and the Philadelphia published it as follows "were you to give your workmen greater wages than other manufacturers do, your goods would be proportionately augmented in price, and would lay on your shelves until your customers were in a humor to take pity on your fellows and reward your stupidity by becoming purchasers." Joseph Dorfman has called this the standard answer of all conservative employers. [9]

William Leggett was a man with strong friends and strong enemies during the Jacksonian era. The poets William Cullen Bryant, John Greenleaf Whittier, and Walt Whitman wrote well of him. When he died, Bryant spoke of his warm and mighty heart. Whittier wrote that Leggett had "labored more perseveringly, and in the end, more successfully" than any other man "to bring the practice of American democracy into conformity with its principles." Whitman coupled the doctrines of "the great Jefferson and the glorious Leggett." The moderate William L. Marcy looked down upon him as a knave while the aristocratic Daniel Hone looked down upon his editorials as infamous and dastardly. Other editors had smarted under Leggett's editorials and denounced him.

He articulately spoke for the radical wing of the Democratic party. As a popular writer, he appealed to the workingmen of New York. The expressions he wrote in his newspaper were liked by the Locofocos of New York. In 1829, he was on the editorial staff of the New York *Evening Post* aiding Bryant. [10]

[1] Eriksson, Erik McKinley, "The Federal Civil Service Under President Jackson," *Mississippi Valley Historical Review*, XIII (March 1927), pp. 517-540.

[2] Belohlavek, *Eagle*, p. 53. Quotes on p. 53.

[3] Satz, *American*, p. 12.

[4] *Niles Weekly Register*, June 13, 1829, pp. 257-258; July 25, 1829, p. 357.

[5] *Ibid., May 4, 1829, pp. 171-172. Quote on pp. 171-172.*

[6] Richards, Leonard L., *"Gentlemen of Property and Standing": Anti-Abolitionist Mobs in Jacksonian America*, New York: Oxford University Press, 1970, pp. 34-36.

[7] *Niles Weekly Register*, August 29, 1829, p. 2.

[8] Bowers, pp. 69, 73, 84-87. Quote on pp. 69, 73.

[9] Dorfman, Joseph, "The Jackson Wage Earner Thesis," pp. 296-298.

[10] Hofstadter, Richard, "William Leggett, Spokesman of Jacksonian Democracy," *Political Science Quarterly*, LVIII, (December 1943), pp. 581-583.

Chapter 6

HOUSTON AND INDIANS

A friend of both Jackson and the Indians, Houston arrived at the Falls, two miles from John Jolly's Cherokee plantation, to find the word had gone out to the Chief that his adopted son had reached his village on the steamboat; it was dark, and Jolly went to greet Houston. In the light of the torchlight, he was home where he was most at ease. He was a Cherokee by adoption and had participated in Indian society when he was formerly with them. He came at a good time when they needed his council. Houston was to write of the venerable old chief that the Indian "had the most courtly carriage ... and never a prince sat on a throne with more fearless grace than that he resides at the council fire of his people. His wigwam was large and comfortable, and he lived in patriarchal simplicity and abundance. He had ten or twelve servants, a large plantation and not less than five hundred head of cattle." His house "was always open to visitors, and his bountiful board was always surrounded by welcome guests. He never slaughtered less than one beef a week, throughout the year for his table." Jolly refused to speak English but Houston had learned Cherokee. Although wealthy, he gained the support of the full-blood because he wore traditional buckskin, a hunting shirt, leggings and moccasins. Some of the Cherokee wore silk coats imported from England and France and used fine glass.

The Cherokee were composed of mixed and full blood, differing in education and economic position. Despite their civilization, they were more Indian than white. The gracious ante-bellum life they lived did not deter them from keeping their ancient native religion ceremonies despite the efforts of missionaries. Although Sequoyah had invented written letters and words of his Cherokee language, many Cherokees could not read or write. They openly warred with the Osage who regarded the Cherokee already in Arkansas and Oklahoma as intruders. They feared white settlement and did not wish the Cherokees still in Georgia and Tennessee to join them as they were to do.

Houston wrote to Andrew Jackson that he would be proud and happy to arrange the preservation of peace among the Indians and between them and the whites. He wished to be an unofficial peacemaker and end abuse and injustice towards the Indians. He would let Jackson know the facts. Especially qualified by his success in both worlds, Houston had great insights into Indian thinking since he had been a Cherokee at one time, by adoption. Houston did refuse the post of sub-agent, however. In effecting his purpose, he joined forces with Pierre Chouteau of St. Louis of the Indian of the Indian trade empire run by the Chauteau family. The French-descended American fur trader was the most influential white man for the Osages, and together they saw to it that the differences between the tribes were settled by arbitration. Houston also arranged for a general Indian peace involving the many tribes of the Plains. [1]

In his first message to Congress, Jackson foresaw friendly relations with foreign countries, concerning his efforts to gain an arbitration of the Canadian boundaries, continued friendship with France and a commercial treaty with both France and Spain. About Russia's recent invasion of Turkey, he hoped that it would promote civilization and human happiness. He hoped that the Black Sea would be unlocked to American commerce. About American trade with Austria, still of secondary importance, he said that it had been on the gradual increase and had been extended with Adams' negotiation, completed with a treaty of amity, navigation, and commerce. Clay's diplomats had done most of the work, and were ready to lay the results before Congress. Minister Poinsett was not receiving happy treatment in Mexico. He suffered from the prejudice of the Mexican people. Plans were made to give him the option of returning when a request was given to the United States from Mexico requesting his recall.

Jackson hoped to effect a change in the electoral law to prevent the reoccurrence of his situation in 1824 when the House of Representatives elected Adams as president. He stated emphatically that the people had the right to elect presidents. With Clay in mind, he stated that one representative might name his reward. He wanted to amend the situation so as to remove the electoral college and the House of Representatives from the vote. He would provide for a slanted vote that would enable each state to vote its present weight of its number of representatives and senators with a second vote to decide upon two leading candidates. He also suggested a single term of four or six years for the presidency. [2]

While the Americans were becoming used to President Jackson, they learned more about the major conflicts abroad. From London, came word of the Catholic question. A bill was to be introduced removing Catholic disabilities in the English nation through an act of parliament. The duke of Newcastle designated it as "a bill for oppressing and injuring the king, and for introducing popery and arbitrary power." The bill would of course do neither but anti-Catholic opinion was still strong in England and this bill came under fire. Its proponents claimed that Protestants were in no danger from the bill, which belief proved to be correct. Later news reported the passage of the Catholic Emancipation bill. [3]

Further news came from Russia and Turkey. A new war season was underway and both nations had their successes in warfare. The Russian emperor celebrated a Russian victory before Varna on the 22d of January and this news was just reaching America in mid-April. It was a lopsided victory for the Russians. Kali fell to them with eighty-two men being killed on the Russian side to 250 men being killed among the Turks. A multitude was wounded and many Turks fell captive to the Russians. Turkish sources reported a Turkish victory in the Balkans. They drove the Russians from their positions into a mosque upon which the Turks fired. There was talk of peace from the Turkish side through the western allies. Elsewhere news came from Rome of the death of the pope Leo XII. An election of a new pope was being prepared. [4]

Bronson Alcott had mixed views on the Owen teachings that he read in the *New Harmony Gazette*. The educator agreed with the Owen view of society and marriage. However, he objected to the Owen attacks upon the Christian religion and his disrespect for religious opinions. Anti-religious sentiments were illiberal. Liberality is that spirit which leads people to respect all opinions and acknowledge the truth that is contained in all. He believed that the socialists would do good work despite them. [5]

As the city grew with their industry, laboring men began to grow in ever greater numbers during Jackson's administration. They were increasingly conscious of their condition. The long hours and low wages, the lack of the ballot for the poorest, imprisonment for debt, insufficient education for their children, the militia system, and child labor were hurting the working class. Class consciences were prevalent among the laboring people because of this. In New York City, 24,200 children of school years were not attending school. This was almost half of the youth in the city. [6]

In Philadelphia after the general election the laboring man continued organizing. At a time when workingmen were urged to go to the tax assessors and be assessed for voting rights, political clubs were formed, starting in the district of Southwark where the Workingmen's Republican Political Association was formed, larger as an educational organization to teach workingmen about the laws effecting them. Pamphlets were to be published in order to promote general intelligence and to achieve society's prosperity.

Southwark's example was followed by Northern Liberties and the city of Philadelphia. The city government used hired men to disrupt the meeting of workmen in the eastern and western wards. The group in the western wards adjourned to another place and passed resolutions that declared the attempt of public officers to prevent lawful assemblies was a violation of republican principles. In New York, the laboring man was interested most in the political cause rather than economic problems as in Philadelphia and its suburbs. To be sure, he fought for higher wages and shorter hours but the emphasis was political.

New York's laboring men believed that they were harmed by inequitable legislation. They believed that a prudent legislature would first find itself devoted to the producing class interest. They saw instead to their alarm that a neglect of labor's interest and consideration of the moneyed and aristocratic interest in New York predominated in the New York legislature. This was a cause to champion and the laboring man felt they needed a labor party. Labor's New York paper, the *Working Man's Advocate* proclaimed that they should go and exercise their privilege to vote and not be slaves. If they did not vote, they were denying the heroes of '76. They risked their lives for the people that could not vote. The laboring men must exercise the vote on their own behalf.

The mechanics of New York thought they would strike, but Thomas Skidmore persuaded them to follow his lead and promote resolutions of a revolutionary nature. Skidmore was a machinist with an interest in Thomas Paine, who felt that this interest could be used to frighten employers. He thought that his plan would alarm those that he called the aristocratic oppressors. I would deal with "the nature of the tenure by which all men hold title to their property."

Five resolutions were promoted. First, that ten hours a day were all that an employer could receive and as much as laboring men should give. The second was that "all men hold their property by the consent of the great mass of the community, and by no other title," and that the masses had an equal right to participate in property. The third was that if those who could give employment withheld it and asked for excessive labor at an unjust price for it, they would be violating the first law of the society and would be subject to the displeasure of the just community. This was also true of those who would ask unjust hours – they would incur disapproval. Should this code of labor be violated by an employer, none of the laboring class would work for him. There would be a labor strike by that method. Skidmore succeeded and the employers stopped asking their employees for extra long hours of work per day. This did not effect slaves, however. The ten hour day became the norm in cities in which Skidmore had influence. [7]

Laboring men also had an effect on land policy, there being two views in the early years of the United States. Those of a liberal viewpoint thought that land should be sold to the masses in satisfactory amounts for low prices. They were usually pioneer farmers, land speculators, and spokesmen for eastern workingmen and women, and those who believed that the sale of land to the public would bring about a true democracy. Conservatives wanted to sell land slowly and for substantial prices, the income of which would be spent for educating all the people and providing for the well-being and happiness of Americans. They were usually owners of eastern lands who feared being undercut and eastern manufacturers who did not want their cheap labor to go west and present the capitalists with a labor problem of insufficiency. [8]

Various groups of American laboring men acted in 1829. Soon after Jackson's inaugural, working men from various Pennsylvanian canals combined to attain higher taxes. They refused to work and acted to prevent others from working, thus obtaining a fuller strike. The law put down the strike and the ringleaders were put in jail. In reporting this, Hezekiah Niles wrote that it was "lawful for every man to make his own bargain for his labor, and whoever forcibly interferes to prevent it, should be punished. Employers have rights, as well as the employed." Thus in a common enough belief, the editor pronounced himself against forced combination. [9]

[1]Gregory, Jack & Strickland, Rennand A., *Sam Houston with the Cherokees, 1829-1833*, Austin, Tx: University of Texas Press, 1967, 1967, pp. 8-21, 61, 69, 96.

[2]*The State of the Union Messages of the Presidents, 1790-1966*, ed. Israel, Fred L., 3 vols., New York: Chelsea House, 1966, I, 294-300.

[3]*Niles Weekly Register*, April 18, 1829, pp. 120-121; May 9, 1829, p. 166; May 16, 1829, p. 177.

[4]*Ibid., April 18, 1829,, p. 121.*

[5]Alcott, *Journals*, p. 20.

[6]Commons, I, 169-184.

[7]*Ibid.*, 200-201, 232-235. Quotes on p. 235.

[8]Zahler, Helena Sara, *Eastern Workmen and National Land Policy, 1829-1862, 1969 reprint of 1941 edition, pp. vii-viii.*

[9]*Niles Weekly Register*, April 11, 1829, p. 101.

Chapter 7

LABOR

In New York City, labor was troubled because of unemployment. Many workingmen were destitute. They were without money to live on and numerous meetings were held to promote charity for the benefit of the unemployed. Jackson was inaugurated in the midst of recession, but he played no part in the labor movement and there was no one to even suggest federal programs. Unemployment relief was only local in the nineteenth century.

While the unemployed sought relief in their city, employers were trying to get more out of their workingmen. Some employers wanted to revive an eleven-hour day, taking advantage of the workingmen. The previous hours had been ten hours a day. Mechanics and others met to oppose this increase in hours at a meeting on April 23,1829. They stayed on to form the Workingsmen's Party. Five days later, a large meeting was held. A large committee was formed to collect relief. The employers, faced with such a stand, retreated and men were hired with a ten-hour workday standard for the city.

The relief committee was also assigned the task of drawing up a report. Thomas Skidmore wrote the report for the committee. It followed along the lines of a book he had written entitled *The Rights of Man to Property*. The book denounced the hereditary transmission of wealth and taught that each generation should transmit the wealth of its citizens on an equal basis to those reaching maturity. Robert Dale Owen's plan for free education was also adopted. Further, the plan was in favor of destroying banks, and ending the tax exemption of churches and church property. Skidmore also favored a slate of workingmen running for legislative positions.

It was now October and the elections were two weeks away. The workingmen had little time for action. In that time the government was attacked for the number of Adams' men in its ranks, its favoritism for national financing for roads and development, and its support of the tariff, also a workers' desire. Tammany claimed to be the true workers' party and there was some disagreement upon events before the election.

Tammany secured the election, but some that bolted from the organization won two positions. One workingman was elected, namely Ebenezer Ford, a carpenter. The Democrats in Tammany tried to secure the workingmen after this election. They believed that they were basically Jackson men and to woo them promised full support for a lien law. This did not destroy the new party of workingmen but got it to exclude the radical Skidmore.

At first, the working men lacked a program. Skidmore's view was taken as too radical and was rejected after the first election. The leading committee claimed that they expected "the reward of our toil, and consider the right to individual property, the strongest incentive to industry." The mass of workingmen was interested in education. The teaching would be in public schools. Education was first of all the teaching of courses that would elevate the working class to their proper position. Some were very interested in trade education. Particularly, the party was anti-bank and had a hatred of monopolies. [1]

Thomas Skidmore had contrived a system for the equal disposition of the wealth of the nation by redistribution of the wealth each generation and proclaiming the rights of individual men to an equal amount of property. It was obvious, according to the view of Skidmore and the thoughts of others, that "as long as property is unequal; or rather, as long as it is so enormously unequal as we see it at present, those who possess it, will live on the labor of others, and themselves perform none, or if any, a very disproportionate share, of that toil which attends them as a condition of their existence, and without the performance of which, they have no just right to preserve or reclaim that existence, even for a single hour."

Next, the radical Skidmore proposed a nation of legislators in which the citizen gave his vote for laws about which he learned by buying for a cheap price the proposed laws. Each could propose his own laws. First of course, every child needed an education of reading and the other r's (writing and arithmetic), so that he could read and participate in his self-government. [2]

Laboring men had several causes for complaint. They were dissatisfied with the system of imprisonment for debt, the competition of convict labor, and numerous small troubles from militia laws, auctions, and minor monopolies. Their chief complaint was the lack of an education for their children. This caused a great deal of resentment and was meet with demands for reform. There were some openings for education, but they had their limits. Laboring men had to declare that they were unable to pay for their children's education to get an education of their children in Philadelphia. The Public School Society taught New York City's poor children. In large areas throughout the states poor and lower class children had an opportunity for education.

Organized labor raised the cry of equal education for all at the expense of all. A committee of workers in Philadelphia attacked the state's legislature for its endowment of colleges for the rich and its failure to provide for schools for the poor. Liberty was nothing, they said, unless everyone had instruction. The results of this cry were the establishment of schools in many Pennsylvanian counties. [3]

During his early weeks in office, Kendall learned also of the petty abuses such as "the great number of letters for private citizens that came under cover to the fourth auditor, as means of avoiding the payment for postage." No longer was that allowed under Kendall and he did not abuse the flanking privilege in the offices he held under Jackson and Van Buren. He could find no justification in the right established in the general post office that one could frank the letter's of one's wife, finding no law allowing it or the precedent thus set in his own office. Concerning small claims disbursement to naval officers in his office, Kendall would not allow them to be made because it was in the law that it should be so. He reformed the Navy Pension Fund manager and gave the House chairman of the Naval Committee the information, he had tried in vain to get during the previous two sessions. He found other points of corruption. President Jackson gave him his support and Kendall continued to act to weld the utmost strictness in the passage of accounts in the sweep of the broom.

For Kendall, federal employees were not lords, but hired help of their fellow citizens. Office was not property. It was a matter of contract for employment between employees and employer-people. Workers in his office held their jobs at the will of the auditor and the secretary of the treasury. Except for this, they had no rights to property in their jobs. Their employment depended upon the industry and the fidelity with which they discharged their duties. They were required to give their minds and work to the service of the American nation. Kendall would live by these rules of office. [4]

Van Buren's position was enhanced by the Eaton affair soon after the administration was underway. As we have seen, the controversy centered around Peggy Eaton. When Jackson was in Washington DC in his senatorial years, he had boarded at the house of a Mr. O"Neal. The now president wrote that O'Neal "amiable pious wife and two daughters, one married and the other single, take ever pains in their power to make us comfortable." He found them to be an agreeable and worthy family, whose leisure hours were profitably spent. Peggy O'Neal or Mrs. Timberlake, "the married daughter, whose husband belongs to our Navy, plays on the piano delightfully, and every Sunday evening entertains her pious mother with sacred music to which we were invited." The local gossips were to have much to say about Peggy in the days ahead. Her husband who was a purser in the navy was away and she was popular with lonesome legislator Senator Eaton, who was in love with Peggy as some others were. When he learned about Timberlake's death and about the rumors, Eaton went to Jackson about advice. The president had just emerged from his election and the slander against his wife. Jackson told Eaton to marry Peggy and defy her detractors. The marriage took place shortly.

The women of the cabinet were very unhappy with Eaton's marriage and caused an uproar followed by those with an axe to grind, those who called themselves friends. These believed that Eaton was a bar to their holding office. Jackson claimed these spreaders of calumny were the tools of Clay set upon preventing Jackson from appointing him. Jackson was making the Eaton appointment for the good of the nation and would not brook any interference. He would rather die than give up the honorable action of supporting Eaton. In the following July, he was saying that he would never abandon a friend for new ones or for slight and trivial causes nor would he be silent when a female character was assailed. Jackson was very much of a man. [5]

There were rumors published in anti-Jackson newspapers that McLane was being instructed by the new administration to make a trade. They would reduce the American tariff if the British would provide reciprocal advantages in the markets of Great Britain. One American newspaper stated that the British would reduce their corn laws and the United States would cut their tariffs on manufactures. [6]

Van Buren sought friends for federal service and he found one for service as a minister to France in William Cabell Rives, a political leader in Virginia, son of a revolutionary army veteran, and grandson of Colonel William Cabell. Born the third child on May 4, 1793, William received his education at Hampden-Sidney College and the College of William and Mary. He graduated and studied law and politics under Thomas Jefferson. Like so many of Jackson's supporters, he was a member of the native aristocracy and man of some talents. Jackson had all kinds of friends and like so many, Rives was a state representative. On March 24, 1819, the young man married Judith Page Walher and lived at the Walher estate before and after his wife became heir to the estate. From 1823 to 1829, the people of his district had him serve in the federal House of Representatives. Following the Jacksonian movement in Virginia during these years, Rives was a good man for Van Buren to suggest in 1829 for diplomatic office. [7]

Not only did Jackson accept Rives for the French post, but he allowed Van Buren to appoint a minister to Spain. A ready Van Buren immediately suggested Senator Levi Woodbury of New Hampshire. Woodbury was interested in the position, but only as a limited mission for a specific mission, but this was not forthcoming and he declined. Descendent of an old Pilgrim New England family dating back to 1623, Levi attended the village school in Franceshorn, the school Atkinson Academy, and Dartmouth College, graduating with honors in 1809. He decided to become a lawyer and studied under Judge Jeremiah Smith, at the famous Litchfield Law School in Connecticut, and in Boston. He was a popular lawyer and speaker who had defended President James Madison's action in the War of 1812. In 1817, a friend, Governor William Plumer appointed him associate justice of the state superior court and in 1823, was elected governor with the support of the "Young America" faction of the Democrats and the Federalists.

While governor, he recommended more education for females, soil surveys, diversified corps scientifically selected, wool production, exhibits of useful invention, country lecturers on agriculture and mechanics, all of which were progressive ideas for his day. Party factions defeated him for a second term, but his political career was just beginning. Elected to the legislature, he was quickly speaker and then United States Senator from 1825 to 1831.

Governor Cornelius P. Van Ness was elected for Spain by Jackson. Van Buren wrote about this appointment, that his relations with the Van Ness family had been for years of an unfriendly character, but he agreed with the appointment. The governor from Vermont accepted the position and went to Spain for almost all of Jackson's administrations. [8]

Rives was well acquainted with the Beaumarchais claims and the French part of the United States-French relations. He had been on the committee that had dealt with these claims. That would give him a set advantage in dealing with the money claims upon the French. There were strong pressures at home for Rives to make an agreement. Mass meetings were held in New York City and other places requesting Jackson to send a special mission to the French Government to gain a definitive answer to American claims. The American press did not think that this was necessary because it expected Van Buren to act in a manner that would find a solution to the problem. The New York *Mercantile Advertiser* felt that it was necessary to have a new system of political ethics, which it evidently thought Jackson would have to give new strength to the exposition of grievances. Strong language was possibly more necessary in order to enable Americans to resist the illegal seizures of property that had taken place during the Napoleonic wars and regain the losses of that time.

Many Americans wrote Van Buren urging a decided attempt to collect the claims of Americans. Most of the writers suggested the sending of a special mission, but a cautious Van Buren thought Rives should do the job. Van Buren would not risk war by appointing a special commissioner. It was not that Van Buren was optimistic because the movement for indemnity for spoliations on American commerce by the French had been discussed thoroughly and often with the French government with no results. There had been over a decade of such efforts. Still he was not hopeless either.

Van Buren consulted three Americans in specific about the claims problem. Charles O. Clapp said that Americans were compelled to the belief that the government had been inattentive to their interest and supine. The United States should include all differences and if this did not work should use arbitration or settlement by a commission. James A. Hamiton suggested a definite sum that was not too high. He thought a sum of five or even four million would be sufficient. The question should be kept apart from other negotiations. This last was different from what Clapp suggested. Samuel Smith, who had been a secretary of state and was now a prominent merchant and politician at Baltimore, wrote that discussion had gone as far as it could and could not be renewed unless Americans gave way. French claims against the United States could after all be greater than claims upon France. A few days later, he suggested the use of a French confidential agent, one Taussaud in particular. Above all, the minister should excel in sociability and pleasantry and to emphasize contacts.

On July 12, 1829, Van Buren finished his instructions for Rives. He was to get what he could and allow the claimants to grumble for the residue all they wished. The tone of the instructions was conciliatory and noted that the United States wished their completion. Jackson, he said, wished the claims of the two nations to be kept separate, but if this was not possible, Rives was to embrace all differences. Jackson opposed arbitration, Clapp's suggestion, but would accept it if the French were insistent.

In France, the *Journal du Havre* felt that agitation should be met with arbitration by third party. The *Paris Constitutionnel* was very conciliatory, arguing that the claims were just and urged accommodation, blaming England for sowing the seeds of dispute. On the other hand, the Parisian *Journal of Commerce* was unfriendly and that there was no hope of resolution of the claims. At this time, the reactionary Prince Auguste J.A.M. de Polignac came to power in France as premier and head of the department of foreign relations. One Paris correspondent wrote that the present state of affairs was not conducive to the claim because the ministry was beset by a powerful opposition with five sixths of the wealth, talent, and energy of the nation and also beset by internal affairs, public discontents, and questions about the conquest of Turkey. [9]

[1]Hugins, Walter, *Jacksonian Democracy and the Working Class: A Study of New York Workingmen's Movement, 1829-1837*, pp. 12-16, 131-132.

[2]Skidmore, Thomas, *The Rights of Man to Property*, 1829, pp. 3-4, 10ff.

[3]Zahler, *Workingmen*, pp. 17-18.

[4]Kendall, *Autobiography*, pp. 309-317.

[5]Swisher, *Taney*, pp. 134-135. Quote on p. 134.

[6]Munroe, *McLane*, p. 263; *Niles Weekly Register*, July 18, 1829, pp. 330-331; July 28, 1829, p. 345; August 8, 1829, pp. 386-387; August 22, 1929, pp. 418-419.

[7]Belohlavek, *Eagle*, p. 29; *Dictionary of American Biography*, VIII (1), pp. 635-636.

[8]Belohlavek, *Eagle*, pp. 29, 260; *"Dictionary of American Biography*, X (2), 488. For Van Buren's early association with the Van Ness family see Wait, Eugene M., *America and the War of 1812*, Commack, NY: Kroshka Books, 1999, p. 6.

[9]McLemore, R.A., 1941, pp. 46-53.

Chapter 8

VITAL EVENTS

New York merchants headed by Preserved Fish wrote up a petition addressed to Jackson, asking for a claim to be presented to the French for spoliations committed in wars of the early period of the nineteenth century. The letter told of the measures of both England and France on the high seas. American shipping was hit by seizures and confiscation. They were asking that the attacks made by Frenchmen be righted; and the value of the goods taken be returned to the shippers and merchants of New York City.

Maritime laws were made in Europe with the purpose of preventing American neutral shipping. According to the petition, "the grasping spirit of European monopoly attempted to impose upon us new shackles in place of the colonial fetters that had been shaken off, and displayed itself in continued efforts to cripple the commerce it could not prohibit, lessen the resources it was not permitted to appropriate and retard the growth of the prosperity it had no longer the power to crush." [1]

In May of 1829, Dr. John Lucius Woodbury set out from San Felipe, Texas, for Philadelphia where he was to promote his Texas colony. He wrote to Stephen F. Austin, who was then at Brazoria, that the house that he was concerned with was very rich. The province he was leaving, had a good year agriculturally and the colonies in Texas were that much abler to withstand the storms and developments of life. Money was scarce however and Woodbury's connection in the city of Philadelphia would hopefully help Texas. There were the usual marriages and children and the colonies were growing in numbers from its small state. As Austin noted in his letter to David G. Burnet, Texas was peaceable and there were only the usual governmental frictions. [2]

On July 4th, the young William Lloyd Garrison made his maiden speech on the evils of slavery. In the colonization meeting at Park Street Church, he touched upon most of the points on which he was to argue for decades. By this time, he was an abolitionist, but the lines were indistinct among the antislavery group of the young nation. Slavery was a national sin he stated, but the Christian establishment had ignored the fact, being racist. Busy searching for potential converts abroad, Christians had ignored the slave in iron chains at home. Garrison believed and said that destruction was almost certain for a republic with slaves. They were ignored because they had black skins.

Born in this country, they had the same rights as other Americans. His countrymen talked about unalienable rights for men. This was hypocritical cant when slaves were denied liberty. Because divine law and natural law were the one and the same and because African Americans had equal natural rights, God did not approve of slavery. This was lost on most of his listeners. Slave owners were sinners denying God and thus, he reasoned were atheists. In closing, he appealed to the churches to pray to God in behalf of the slaves. Boston was unmoved, but Garrison had only just embarked upon abolitionism. Garrison shortly left for New York and another meeting with Lundy. [3]

Charles Stuart, Anglo-American abolitionist, was born in 1781, in Bermuda, to a British army officer and his wife, to be educated, perhaps in Belfast. He did not discover the Bible until early manhood, perhaps in India where he was an officer in the Madras army of the East India Company. A cadet officer in 1798, Charles was promoted to lieutenant in 1801. Learning the Hindustandi language, he taught it to the cadet officers at Coddalore and wrote a manuscript on the subject that was transcribed for use in his classes. Promotion came his way to lieutenant-captain, but he ran into conflict with is superiors. Stuart returned to London and then immigrated into Canada and gained a land grant of eight hundred acres of land. His religious impulses sustained him and he became a lay reader at York. Next, he wrote his first book, *An Emigrant's Guide to Upper Canada*. He used it to express his opinion, moralizing and reminiscing. As an entrance to the future, he took a helping hand to Indians and to black refugees from the United States. Soon, he became a Presbyterian preacher.

At this time, Stuart and the youthful Theodore Weld started and developed a friendship in New York State. He became particularly devoted to the whole family, Weld's parents and sister Cornelia in upper New York State. Revival evangelist Charles Grandison Finney converted Theodore Weld to his form of Christianity. Stuart found himself in agreement with the evangelist; both having already plenty of grounds of belief. He joined Finney and his preaching team in revivalism. A ready help, Stuart paid for some of Weld's educational expenses, as he studied for the ministry. In August of 1829, Stuart returned to the British Isles. [4]

Jackson left the White House and the capital soon after the fourth of July of 1829 for a trip down the Potomac River to the Chesapeake and points south. With him were the secretaries of war and navy and the postmaster general, the ranking general, two other generals, two commodores, two majors, Martin Van Buren, and several ladies. On the ninth of July, the expedition reached Fort Monroe at Old Point Comfort, at the mouth of the James River. They had traveled on the steamboat *Potomac*. The greeting party was headed by Colonel House, who was commander of the fort, and included other officers as well.

After a night's sleep, the touring party went across the river's mouth to Norfolk, Virginia. There, Jackson visited the naval yard before going on to see the Dismal Swamp canal and other points in the vicinity. He greeted the crowds, replied to the Norfolk address, and found a warm and enjoyable reception. From there, he returned to Washington. [5]

Another trip followed Jackson's trip to southeastern Virginia. The president went in late July to visit Charles Carroll of Carrollton at the venerable man's estate. Carroll had signed the Declaration of Independence and was the last signer to survive to that time in the nation's history. Martin Van Buren went with the president. [6]

Rumors spread rapidly in Georgia and Alabama that the Creeks were becoming hostile. To counter such falsehoods, fifty chiefs and headmen of that Indian nation issued an address to the alarmed citizens. They were sorry to hear such accounts. There were no truth to such rumors, they said. They suspected that some malicious person was inventing such statements to stir up bad feeling among the white citizens of the nation and their president to move them out of their lands. The Creeks wished to live in peace with the whites and bring up their children in white ways. Cherokee actions in such ways were a model for the Creek to follow. They would do the same as the Cherokee. They appealed to the whites for justice and magnanimity. The Creek wanted the same rights and privileges that the white man had. No blood would be spilt by the Indians against the whites of the Southeast.

This quieted things. Actually the whites did not want the Indians to have their rights. They wanted their land pure and simple. Frightened of Indian attacks, they were eager to see in the Indians a menace. No one knew who started the rumor, but the Indians had a good idea about its origin. It was probably a white one and the Indian was meant to be the victim. After the War of 1812, the Five Civilized Nations were certain that they could not fight the whites and win. Their only avenue was to resist peacefully. [7]

On August 12, 1829, McKenney and his New York Indian Board held a public meeting at which he delivered an eloquent and judicious address that was successful in getting the ball rolling. The administration used Indian educational funds to publish about two thousand copies of a forty-eight page long tract with the proceedings, the talks to the Indians, and the McKenney address. McKenney had the board openly solicit the views of the president. The Indian office official provided Democratic editors notes about the board's proceedings and the official organ of the Dutch church published most favorable articles. A lobby plan was unrolled and Lewis Cass wrote a pro-removal article for the influential *North American Review*. While the Baptist, with its western and southern membership, got aboard the bandwagon, they were countered by articles by Congregationalist leader Jeremiah Evans who denounced the Indian removal because it would drive the Indians out of their lands.

Wishing public support, Jackson became cautious. Informing southern governors that he shared their views on the Indian question, he nevertheless continued to use the army to keep settlers and gold miners off Indian lands. He genuinely wanted peace and a consensus of white support for removal, while he tried to get the Indians to agree to removal. Eaton cautioned the governor of Georgia and told him that action on their point would mean a setback to Jackson plans. [8]

Nearly six months had passed since the inaugural when Jackson had Van Buren write Poinsett to press for a boundary line between the Nueces and the Rio Grande if he could. There were other possibilities. For a smaller payment, Mexicans might draw a line following the Lavaca River, or the Colorado, or the Brazos. The maximum sum was five million dollars. Van Buren and many Americans rationalized this offer to be essential to guard the frontier of the United States and the emporium of New Orleans, which was hardly under threat. There were numerous reasons why Mexico should snap up the offers, but none as far as the Mexicans were concerned. Colonel Anthony Butler of Mississippi influenced the ideas with his report on Texas. Poinsett had too many enemies in Mexico by now and would hardly promote the offers, so Jackson had him recalled, replacing him with Anthony Butler, who soon realized that he must wait to promote the sale offers. [9]

There were several possibilities of a boundary line as if the Americans could not make up their mind. Of course, there were several prices depending upon the territory to be granted. The most inclusive and the most desirable was a line in the desert country between the Rio Grande and the Nueches to the north. Moving northeastward were lines of the Lacava, the Colorado, and the Brazos. Jackson was ready to spend millions to secure a guard for the Mexican frontier, to protect New Orleans, and to secure the navigation of the Mississippi Valley, including the Red River between Texas and Indian territory. This new treaty would also settle a controversy over the Sabine and Neches in east Texas. Neches was in the east and Nueches was in the south.

Americans argued that there would be problems left in case of the settlement of the disputed boundary. The United States would need a large army on the border to prevent large-scale smuggling and to control the Indians. Further, they brought up the disagreements between Texas and Mexico in political issues of the province. Mexico, it was claimed, would not miss the territory desired by the United States and would need the money to be paid. The Mexicans could be persuaded, Jacksonians thought, because they were faced with Spanish hostility and the danger of dismemberment at any rate.

Jackson was kept informed about events in Texas through Colonel Anthony Butler, who was usually accurate. The president replaced Poinsett with Butler shortly afterwards. The former had long ceased to the effective in Mexico City because of the large number of enemies he had made, but still it was a mistake to send the Mississippian Butler. He could do no more. The Mexicans did not wish to lose their province and no one could persuade them otherwise. Both public and press deeply resented Bulter's attempt to buy Texas. It was not for sale. Newspapers in Mexico considered the offer to be an insult to national honor. Still Butler was optimistic. Soon he was to write that General Santa Anna had seized the custom house of Vera Cruz, a leading source for national revenue and led to revolt against President Bustamante. [10]

Governor William Carroll wrote John Ross, Cherokee leader, a letter on August 29, 1829, explaining the president's Indian policy under instruction of the secretary of war. Ross was told that Jackson, as was known, had told them that he wanted the Cherokees to move across the Mississippi to new lands. The idea of this letter was the establishment of a commission to talk to the Indians. Carroll want them to agree to a meeting of such a commission in the near future at such times as was convenient to the governments of the United States and the Cherokees.

Answering Carroll, Ross stated that an executive council had met to discuss the issue. The Indian wishes were to stay in their southern lands. They did not want to leave, Ross wrote. Indeed, they hoped to remain, on the basis of previous agreements made between Indian and whites. Ross was careful to stress the loyalty of the Cherokees to the Americans. They had been loyal throughout the War of 1812 and remained so. [11]

Americans still remember the dangers of the Indians during the War of 1812 and could still be alarmed at the position of the British in relation to the Indians living in the United States. In the September 5, 1919, issue of *Niles Weekly Register*, the editors inserted a news item of the expensive gift giving of the British in Canada and the United States. Some sixty tons of Indian presents were underway for distribution at Amherstsburg and Drummond's island, made up of blankets, striped cotton goods, vermilion, brass kettles, tobacco, guns, trinkets, and items for ornamentation for British Indians. Indians from the United States also appeared to take advantage of gift giving.

Niles editorialized in brackets that "a large body of Indians had passed through Lower Sandusky, Ohio, to receive the presents which are annually provided for them at Malden, in contravention we must believe of those bonds of good faith which the respective governments are bound to observe toward each other. The policy of the British government should be checked by prompt measures, or else the harmony of our Indian relations may be speedily disturbed, and our frontiers rendered to a scene of hostages." This was a disturbing factor given the British use of Indians fifteen or so years earlier, especially in the fall of Detroit. [12]

Rives reached Paris in August of 1829 and discussed the claims with Polignac on the second of November. He noted that the claims have remained long unsettled and if any more time was Ross, they would create dissatisfaction in America and impair Franco-American relations. Polignac said that he feared it had been decided that they had nothing to do with the acts of Bonaparte, but this was false. The American said that it mattered not which government ruled a nation since its acts applied to subsequent governments. The Frenchman noted that he was not familiar with the subject but that what was just must be done. This was to be another conference, but the French did not seem to be in a hurry.

Meanwhile, Rivas attempted to impress the seriousness of the matter, but it took Jackson to stress the point to the attention of the French in his annual message to Congress. He would he said ask nothing that was not closely right and would not submit to that was wrong. The claims were unsatisfied and must be discussed. He sought redress. American newspapers found it too imperial and too bellicose. The London *Morning Herald* was critical and saw in the discursive essay as it said a virtual declaration of war against the French. Jackson had talked of a possible collision between the American and French governments. At this point, the French became cool to which

Rives told Polignac that the American government had no "intention of holding a menace over the head of a foreign power." Polignac was satisfied.

On January 11, 1830, there was some progress. Polignac stated that the United States could not claim compensation under the Berlin and Milan decrees because although they were unjust, they were the law of the land. If the United States considered Napoleon's government to be the lawful government of France, its decrees must be respected. Otherwise, if they were nullities so would be the cession of Louisiana. Rives said that Napoleon was recognized as lawful sovereign of France, and succeeding governments were responsible for its acts. There were two kinds of acts. Some were right and others should not be performed. In the second case, the illegal lows must be corrected and redressed. The Louisiana treaty was first and the Berlin and Milan decrees were of the second case.

Polignac replied that none of the other nations had been recompensated, but Rives was able to say that the effects of the decrees fell almost exclusively on the neutral commerce of the United States. The French premier said it would be impossible to redress all the wrongs of Bonaparte, but suggested discrimination to provide redress to some. Rives said this could not be done. The Frenchman took his stand on this point which the American gave leave for a delay to suit the financial abilities of the French, which were a problem at this time. A partial agreement might have been reached had not Polignac become ill and then was beset by a press of other business, according to one author. Rives obtained the help of the Marquis de Lafayette to get the American case considered in a friendly light in the Paris *Courier Francais* after hostile arguments in the Paris *Constitutionel*.

The American envoy believed that Polignac would not acknowledge the validity of claims under the Napoleonic decrees because he feared that would set a precedent and the French government would be beset by unlimited claims. However, the French leader felt that the payment might be made under peculiar circumstances such as those which were not made by regular prize tribunals or as prescribed by law and so forth. These were to be determined by a mixed commission. When Rives presented claims Polignac noted that they did not take into effect French claims, which should be founded upon the same principles. [13]

---

[1] *Niles Weekly Register*, May 23, 1829. p. 203. Quote on p. 203.

[2] Austin, Stephen F., *Fugitive Letters, 1829-1836: Stephen F. Austin to David G. Burnet*, comp., Tomerlin, San Antonio, Tx: Trinity University Press, 1981, pp. 13-15.

[3] Thomas, *Liberator*, pp. 96-101.

[4] Barker, Anthony J., *Captain Charles Stuart: Anglo-American Abolitionist*, Baton Rouge: Louisiana State University Press, 1986, pp. 2-37.

[5] *Niles Weekly Register*, July 18, 1829, p. 334-335.

[6] *Ibid.*, July 25, 1929, p. 345.

[7] *Ibid.*, August 29, 1829, pp. 12-13.

[8] Satz, *American*, pp. 16-18.

[9] Barker, Eugene C., "President Jackson," *Texas Democracy*, 1936, pp. 36-38.

[10]Barker, Eugene C., in *American Historical Review*, 1907, pp. 789-792.

[11]*Niles Weekly Register*, October 3, 1829, p. 94.

[12]*Ibid.*, September 5, 1929, p. 19. Quote on p. 19. See Wait, Eugene M., *America and the War of 1812*, Commack, NY: Kroshka Books, 1999, for the stirring details of the war and much on the Indians during the war and the rest of the Madison Administration. This is the definitive book on the war and its period and reading it is a fine event in history reading. If you like this book, you will enjoy 1812 even better. Poet Sarah Patton, one of the leading poets of her generation found it vivid and moving. One can smell the gunpowder of the Battle of New Orleans, according to her. There are other fine books in the Age of Lincoln series, the titles of which are tentative at the time of this writing. More still are due out in the future.

[13]McLemore, pp. 53-64.

Chapter 9

California

In August of 1829, Captain Ewing Young led his party from Taos to the land of the Gila, where his earlier trapping crew had been beaten in a battle with the Apaches and turned back. He was now determined to teach the Apaches a lesson, reopen the trail, collect a quantity of furs, and reach California. There were forty-odd men with him when he set forth. Since he had earlier had furs seized by the new governor, Manuel Armijo, who did not recognize the previous governor's license to Young, he decided to avoid as best he could any license or seizure. He had then passed as a trader, but lost his next furs anyway. Now he got a passport from the Mexican minister at Washington and another from Secretary of State Henry Clay. This should safeguard his arrival in Mexican territory in New Mexico and in California with furs.

In order to mislead authorities in New Mexico about his intent and destination, Young took his men north of Taos as if to head for the mountains and the upper Arkansas river. Once in Colorado, he swung into the San Luis valley and went into the southwest, avoiding Santa Fe altogether. Next, they passed through Navajo country and then Zuni land. When they reached the headwaters of the Salt River, the Spanish Salcedo, they had reached the vicinity of the earlier attack. There they stopped and a trap was set. Young had the baggage piled high and his men concealed behind them. The Apache saw the supposedly weak defense as well as could be seen and wanting the goods and weapons, as well as the munitions and the animals, so they attacked from the hills. There they maneuvered to overflow the camp and the Americans rose and fired into their ranks killing from fifteen or twenty Indians before the survivors fled. Blood atonement had been achieved; the trail had been cleared.

They passed various remains of old stone towns, with broken pottery, aqueducts, and disused irrigation ditches down Salt River and laid out their traps for beaver. It was an sometimes narrow river passing through canyons and down from ranges, but when it passed wooded flat land, there were beaver. It was a rich haul there. Before reaching the Gila, they came to the Rio Verde or San Franciso River that they ascended for more beaver pelts. There too they found the ruins of stone houses, fortifications and irrigation ditches, abandoned for centuries. On this stream, Indians stole their traps and killed their animals, but it was a profitable sojourn. At the head of the San Francisco, Young sent back a crew of twenty-two with the pelts to sell in Taos and to buy traps for future operations. He and twenty-one others, including the youthful Kit Carson, continued in the field, to go on to California.

From friendly Indians, Young learned of the stretches of California and of the dry march that would have to be undertaken first and he and his men made their preparations. They hunted and made jerky of their meat. They filled pouched hides with water. Driving their pack animals before them, the men were soon underway through Arizona following the edge of the Colorado Plateau well south of the Grand Canyon. The route was desertland with tableland, rimrock, buttes, and mountain spurs; it was filled with desert vegetation; with its cactus prominent and troublesome. They had a dole of water and were frozen at night; the way was difficult. Their mules led them to water on one occasion. They rested there for two days.

On the desert, they met the hardy Mohaves whom the Patties had met once before and more earlier and later. Then they went further on through more desert until early in 1830, they reached Mission San Gabriel, out from Los Angeles, a welcomed stop after months of hardship. Everything was not clear for they had Mexican officials to deal with and could end up in jail like the Patties had a few years before; following the paths of Jedediah Smith. He tarried shortly at the various missions taking care to avoid the actions of Mexican officialdom. They went up the central valley, and got trapping along the way. Suddenly, they saw signs of other trappers. They then met Peter Skene Ogden with his Hudson Bay Company crew. Since neither would cede the field to the other, they cooperated.

Early in June of 1830, an Indian overseer from Mission San Jose appeared at the trapper camp with his mission Indians. They had just returned from an attempt to gather back some runaways from a village of unchristianized Indians and had been driven out. Coming back, they saw the trappers, and stopped by. After telling his tale, the overseer received a ready response. Young and his men were eager to join in the fray. Half the band, some eleven out of twenty one men with Kit Carson heading it, were detailed to join the overseer's posse and carry the day against the recalcitrant natives. The Christian Indians and Kit and his men headed up the trail and fired upon the village. It required a day of fighting. Before the day was over, the Christians seized and burned the place down. Under fear of death, the defeated natives surrendered the runaways.

Captain Young, Carson, and three others went with the overseer, his men, and his captives to the mission. He showed his passports, told of his numbers, and the addition of one other from the Ogden company, and said he wanted to sell his furs and buy horses. The padre was favorable. A naturalized Mexican, the former Captain John Roger Cooper, met with Young and helped out. Either he or the mission officials arranged the sale of furs to a trading captain at Monterey. They were stored in the Jose Asero ship and money was paid out. Young bought his horses and readied his men for the trip home.

The recently defeated Indians used the cover of night to frighten and steal the horses while they were grazing. Fourteen were recovered on the next morning. Carson and his men were sent out to regain the horses and they followed the trail for one hundred miles into the sierra country. Carson's band charged at the Indians while they were eating horse flesh. Eight natives were killed. The rest escaped and all but five or six horses were captured. The others had been butchered. Three captive children were turned over to the mission. This was the last these Americans saw of those Indians. [1]

Young had his troubles in California after that series of successes. First three Frenchmen tried to mutiny to avoid the debts they had run up with Young. Second and more dangerous, on the way back to Los Angeles, his men had their break and most of them got drunk. By this time, Sergeant Jose Antonio Pico had his orders from San Diego to arrest and hold the Americans. At the time, the Mexican officials had insufficient force to gain the point when Young could not produce a trapper's license. Young had to act quickly before Pico got his reinforcements.

He sent a sober Kit Carson and three fit men with horses and baggage for the trail east. Next, the captain began rounding up the rest of his men. Soon, they were underway but too drunk to obey orders and it was only when one trapper shot a pursuing Irish-Mexican to death, that the pursuers decided to let the Americans go and prevent their individual murder, by the quick killing Americans, good shots as they were from their horses.

The American followed their trail back through the desert. Back in beaver territory they trapped one again. One day, they had a large band of 500 warriors in their camp versus a squad of Americans still in camp while others were trapping. They looked suspicious and had long garments on to conceal weapons. Carson was in charge and decided immediate action was necessary. He briefly prepared his men with a few words. They fingered their rifles. Kit told the Spanish speaking native interpreter that he had to clear out with his men within ten minutes. Any Indian still in camp would be shot. The natives saw the ready weapons of the whites and quietly departed.

Young's group continued trapping, covering the Colorado of the West, and the Gila upstream, where the beavers were. They returned to New Mexico ambushing one Apache band of cattle rustlers and released the horses they could not take or butcher for emergency food. Young sold the beaver with a trader's (not a trapper's) license. Misfortune played its role during the rest of Young's life. He ended up in Oregon and took a civilizing role there before dying on his farm on February 15, 1841. [2]

On September 15, 1829, Mexican President Vicente Guerrero signed a decree liberating slaves in Mexico. He wrote that it was an act of national justice and beneficence. He expected that it would help public tranquillity. It would return to the slaves their natural rights and give them protection under wise and equitable laws. The Mexican government would indemnify the slaveowners in the future when the nation could afford it, but meanwhile, the blacks of Mexico would be free in the confines of the Mexican country. The Anglo-Americans in Texas learned of this new law, but were able to keep their slaves under the idea that the blacks would be contact laborers. Actually, they were still slaves in all but name though the loop hole of this understanding. They would have to wait thirty-six years except for those who escaped to Mexican property.

Slaves in Mexico property were free but they were still subject to debt peonage. The more things change the more they remain the same. Still it was better being a serf rather than a slave. They were serfs in Mexico, but slaves in Texas. Serfs belong to the land, while slaves could be sold. Serfs stayed with their families, but a slave could easily be taken from his family. This was the main difference between serfs and slaves. Mexican serfs were tied down by the debts they incurred and there was no way they could avoid the debt peonage since the situation was arranged so that they paid higher prices than their pay allowed. They were overcharged at the hacienda store. [3]

The president and Van Buren were riding on horseback in Virginia when the question of a minister to the Russian court came up. The assets of the secretary of state were improved by these frequent rides and Van Buren made good use of his time. Since there was no burning issue at the Czar's court, Van Buren suggested quixotic John Randolph of Roanoke for the position. The brilliance of Randolph was beyond question as was his eccentricity. Conservative Old Republicans in Virginia liked Randolph and he was also a favorite of Van Buren's, but however he liked John Randolph, he felt that he could sooner or later turn on Jackson and should be safest abroad at the far reaches of Russia's St. Petersburg. [4]

Randolph's family was the most notable of Virginia families on both sides of the family. His father John Randolph (1742-1775) was the second cousin of his mother, Frances Blad (1752-1788). The elder Randolph died early, before the child was out of infancy. John Randolph of Roanoke was born on June 2, 1773. His mother married again and although John idolized his stepfather at first, his natural bent of alienation was prominent and he was estranged from this amiable man. He was subject to heavy discipline at school, but he was never humbled. During these years, he read heavily in English literature.

In March of 1787, he went to Princeton at age thirteen, but his mother terminal health brought him home in the following year and he did private studying and took up the study of law with Edmund Randolph. With lack of supervision, he drifted off and his education became more and more desultory. His career opened up for him, however, in 1799, he ran for Congress as a Jeffersonian. He did well in a debate with Patrick Henry running for the state senate. John ran the first of a series of elections, remaining in Congress until 1813. Once there, he rapidly became Jefferson's leader in Congress and showed great talents. He supported the Louisiana Purchase, that great opportunity well taken. Eventually here was a breach with Jefferson. By August 15, 1806, he ranged with the open opposition to Jefferson. He opposed the Embargo and the War of 1812. Most importantly, he was suspicious of Clay and bitterly hostile to John Quincy Adams and was the leader of the opposition in an Adams administration. Unwisely, he accepted the ministry to Russia from the hands of Jackson. [5]

On the other hand, the mission to The Hague was significant because the king of the Netherlands was arbiter on the issue of the boundary of Maine-New Brunswick. William

Pitt Preble had been actively involved in that controversy and was a logical choice to continue this work in the Netherlands. Unfortunately Preble came from Maine and had the interests of his state so much at heart that he was injudicious when the king made a decision which was a compromise. Preble was born on November 27 1783. The blind clergyman Rosewcle Messinger prepared him for college and he went to and graduated from Harvard in 1806. He tutored in 1809 and studied law. Next, he was U.S. district attorney and advocated the separation of Maine from Massachusetts. Following this, he was a judge and aided Albert Gallatin in preparing the Northeastern boundary case mentioned above. [6]

Despite his well-known Anglophobia, Jackson handled Great Britain well and with warmth, which took the British by surprise. The relations between the two countries had not recovered from two wars. The British were aware of Yankee expansionism, their desire for Canada, and their acquisition of territory since 1783 in the purchase of Louisiana and diplomatic acquisition of Florida. There was a time of identical interests in Latin America when the British and Americans could go almost hand-in-hand at keeping the rest of Europe out of the Americas. The North Americans had taken the bit in their teeth, but the Europeans were kept out more by British power on the seas than American declarations.

There was, however, above all a competition in commerce between the two peoples and this kept the two, unfriendly rivals. There was enough hostility abroad in the United States and Great Britain to make a third war a possibility. Indeed in 1828, no less a person than the Duke of Wellington expressed his fear that the greatest danger facing Britain was a conflict with the United States. Jackson did not want a war however, and steered away from conflict.

According to some sources, people in Great Britain did not respect America and her political institutions. Democracy was looked upon as a weakness. They had only to look at federal mismanagement in the most recent war to believe that the American system was inherently inept. To them and also to some Americans, Jackson was looked upon as the leader of the mobocracy. Also there was the possibility that state sovereignty could split a fragile union.

On his own part, Andrew Jackson surprised people with his friendly maneuvers, because he made Anglo-American relations his high diplomatic priority. Adams the diplomat had failed to resolve the important questions of the West Indian trade and the Canadian boundary. Jackson did have some advantages. His agents included three capable men. Louis McLane, Van Buren, and Andrew Stevenson. Jackson also had the right attitude of calmness and dispassion.

In a maneuver which irritated Adams' followers, but not the British, Jackson and his team repudiated the Adams position. They would accept the British restrictions of 1825 and settle the question by statutory law. McLane reached London in September of 1829, where he was assured for awhile by rumors of the favored disposition of the Ministry of Earl Grey, but he was disabused when he consulted with Foreign Secretary Lord Aberdeen in mid-October. The two men discussed the protectionism of the West Indian trade and British Corn Laws and of the American Tariff of 1828. The obstacle to talks, Aberdeen said, was the tariff. McLean did not know if it would be lowered or not.

Jackson talked of peace and fair competition. He suggested that there would be mutual respect between the United States and Great Britain. He wanted cordial relations. The American voters, he thought, wanted the same things as he did. *The Times* praised these public sentiments of Jackson. However the Aberdeen-McLane dialogue remained weak and unsatisfactory. McLane gathered information, lobbied, and learned about the problems he faced. [7]

In mid-1829, the trapper James O. Pattie and his father Sylvester Pattie set out on a new expedition into the interior of Mexico, after an accountant had taken the profits of the elder Pattie's profits in managing the copper mine facility and run. He was now starting out all again from square one. The expedition heading out from Santa Fe was made of thirty men and the Patties joined them as individuals. Sylvester gained a license for the company for safe transit through Chihuahua and Sonora provinces. On September 23, 1829, the company named Sylvester Pattie their captain. They found Helay River to be trapped out and sought more beaver on Beaver River.

Early on in the trip, they began to suffer from want of provisions and had to shoot some horses to live. Then, one man and his horse drowned in the river and they had to build a canoe to do the trapping from. James and another trapped the river in this manner, while the rest rode along the banks. On the 26th of October of 1829, a majority split off from the Pattie's and a few others' group. All who were young with the Patties became partners and they took great precaution against an Indian attack, having seen Indian tracks and smoking fires.

The Indians were ready to make an attack if given an opening against the eight outnumbered and not knowing the territory, although better armed. This was insufficient as on the darkest of nights an Indian brave cut the ropes holding the horses and the cries of the Indians frightened them off. The Americans were stranded. Chasing the horse thieves was fruitless since they had divided the horses among themselves and took out for different parts, those clever Indians. The Americans then destroyed the empty village and later happened to kill two of the thieves.

At this point, they built a little fort and set to making canoes enough to carry all that they needed. Along the way, they found it easy to trap a large number of beavers. They met other Indians who knew nothing about clothes or the guns of the trappers. Some of the natives they saw were friendly and some hostile, but the guns made up the difference and more. They had to bury their furs and take forth on foot to discover Mexican settlements. They left behind a tide-struck river mouth, looking for California villages somewhere in the area. Thirsty and tired, they reached the village of a friendly Indian tribe and smoked the peace pipe.

They gained guides to go to California, since one Indian knew Spanish and they knew about the Mexicans. Again they had a raging thirst and had trouble keeping up with the Indian guides. This journey became unbearable and dreadful. Finally, the Americans reached snow water at the foot of a hill and were soon in high spirits. It was then late in

February of 1830. In early March, they reached St. Catherine's in California and were put in jail.

After a week of corn mush once a day dinners, the Mexicans moved them to St. Sebastian mission, in a delightful valley with rich vineyards, a variety of orchards, and many cattle. They protested about the bad food and received better. They were then allowed to hunt for deer, while awaiting a decision about their request for horses with which to return to their own country. Seeing an ocean as a delightful thing with its sea creatures, they had a lot of fun examining the seashore from atop high cliffs. On the second of April, the Mexican official at San Diego to the north, ordered the American to be brought to him, and they saw many rich and cultivated missions where they were entertained. One priest gave Sylvester Pattie a saddle mule.

The general at San Diego accused them of being spies for the Spanish who wished to reconquer the country. He tore their passports from the governor at Santa Fe into pieces. Pattie and his men denied this charge. Despite or perhaps because of their denial, they were all put in separate cells. While still in imprisonment, the elder Pattie died and was buried. Finally, they were released to go pick up the furs at the mouth of the Colorado River and return to sell them to the Mexicans, all to no avail because the furs when found were spoilt. They had to return to San Diego, where James Ohio Pattie was kept as a hostage. A smallpox epidemic hit California and the general released the American in order to get Pattie to vaccinate the people of California. In time, he returned to the United States by ship and land. [8]

---

[1]Sabin, Edwin L., *Kit Carson Days, 1809-1868, Rev ed, New York: The Press of the Pioneers, 1935, pp. 37-56.*

[2]*Ibid.*, pp. 56-64.

[3]*Niles Weekly Register*, November 28, 1829, p. 219.

[4]Belohlavek, *Eagles*, pp. 29-30.

[5]*Dictionary of American Biography*, VIII (1), 363-365.

[6]Belohlavek, *Eagle*, p. 30; *Dictionary of American Biography*, VIII (1), 184.

[7]Belohlavek, *Eagle*, pp. 53-57.

[8]Pattie, pp. 132-176, 183, 191ff.

Chapter 10

WALKER'S APPEAL

There was at this time, an old clothes shop in the city of Boston, whose owner was to stir up proslavery feeling in the South. He was the free-born African American David Walker, who had come to that city from Wilmington, North Carolina. In September of 1829, he published his *Walker's Appeal* that called upon black men to rise up from the depths of their degradation and kill the whites in mass. It was necessary to kill or be killed to establish their freedom. Slaveholders had been most cruel and now was the time to overthrow slavery. Southerners had feared a servile war and when they found copies of this in African American hands in several Southern states, they overreacted with laws to combat any distribution of such writings among the slaves and freemen of their section. They put further restrictions on free African Americans in their states.

William Lloyd Garrison spoke out against Walker's program of insurrection. He was a peaceful man and in the second issue of his newspaper, he was to deprecate both the spirit and tendency of the appeal. Being against rebellion, he advocated submission and peace. Since many free African Americans read his new journal, he was striking for an audience who might read Walker, but whom he probably knew would not act for they were law-abiding Christians. Garrison's appeal was to conscience on the emotional plane. However, like Walker, he wanted immediate action and even urged the slaves to strike for God and vengeance now. Whether this meant violence or not, the Southerners could see no difference in Walker and Garrison, especially after Nat Turner. There was a conflict in Garrison's views but he did not as the Southerners thought wish for mass murder by African Americans like Walker. [1]

For more on Walker, we have the following. Walker distributed his *Walker's Appeal in Four Articles together with a preamble, to the Coloured Citizens of the World*. Walker was born to a free black woman and a black slave. Because his mother was free, David was free. He learned to hate slavery and as a young boy went north to Boston where he gained an education, helped his fellow man, and finally wrote his pamphlet. Walker began by showing that the Egyptians treated the Hebrews better than white Americans treated their slaves. He next proved that the whites of America treated the black slaves more cruelly than the Spartans did the Helots and that Roman slaves had more rights and opportunities than American slaves. Still, he recognized the injustice of all slavery.

In his second article, Walker noted that the slaves were kept divided and noted the consequence of that in Haiti where whites slaughtered blacks. He deplored the cruelty of the whites and the method of setting blacks against one another. Particularly offensive was black injustice against blacks, created at the command of whites. He preferred death to slavery and knew that the whites wanted them for slaves and would kill to secure them. American whites had wanted African Americans kept in ignorance and wanted the slaves to believe that God made them to be slaves for all time. Next, he told about the suppression of religion for the slaves except for sermons stating that God made blacks to be slaves.

There were many reports of African Americans having copies of the Walker work. Noteworthy were those in Savannah, Richmond, Georgia, and New Orleans, but there were others. Two missionaries were jailed because they had a copy and had admitted some African American children into their Indian school. Southern legislators reacted by passing laws against the education of African Americans and penalties for passing pamphlets such as Walkers were made. Quarantine laws against the arrival of free blacks were passed. Various emancipated slaves were required to leave Louisiana and North Carolina. [2]

That fall, Captain Nicholas Brown sailed the brig *Francis*, which belonged to the merchant Francis Todd from Garrison's home town of Newburyport. It carried a cargo of slaves bound for work on a Louisiana sugar plantation. The African Americans had been terror struck over their destination towards the slave gangs in that Southern state. Indeed, it was terrible work. They had fled to the woods, where they were recaptured and driven to the ship. The abolitionist editor, Garrison attacked Todd and Brown in the *Genius of Universal Emancipation* of that November, but he did not know about the attempted escape. Garrison used harsh words such as "thick infamy" and "nefarious business" in describing the shipment of slaves. Todd sued Garrison and Lundy for libel.

In February of 1830, the state of Maryland acted and brought the two men to trial. Garrison and Lundy found a liberal lawyer in Charles Mitchell who donated his services. The prosecution argued that the slaves had been well treated aboard the ship with freedom below decks and allowed prayer meetings. Todd and Brown, the prosecution argued, had broken no law and the only reason for the Garrison press attack was his fanaticism and virulence. Michell spoke of a higher law and attempted to gain the sympathies of the jury, but they came back in fifteen minutes with a verdict of guilty.

The judge fined Garrison, who was the sole author, fifty dollars and cost. Lacking the money necessary, Garrison was imprisoned for six months. Lundy tried to get the money for the fine but failed and his friend accepted the martyrdom with meekness. It was not an unpleasant confinement since he had the freedom of the jail and ate with the jailer and his family. Garrison wrote an eight-page pamphlet on the trial, about its unfairness, the prosecutor's vindictiveness, and his own determination to continue with his anti-slavery crusade. By June, he learned that over one hundred newspapers and magazines had praised him and the idea of the freedom of the press. Shortly, Arthur Tappan paid his fine and the jailer released Garrison after forty-nine days of jail. [3]

Jackson was asked to attend the opening of the Chesapeake and Delaware canal on a date decided by the president, but Jackson replied that he was unable to come. In his letter, Jackson wrote of the importance of the occasion and the happiness of the event. Unfortunately he could not attend because of the press of work. He needed full time for work on public business, particularly upon congressional matters pending the opening of Congress in several weeks. Mentioning the goodness of the project, he assured the managers of the canal that he wished for its success. [4]

Elections were held in Maryland in October of 1829 both for Congress and the state legislature. In the House of Delegates some thirty nine Jackson supporters and forty anti-Jacksonians were elected to high offices. In the city of Baltimore, a stronghold of Democratic beliefs, Jacksonians won the two seats at stake. For the state senate, eleven Jacksonians and four anti-Jacksonians gained election. It was a close election. For Congress, six Jacksonians and four anti-Jacksonians won election to the national House of Representatives. [5]

Two anti-Jacksonians won election in Vermont. Running for governor, Samuel C. Crafts won 14,325 votes against Anti-Masonic Heman Allen's 7,346 votes and Jacksonian Joel Doolittle's 3,973 votes. In his race for lieutenant governor, Henry Olin won 19,973 votes as against the Jacksonian candidate's 4,481 votes. Meanwhile, in New Jersey, ten Jacksonian councilmen were elected to four anti-Jacksonian men. Thirty-three assemblymen favoring Jackson won election there versus ten anti-Jacksonian candidates for the state assembly. Elections were also held elsewhere. [6]

The general assembly of Virginia had passed an act calling forth a convention for the winter of 1829-30 in the state. Each senatorial district was to send four delegates to meet in Richmond on October 5, 1829. This was done in a fashion to bring forth the best citizens of the state and when the convention first met on the fifth at noon, the galleries and the lobby were filled with distinguished men from the South and foreign countries. James Madison called the meeting to order and nominated James Monroe as president of the convention. John Marshall seconded it. The distinguished choice was unanimously voted and confirmed. [7]

There were a number of diplomatic moves at this time. The first was the drawing up of a treaty with France on claims. A large amount was decided upon and the Beaumarchais heir claims against the United States were deducted. The final offer of $4.6 million was satisfactory. The heirs got $270,000 and all seemed well. The American Senate ratified the claims treaty and most Americans were overjoyed. Rives returned to the United States a hero. He arrived in October of 1832. The French parliament refused to ratify the treaty. It resisted pressure until 1836 to get the treaty passed and to make payments. Charge d'Affaires Thomas L.L. Brent of Virginia negotiated a small claims treaty with Portugal, two years before the fall of Miguel. Because of the revolutionary turmoil of Portugal, payment was delayed over five years. The government of Queen Maria II paid it off. [8]

In late October, Americans read about Lafayette's triumphant trip in France. The French and American hero had gone across several provinces to see his granddaughter in Lyons. The trip showed he was as much a hero in his own country of France as he had been in the United States where he had fought for the Americans in the Revolution. They also learned of Russian advances in the Russian war against the Turks. It was reported that Adrianople, Iniada, and Rodesto had fallen. Russians under General Paskewitch were besieging Tokat and Choumla and had their sights upon Constantinople. [9]

[1]Sydnor, C.S., *Sectionalism*, 1948, pp. 222-225.

[2]*"One Continual Cry" David Walker's Appeal to the Colored Citizens of the World*, ed. Aptheker, Herbert, New York: Humanities Press, 1965, *passim*.

[3]Thomas, *Liberator*, pp. 107-113.

[4]*Niles Weekly Register*, October 24, 1829, p. 131.

[5]*Ibid.*, October 17, 1829, p. 122.

[6]*Ibid.*, October 24, 1829, p. 132.

[7]Grigsby, Hugh B., *The Virginia Convention of 1829-30*, 1854, 1969 edition, pp. 4-6.

[8]Behohlavek, *Eagle*, pp. 81, 91-125.

[9]*Niles Weekly Register*, October 24, 1829, p. 133.

Chapter 11

CONTEST

There was a contest between two good Democratic Republicans in the Tennessee Valley of Alabama in the fall of 1829. They were in opposition on the issue of donation of land for the Muscle Shoals canal. Clement Comer Clay, a lawyer and large planter, was in favor of a canal around the important rapids of the river. He would not give favor to the residents who had lost the land. Before this, he had been for land relief and settlement of the land, supporting Henry Clay. Now he was a Jacksonian.

Captain Nicholas Davis was still for land relief in that election. He opposed the canal in this election although he had been a director of the canal company and was later to become an internal improvement Whig. His views were not contradictory, however, since he was against the canal for the reason that it took land away from those who would pay to repossess it and restore their farms lost to the government because of their defaults on debt. The two newspapers supported the canal. Clay was shortly to win the election and later a canal began being constructed only to be abandoned after a few years. [1]

In the *Working Man's Advocate* of the seventh of November in 1929, the editor wrote in an editorial that Americans were "fast approaching those extremes of wealth and extravagance on the one hand, and ignorance, poverty and wretchedness on the other, which would eventually terminate in those unnatural and oppressive distinctions which exist in the corrupt governments of the old world." Working men in Philadelphia had voted for the anti-Jacksonian part. They did not see him championing their interests and indeed Jackson did not. He was a planter and a frontiersman and had those views for most of his life. He knew little of the labor of the cities and industries. Their views were too radical for him and he stated little in regard to their needs during his eight years. [2]

The editor of the *United States Gazette* offered a prize for the best essay on the "inadequacy of the wages generally paid to seamstresses, spoolers, spinners, shoe-binders, to procure food, raiment, and lodging." These workers were female and the poor payment in return for work was based upon their happiness and morals, an idea which was to be the subject of much of the essay. Also, the editor wanted to test the accuracy of the idea that young working women were forced to choose between dishonor and a want of common necessaries. He wanted to hear of the essayists' views of answers to the problem if there were any. Writers had the deadline of the end of the year of 1929. [3]

Upon reading Jackson's message to Congress, New York Federalist intellectual John Pintard reacted strongly to the segment on the Bank. Jackson had "thrown an apple of discord into our moneyed market, by recommending a National Bank on the expiration in 1837, of the charter of the existing U.S. Bank. He has taken unwarranted ground in expressing an opinion the exercise of which cannot fall to his lot, and prejudging a question fraught with, at best, great difficulties. The instant effect in this city was to depreciate the value of the U.S. Bank stock 5 to 6 1/2 percent. A National Bank would become a political engine subject to the control of every successive administration, and would become a curse instead of a blessing. The country can never submit to such a measure. Other parts of his long talk are speculative and objectionable. But to these subjects, I can only give a passing review, and leave to politicians the field of censure or of praise, looking forward to a better world, where all is perfection." [4]

Jackson and the governmental agents involved thought Indian removal would give the Indians four major benefits. First, those, who could not realize that the Indians certainly would be pushed backward across the continent in the future, stated that the Indians would have a fixed and permanent boundary far from the white man's civilization. They would be isolated from corrupt influences from gamblers, prostitutes, and whiskey vendors. The Indians would have self government and it would give them opportunities to acquire ideas and knowledge of civilization and work.

When it came time to remove the Indians, the Americans were not interested in the rights of treaties with the Indian. The government reacted rather harshly, selling contracts to feed and transport the Indians to the cheapest contractor that would often almost starve the Indians to death in order to make a large profit and go to church on Sundays. Nothing was done to provide medicines in advance either.

Permanent and fixed boundaries could not be designed since expansion continued. The Indians could not be protected against corrupt influences. Many Indians were wed to liquor and could not be protected. The war department tried to interfere with Indian self-government. Indians could not adjust well to civilization because many were hampered by always living in temporary locations and it was easier to just collect interest on annuity. The Chippawa Indian George Capway complained that "no sooner have the Indian gone on and made improvements, and our children began to like to go to the school houses which have been erected, than we hear the cry of the United States government" that they wanted the poor Indian's land. The Indian thus lost all that he had earned or learned. [5]

President Andrew Jackson presented his speech to the Congress before this body through his private secretary Andrew Donelson. Donelson, who had been named after the president and remained most of the rest of his life a close friend. The secretary later became a diplomat for some years. In the opening of the speech, Jackson noted happily that America was at peace and was doing well in the field of "general welfare and progressive improvement." The various difficulties in foreign affairs were expected to undergo successful negotiation. He saw a friendly competition with Great Britain.

The differences between the United States and France on the matter of reparations would need further discussion to find redress. Discussions with Spain, he hoped, would end in commercial settlements for the future of Spanish American trade and for indemnity. Relations between Russia and America were good, although "her recent invasion of Turkey awakened a lively sympathy for those who were exposed to the desolation of war." Showing a tinge of support for the Russians as the civilized country in the war, he anticipated "that the result will prove favorable to the cause of civilization, and to the progress of human happiness."

With the experience of 1824 in view, the president proposed an amendment to throw out the electoral college and the use of the house in cases where no one had the superior electoral vote in selecting a president. He wanted a direct election with run-off campaigns of the two leading candidates in cases where one did not get a clear majority. Tied to this was the provision that the president should serve only one term. The term might be either four years or six years.

Following this, he spoke in favor of rotation in office of officials, justifying changes in offices and in favor of free enterprise in areas of agriculture, commerce, and manufactures. Excessive regulation would harm the economy, he felt. Caution was necessary in this important area of the peoples' efforts for business in the three basic fields. He was for the benefit of the whole according to this speech.

Jackson could speak also of the governmental surplus and the payment of the public debt since government was bringing in more than it was spending. Indeed, this became somewhat of an embarrassment, but Jackson saw in it strong advantages. Once the debt was taken care of, Jackson felt that the federal government could do more to benefit the well being of the nation. The president said highways and canals could then be built by the central government, while the states could spend money on education. In a seeming contradiction to this, he foresaw the use of surpluses to be turned over to the states for their public expenditures.

Next, Jackson stated that delinquent accounts in the treasury should be moved to the attorney general's office for collection. There were some extenuating circumstances in these debts. He would not have the attorney general press for debts when the result would be to devastate the poor with debts out of proportion with his finances. In addition, the limitation of law should be changed so that accounts could be collected with two years from the time the debtor was accused or left office. These would prevent many scoundrels from escaping collection of their fraudulent debts.

In this address to the Congress, Jackson gave his view of the Indian problem. In clear terms the president stated that the Choctaws, the Cherokee, and the Creek should be moved beyond the Mississippi River for their own protection. He felt that this would preserve the tribes from extinction. White influence had killed other tribes and these three tribes would be safer beyond the river. [6]

Jackson had not been president a full year when talk was raised about the next election and who would follow that general in his high office. The president had expressed his opinion that one term was enough for any president to serve and for this reason some of the discussion of the next presidency was about the 1832 election. A writer in the New York *Courier and Inquirer* tried to dampen the talk. It was too easy to discuss the question of presidential elections. Such agitation was unnecessary. Indeed, Jackson was unquestionably the choice of most of the people over anyone else. If Jackson's health allowed it, the editor felt that Jackson would no doubt consent to running and administrating the nation for another term.

Westerners expressed the hope that New York would ignore her claims for a piece of the political pie and not promote Martin Van Buren, then secretary of state and the logical successor. The *Courier* dealt with this idea strongly and editorialized that when the time came to act, the politicians and people of New York State would be true to New York and the party. New York claims were great and well understood. They would promote Van Buren and expected help from other states whom New York leaders had long been in concert with. Whether these claims were followed or not, Van Buren could stand on his own two feet because of his talents and qualifications. The reader was informed that Van Buren's ability and his "stern republican principles and unwavering consistency; his industry and legal acquirements; his knowledge of men and measures-- unite to place him before the people as a suitable candidate for the presidency, when the proper time shall have arrived." *The United State Telegraph* responded that this article in the New York paper was indiscreet. [7]

Word reached the American people by way of *Niles' Weekly Register* of the progress of industry in March of 1829. The Dismal Swamp canal was renewing the business of Norfolk and providing contact to internal Virginia with other seaports through Norfolk. Nearby on the James River, the boiler of the steam boat exploded, killing one man and critically wounding three others. The accident was a relatively rare one considering the large traffic on the river.

The editors reported on advances on the making of spikes. Recently invented machinery was manufacturing spikes at Troy, New York. The machinery produced cheaper and tougher spikes than those previously made by hand. One man with the new machine could make a ton of them, instead of fifty pounds in the old way. In Pittsburgh, at the same time, a factory at Beaver Falls was making iron wire of varying sizes from the finest to the thickest. Production reached a full ton a week. It was located at a good site for the use of the right materials. Previously attempts at building iron wire factories failed because of the lack of the right materials for its production. [8]

As a young man, Jackson had been an important land speculator in the west and allied himself with the party of the great speculator William Blount. He gained control of large grants of land on credit and could look forward to great success when the panic of 1797 swept away his land holdings. His mercantile business had led him into debt until in 1804, he lost even his home plantation and moved to a new plantation. He labored for years to regain his equilibrium and restore his financial fortunes. Having lost heavily, he was a very chastened young man and was promptly alienated against speculation and credit. This stayed with him the rest of his life and was his personal reason for being against paper money and the banks, although he never admitted it.

His subsequent alliance with banking interests was circumstantial. The Blount party had control of the two banks in Tennessee and although Jackson was anti-bank, he stayed with this group for personal and political reasons. They later tried to influence him in favor of the United States Bank, but Jackson would have none of it. He opposed the paper economy and banks as a matter of principle and thought banks favored the rich class whose interests he was not favorable toward, although he had been tied to an aristocratic party in Tennessee. He was a planter and thought much as that class did, but those above him were villains in his philosophy of life.

Jackson was a hard money man ever since his unfortunate brush with bankruptcy and this determined his personal attitude although the anti-bank interests he was to support had other reasons. These reasons he was to support for political reasons, but his primarily motive was personal. He took his people with him. Those who opposed Jacksonian banking policy were soon to oppose Jackson himself. Living in a world of black and white and not colors, Jackson was a friend or foe and not indifferent.

He was particularly opposed to the United States Bank because he did not see a need for a national bank and he thought it was allied with the rich business interests of Philadelphia, his particular enemies in his democratic view. The people were not represented by banks and were not benefited by banks. Paper money and banking was odious. Unfortunately, Jackson's experiences blinded him to the reasons for the existence of the United States Bank. He failed to follow his dislike of banks by an attack on state banks because in his view of government that matter was up to the states themselves and because he needed them for reasons of government financial activities as well as Van Buren's pro-bank policy. Jackson was very considerate of Van Buren's view throughout and Van Buren was one of the few strong influences upon the president. [9]

Closer associates were Kendall and Blair, who "favored currency inflation only as a necessary expedient to aid hard-pressed farmers and mechanics. They were moderates who sought to ensure public control over the money supply through government operated banks or private banks subject to governmental regulations. Indeed, both men had latent misgivings about all paper currency, a hard money bias that was of necessity suppressed during the emergency of the depression years but which became increasingly manifest during the 1830s." Both men had great influence with Jackson who also was anti-bank in economic philosophy and proved of good use to him in combating the Bank. The rest of the Jacksonian adviser wanted him to leave the Bank of the United States alone. [10]

---

[1]Dupre, Daniel, "Ambivalent Capitalists on the Cotton Frontier: Settlement and Development in the Tennessee Valley of Alabama," *The Journal of Southern History*, LVI (May 1990), 228-229.

[2]Sullivan, William A., "Philadelphia Labor during the Jackson Era," *Pennsylvania History*, XV (October 1948), 308, 317. Quote on p. 308.

[3]*Niles Weekly Register*, November 14, 1829, p. 178.

[4]Pintard, John, *Letters From John Pintard to his Daughter Eliza Noel Pintard Davidson, 1816-1833*, 4 vols., New York Historical Society, 1941, III, 111-112. Quote on pp. 111-112.

[5]Satz, Ronald N., "Indian Policy in the Jacksonian Era. The Old Northwest as a Text Case," *Michigan History*, LX (Spring 1976), pp. 73, 82-92. Quote on pp. 91-92.

[6]*Niles Weekly Register*, December 12, 1829, pp 247-248 (Quotes on pp. 247, 248); *Dictionary of American Biography*, III (1) 363-364.

[7]*Niles Weekly Register*, January 2, 1830, p. 300. Quote on p. 300.

[8]*Ibid.*, March 21, 1829, p. 55; March 28, 1829, p. 66.

[9]Sellers, Charles G., Jr., "Banking and Politics in Jackson's Tennessee, 1817-1827," *Mississippi Valley Historical Review*, pp 61-84.

[10]Latner, Richard B., "A New Look at Jacksonian Politics," *Journal of American History*, LXI No. 4 (March 1975), 945, 951. Quote on p. 945.

Chapter 12

THE BANK

Jackson's hostility to the Bank of the United States requires these observations. First was his western dislike for the east and nothing typified the most objectionable aspect of the east more than the Bank. Philadelphia and New York City were the big city business communities on which the westerners could blame their ills. Second was the state banks' dislike of the limitation set upon them by the operations of the Bank of the United States. The smaller banks wanted a big boom atmosphere all of the time and their officials were great speculators and wanted to see the conservative competition they saw in the Bank ended. The third observation was perhaps the most important. Martin Van Buren and his New Yorkers were moved by opposition to the bank and had their effect upon the president in strong hostility to the Bank.

It was a matter of rivalry. The state banks and their supporters wanted to do away with the competition and the Bank was their chief rival. The state banks proprietors controlled the newspapers and got support for their aims. The Bank's curb on the smaller banks created an intense jealousy. The chief curb was to prevent and enlargement of banking issues beyond the limits of prudence. With certain advantage including the governmental depositing of funds, the Bank would throw its weight around. The smaller banks wanted these advantages too and eventually were to get them. Bankers opposed to Jackson gave him their support to bring down the wrath of government on the Bank of the United States. [1]

Nicholas Biddle, at the helm of the Bank had been led to believe that Jackson was friendly toward the Bank, although the president had already tried to get Jacksonian Democrats on the board and Biddle had opposed the idea. The bankers around Biddle tended to think in rosy terms. They thought the bank to be well managed and high in the esteem of important and acknowledgeable men. For them, their enemies, including Duff Green of the *Telegraph,* were mischief makers. Green was popular and the bankers of the United States Bank and their friends did not take ample warning from his pro-Jackson attacks on their bank. Biddle did not fear anything from Jackson and could not see why anyone in power would want to turn back to the pre-Bank days. Contrary to what Jackson was told, the Bank did not meddle in politics. [2]

Jackson had stated that he always had been against the Bank of the United State and this was probably true. It was equally true that his administration tried to gain political control of the Bank. Biddle's refusal to bow to pressure resulted in a greater opposition from Jackson and his men. There was a meeting in Richmond in October where there was an attempt to commit the party to an attack on the Bank. Jackson was careful, because there was not enough anti-Bank sentiment to be bold.

Meanwhile, Biddle had been reassured. Major William B. Lewis had written Biddle for Jackson that the president was gratified that Biddle would not tolerate making his bank political and he was glad to learn that there had been no partiality in the election campaign from the Bank. Jackson made great efforts to lull Biddle, who believed Jackson, not being a liar himself. Biddle met the president and was impressed. An official of the Bank visited next and reported back that Jackson was mild and friendly. William B. Lewis tried to get Biddle support in the H. Toland matter, but Biddle would not fall for that. Jackson soon acted. [3]

President Jackson submitted his condemnation of the Bank to Congress and was surprised when both committees rejected his attack. They were close to the subject and disagreed with his hostile statements. They listened instead to Biddle. The bank president was not without important allies. Samuel Smith had been an opponent of the Bank, but had since changed his mind. Now he was chairman of the Senate committee with jurisdiction over banks. He found Biddle's bank good for the economy. He was right. [4]

An early ally of Jackson in the House, James Buchanan had early sought opportunity. On February 6, 1813, he had written a letter of application to Pennsylvania Attorney General Jared Ingersoll. Later, in a fourth of July oration of 1815, he said that the Jeffersonians had "begun with the destruction of the navy. It had been supposed by the federal administrations, that a navy was our best defense. From the locality of our country, and from the nature of such a force, they knew it would be particularly calculated to protect our shores from foreign invasion, and to make us respected by the nations of the world; without, like a standing army, endangering our liberties. It was also foreseen by them, that without a navy, our commerce would be exposed, as a rich temptation, to the avarice of all nations; and in consequence of our own weakness, we would be subjected to constant insults and injuries upon the ocean, without the power of resistance. It had, therefore, been their policy, gradually to erect a navy, and they had built a great number of vessels at the time when the first democratic administration came into power."

"At that moment the scene changed." Jefferson had promised an end to taxation. If they could not follow this promise with results they would lose public favor. They cut expenditures by selling the national ships. In this disarmament they "left commerce unprotected and invited insult and injustice from abroad." By now this had subsided and the War of 1812 had taught the need of a navy.

"The democratic administration next declared war against commerce." Jefferson's acts hurt the economy. Prosperity was given a serious blow as we have seen in an earlier book. At this point, Buchanan exaggerated and saw the hand of Napoleon in all of this. He blamed the partiality toward France as the reason. This was not true. It was the peaceful aims of Jefferson that led the way. When there was war, there had been a disaster. It is clear that at this time, Buchannan was a Federalist, just like in Jackson's years he was a Democrat.

He closed with a peace that required Washingtonian policies to enjoy it. He was for a strict neutrality and a strong navy. We must no longer follow a visionary like Jefferson. Commerce must be protected. Americanism must be exalted and followed. There must be no more foreign influence of any kind. Foreign influence had always been the bane of republics. Experience should teach something. Washington's policy would bring a national wealth and greatness. He ended in a reference to the Fourth of July.

On January 9, 1823, Buchanan spoke in Congress, of which he was now a member, against the rivalries of the government. He stated that "nice distinctions have been drawn between a just confidence in the Executive departments, and an unreasonable jealousy of their conduct on the one side; and, on the other, between that, confidence, and a belief in their infallibility. Extremes in such a case are very dangerous. Whilst unreasonable jealousy of men in power keeps the public mind in a state of constant agitation and alarm, a blind reliance upon their infallibility may enable them to destroy the liberties of the people before they are aware of the existence of danger. At the same time, therefore, I trust that I am one of the last men in the House who would consent to establishing the office of dictator in the Commonwealth, or to believing in the infallibility of mortals in politics more than in religion. Yet, I should think it wrong to withhold from a public officer that degree of confidence when he assumes that he has acted correctly, until the contrary appears. It ought to be a maxim in politics, as well as in law, that an officer of your Government, high in the confidence of the people, shall be presumed to have done his duty, until the reverse of the proposition is proved."

For him, the bankruptcy bill was of an important issue. He was against extending it to everybody since it would sanction the violation of contracts. He was against it even as protection for merchants. He did feel it might become war sometime in the future. It failed then, but in time became law. He became a supporter of Jackson and wrote to him, in a friendly letter that "in Pennsylvania, amongst a vast majority of the people, there is but one sentiment" about the election of 1824. They submitted patiently and prepared for a major change in the next election. Jackson was more popular than before in the state as events were to go. The only thing about Jackson that worried them was news and rumors of his temper. However, his prudence before and after the election had dissipated that fear.

He was for reform but he did not think it was time for it in January of 1828. He probably expected it to come with Jackson's election. Reform would not come in a big sweep. Each abuse would have to be rooted out one at a time, until there were no more of them left. On this account, he was against a resolution for reform in the Senate. [5]

Looking ahead in 1826, the statesmen of the Republic foresaw the creation of a governmental surplus by rising government income. In late 1826, Senator Mahlon Dickerson of New Jersey proposed the distribution of federal funds to the states, expecting them to aid internal developments and education. Dickerson and others feared the institution of lower tariffs (the other alternative). In his December 1829 message Jackson proposed the granting of excess funds to the states on the basis of the ratio of their representation.

There was some criticism of Jackson's suggestion, but these were limited to the method of distribution. The president was soon to change his mind. He next proposed governmental economy and a reduction of the tariff. This was in line with his views on limited government as the previous idea had been on his western general favoring of internal improvements. Jackson's difficulty was that of surplus money would be embarrassing to his administration. Large government distribution or expenditure was basically objectionable and Jackson took what was to him, the easy way out. Opposed to a low tariff bill wanted by Jackson, Henry Clay finally got a bill for distribution passed Congress only to find it vetoed by Jackson. [6]

In New York City, the common people did not have the power to elect the mayor in 1829, but gained that right in 1834. Even after 1834, the people elected their mayor and other top officials from among the wealthy merchant and professional class in the city. There were a few artisans who were councilmen, but they amounted to less than ten percent of the total. As the years progressed, the city council contain a smaller percent of rich men in its numbers, but still large. In 1826, the rich made up two-thirds of the council, in 1831, one half, in 1840 two fifths, and in mid-century one quarter. This change was due to declining interest among the wealthy for public service. The well to do took a larger interest. Ordinary men took less interest in political affairs and had less time for the work involved in politics.

One of the big results of rich man control were the low taxes which provided New York City with insufficient funds to meet the problems facing the city. The elite would not tax themselves heavily, but they would lease city property to their members at cheap rates. In addition, the wealthy made sure that the districts in which they lived had the best streets and city services. Public interest paid second fiddle to private interest. [7]

In the years that Jackson spent in the presidency were years spent in a sparse city with large open spaces in which serious business was performed among a citizenry which also had a social life. The roads were muddy and dusty depending upon the season, hard for a newcomer to find his way around. They were also unlighted and at times had to give way to traveling across vacant lots in Washington.

There were three hotels in town. Gadsby's was the most popular among men who preferred comfort. It was near the capitol and was noted for clean beds, excellent service, and lordly hospitality. There were plenty of servants and fine wines were available. Next was the Indian Queen run by Jesse Brown. The cost was a dollar and a quarter a day including access to a table of decanters of brandy, rum, and gin. Fuller's was the third with a main house and annexes.

The families of congressional members usually stayed at home in the states and away from Washington. Sometimes families would lease a house for from $50 to $800 a year. Most formed messes at rooming houses for men of like views. They slept and ate in such messes and conceived plans of strategy for fights in Congress. The friendships made there lasted a lifetime. Because sessions did no last all year, the congressmen could spend part of the year at home with their families in their native states.

Congressmen, presidents, and justices found racing, cockfighting, and gambling great fun to be indulged in at all times. The leaders of this particular administration drank heavily. Liquor was available at messes, hotels, and bars strung out on thoroughfares. Drunkenness on the floors of Congress was at times commonplace. Women had a strong place in Washington and keeping up with Paris fashions was a main interest in their lives. Hair dressers were in demand for the women also. [8]

[1]Hammond, Bray, 1957, p. 305, 355, 357.

[2]Biddle, Nicholas, *The Correspondence of Nicholas Biddle dealing with National Affairs, 1807-1844*, ed. McGrane, Reginald C., Boston: Houghton Mifflin, 1919, pp. 61-62, 66-72, 75-79.

[3]Hammond, pp. 370-373; Biddle, *Correspondence*, pp. 79-88.

[4]Hammond, pp. 374-377.

[5]Buchanan, James, *The Works of James Buchanan*, ed. Moore, John Bassett, Philadelphia: J.B. Lippincott, 1908, I, *passim*. Quotes on pp. 2, 3, 12.

[6]Bourne, Edward G., *The History of the Surplus Revenue of 1837*, New York: G.P. Putnam's Sons, 1885, pp. 6-11.

[7]Pessen, Edward, "Who Has Power in the Democratic Capitalistic Community? Reflections on Antebellum New York City," *New York History*, LVIII No. 2 (April 1977), 129-156.

[8]Bowers, Claude G., *The Party Battles of the Jackson Period*, 1922, pp. 1-30.

Chapter 13

PARTY STRIFE

D aniel Webster believed that party strife and the resort to the people were not desirable in the Republic. Instead, he wanted a government by private, respectable and respected men who would be chosen from among the elite to lead the Republic. He believed he was that special man who should lead in an era which became known by the name of another leader, Jackson. Not elected to give in to the concept of a party government, he struggled during the Jackson years for his concept of an elitist government. It was not until ten years afterwards that he bowed to reality and used party methods and public canvassing, assured at last that by then he had no other alternative if he wished to become president which he most certainty, did. As late as 1833, Webster considered himself "one of the great before his country." Eventually, he became one of the humblest in order to obtain the presidency. He was never able to manage it, but in 1829, there was a good chance that he might follow Jackson or Jackson's successor into the office of the presidency. [1]

Webster counterpoise was the elitist Virginia in the South. Virginians were divided at the opening of the years in which Jackson was in the White House. Not only were there various classes ranging from the plantation few through the slave many, but different views on economic and politics. There was the quest for wealth, well-being or power, and as a result principles and hopes, and various private and public interests clashed. There was a difference between westerners and easterners in the state and between political groups and economic interests. The number one issue was political representation. The western Virginians wanted representation based on white population and not a weighed one based upon population which gave additional votes to Virginians in areas in the east filled with slaves. The slaves were represented but could not vote. Easterners wanted to include slaves so that landed property would have the best of representation, it being believed that propertied men were better and more conservative than the poorer farmers or the landless. Fear of the people or masses and the changes that these poor might demand underlay the ideas of the plantation aristocracy of land and money in the east.

In his January 22, 1829 issue of his *Richmond Enquirer*, editor Thomas Ritchie warned the plantations in the East that events and principles required that all whites have equal representation. This was the basis of all representative government. Ritchie found that the planters had no excuse to give free men in the east more power than free men in the west or to give Warwick votes twelve times the voting power as it did Shenandoah voters. They should not maintain an oligarchy in a democratic disguise. It was necessary to arrange the voting of one man equal to any other in the decisions at the polls. To do otherwise would make representative government a mockery and harm the influence and integrity of the state of Virginia. Representation must be equal and just.

Ritchie then proposed adding non-freeholders to the rank of voters, considering them to have the same equal rights as those who owned land. Still, Ritchie supported the planters in their use of slavery as necessary and right. At the time and especially in the western counties, many Virginians wanted to see slavery abolished. Westerners did give Ritchie support by subscribing to his newspaper. Easterners reacted to the Ritchie voting platform by attempting to erect a pro-eastern press in Richmond and drive Ritchie out of business. The friendship of C.W. Gooch protected Ritchie and the decision in favor of a compromise in the convention of October of 1829 cooled the ardor of Ritchie's opponents and easterners dropped their plans of driving Ritchie out of business.

Early in the Jackson administration, Ritchie was concerned with the situation in Washington. He worked for Democratic unity and advised that Jackson ignore the hordes of office-seekers and establish secretaries to investigate and make recommendations. The Virginian wanted Jackson to buy Texas from the Mexicans in order to gain new lands for slavery and as a step to allay interparty discord. Seeing that a protective tariff was inevitable, Ritchie wanted Southerners to establish factories manned with slaves. He opposed nullificationists, but wanted strict constructionism to prevail. Van Buren was informed by Ritchie that the Maysville veto was a glorious Jackson victory, better than New Orleans. [2]

In South Carolina, political and personal ties determined the affairs of state. There was a unity in the state unlike anywhere else. The same views were shared by most. Friendships were cemented through schools--for the minority that attended schools--and inter-marriages created a community of interests in the ruling class, both rich and middle classes. The rest of the men in the state accepted the power of the few and readily adhered to views established for the benefit of the great planters. A few men, the merchants of Charleston and mountain yeomans disagreed with planter philosophy and power, but they were in the minority and divided.

The dissenters in South Carolina could do nothing. The chief issue of the upland planter and farmer was their aversion to the high tariff necessary for northern industrialization, The chief issue of the tidewater planter was the hatred of the abolitionist campaign. Economic hardship felt by some, relative it might be, caused them to oppose the federal government. The upcountry cotton planters, Charleston mechanics, and Charleston retailers were hurt by bad times and expressed their dismay by fighting for nullification. Prices for upland-cotton dropped faster than consumer goods and the planters dealt with lower purchasing power by borrowing more. Most planters and especially the younger generation were spendthrifts. They lost what the hard work of the blacks earned for them. The oppressor class lived well upon the subjected slave, even in hard times.

However hard times created dangers to the planters of losing their plantations. They had to blame something, so they made a scapegoat of the protective tariff when the real problem was that they could not live within their rich means. White mechanics were angered at competition from slaves but they blamed them instead of the slaveholders. All classes except the slave prayed that tariff reform would save them financially. [3]

The departments of the government were filled with old men who had political pull and the young and vigorous were denied employment. Mrs. Smith wrote the following about a person she was trying to get a job for: "I have tried and other friends had tried, to procure a clerkship for him. Mrs. Porter did her very best and I pursued all manner of persuasion and argument with the kind, good natured secretary of war.--'My dear Madam, what am I to do? When we ask Congress for more clerks in the department and tell them the present number is insufficient for the duties of the office, the reply is, If you continue to fill the offices with *old men,* no number will be sufficient. Get young men and fewer will answer and the work will be better done.' This is too true, the public benefit is sacrificed to private interest and charity. The departments are literally over-stocked with old, inefficient clerks." [4]

Jackson relied upon his friends for his best counsel and they in turn were willing to aid him. The idea of the general being influenced by his aides was discussed at the time of his election. His precarious health and inexperience in government caused some of his supporters to feel that he was not fit for the presidential office. The need of the new president for more experienced hands gave a position of closeness to the president of greater importance in the White House than most presidents. It was to end in a race for influence by Van Buren and John C. Calhoun. [5]

In 1829, a mulatto woman named Elizabeth Cunningham was seized in New York City by a policemen on the claim that she was the escaped slave belonging to Henry Hubbard of Mobile. She claimed that she was free, but the court listened to Henry A. Holmes, her denouncer, and put her in detention for a return to Mobile. It was while there that she received good legal counsel and was released on legal processes. Once more, she gained her freedom.

Her story was that she was a native of Wilmington, North Carolina, born into slavery and freed when she reached adulthood. Living with various families in the Carolinas, Elizabeth was seized and auctioned off as a slave in Mobile. The successful bidder soon discovered that her title was defective and refused to turn over her purchase price. Hubbard was stuck with her as the clerk of the auctioneer. Escaping on a ship to Boston, she was seemingly befriended by Holmes who talked her into visiting New York City while the ship was stopped there. There she was seized and never reached Boston. At her trial Elizabeth had various New York African American freemen testify that they knew her as a free woman in the Carolinas. [6]

In the same issue of *Niles' Weekly Register* for the twenty-third of November of 1829, the editor was enthusiastic about the possibilities of fast travel. The recent development of railroad speeds of 28 miles per hour in England brought about a happy editor filled with the possibilities of the machine age. When he looked abroad he saw not only the railroad between Liverpool and Manchester, but the plan or idea for a canal between the Rhine and the Danube in southwestern Germany. He could envision steamboat travel through Europe from London to Constantinople.

At home, the Baltimore and Ohio railroad was a building and a canal made river traffic possible on the Connecticut River around the falls at Enfield. America and the world were truly moving into a great new age. Canals were already presenting the nation with a transportation revolution and railroads were just beginning to add to that in a solid way. After imagining eating one's breakfast in Baltimore and one's supper in Pittsburgh, Niles concluded: "what revolutions in the condition of society, are soon to be brought about by science."

Railroad building began in the east to tie eastern cities to inland cities across the mountains. Eventually there would be added north-south lines, but this is getting ahead of the story. Right then river transportation predominated because of its cheapness and availability. New Orleans was the key city because of its location near the mouth of the said river system. Transportation of goods into New Orleans was on the rise. A sharp addition in trade there was developing. In the years of 1827, 1828, and 1829, bacon, hams, beef, flour, lard, lead, barrels of pork, tobacco, and whiskey, all of those were on the increase of trade into the city. The same was true of a multitude of other products. Bulk pork was on the decrease.

Development elsewhere helped the economy. The Ohio town of Chillicothe was in line to become a point on the new canal in the state. This would boost the economy. Already manufactures were busy in the production of goods. Soon would come the canal and water power would be created in the locks. This would further benefit the town. Already manufacturers were making iron and selling it for 6 1/4 cents a unit. Twenty years earlier iron was brought into the town from distant parts and cost 18 cents. The same was true for nails. They were now selling for seven or eight cents a pound versus 25 cents in the previous date. [7]

Locke's influences in philosophy and psychology, once so strong, had waned so, that the president of the University of Vermont, the Reverend James Marsh, could write Coleridge that he had been replaced by college courses in the United States. He had been supplanted by Stewart, Campbell, and Brown, who in time became known. Locke is now a historical giant, although little read except by those who wish to understand the period and the basis for the American system that Locke laid the groundwork for in the late seventeenth century.

Joel Giles restored the *Essay Concerning Human Understanding* as part of coursework in 1833 and used Locke for the next eight years or more. There were still those who read him after that because a whole generation trained in Lockean philosophy were ever active. Locke survived for the next centuries, but as Americans took the Lockean ideas for granted he was never prominent thereafter. His influence lived on in the great processes of American historical development. He was always the foundation stone of American philosophy, especially political philosophy. He was always the basic authority in back of all the others. [8]

Although the people of the time reported an anti-intellectual mood during the Jacksonian era, there was no over-all diminishment of college-educated men among the officials of the country. The anti-intellectualism of the frontier was never paramount and Americans continued to elect college-educated men to their public offices. Education was still important and college educated men were in demand. Able men got an education and were trained in ways that gave them a skill in writing and thinking, prerequisites for public office. However, the day of the gentleman was over, lost with the highly intellectual first six presidents, but that was because these six men were born of a generation that was exceptional in its most important leaders. This did not mean that there were no more educated men in high office, but that the happenstance of history had past and the special touch was lost.

The Jacksonian administration was the beginning of a new world in which the gentleman was not the only man recognized as valuable to society. The teaching of the Enlightenment with its human values had lead to a new feeling, a feeling that a man of any class could prove important in life. More men and women of the lower and middle classes were rising to great position and most of those sought a formal education. Even when men of little formal education, such as Lincoln, rose to leadership positions, they sought the help of educated men of all classes. Men had risen through the classes before, but now they were more acceptable and numerous and even those lacking a formal education, sought an education in law offices and elsewhere. [9]

Sumner Bacon was a wandering man. Born in Auburn, Massachusetts on January 22, 1790, Bacon was slated to become a lawyer, but his father died and with a loss of income, Sumner never did get his education. When he reached manhood, he went traveling westward through Pittsburgh. At Wheeling on the Ohio River, he stayed almost a year. By river boats, he went down river and was soon in Little Rock, Arkansas. Bacon served in the army many years at Fort Smith, Arkansas. In the fall of 1826, a non-believer before without religious training in childhood, he was converted by a Cumberland Presbyterian revival preacher. He tried to become a preacher but he was making little progress in the minimal educational training that he required. After preaching to the Indians without ordination, he traveled south.

In the fall of 1829, Bacon went to Texas, where there were few ministers and where Stephen F. Austin, in his efforts to please Roman Catholic Mexican authorities, did not want any fiery preachers who would harm his effort. Religious toleration was weak and preachers in Texas would cause the Mexican officials to react. Bacon held secret religious meetings in Gonzales and San Antonio until forced to leave by Mexican displeasure. [10]

[1] Nathan, Sydney, *Daniel Webster and Jacksonian Democracy*, Baltimore: Johns Hopkins University Press, 1973, pp. 1-4.

[2] Ambler, Charles Henry, *Thomas Ritchie: A Study in Virginia Politics*, Richmond: Bell Books, 1913, pp. 119-132.

[3] Freehling, William W., *Prelude to Civil War: The Nullification Controversy in South Carolina, 1816-1836*, New York: Harper & Brothers, 1966, pp. 21-37.

[4] Smith, *Forty Years*, p. 276.

[5] Latner, Richard B., "The Kitchen Cabinet and Andrew Jackson's Advisory System," *Journal of American History*, LXV No. 2 (September 1978), p. 369.

[6] *Niles Weekly Register*, November 23, 1829, p. 208.

[7] *Ibid.*, pp. 209, 212. Quote on p. 209.

[8] Curti, Merled., "The Great Mr. Locke, America's Philosopher, 1783-1861," Curti, Merle, "The Great Mr. Locke, America's Philosopher, 1783-1861," *The Huntington Library Quarterly*, No. 11 (1937), 117-119.

[9] Cobun, Frank E., "The Educational Level of the Jacksonians," *Historian of Education Quarterly*, VII (Winter 1967), 515-520.

[10] Brackenridge, R.D., 1968, pp. 13-20.

Chapter 14

CHEROKEE GOLD

The discovery of gold in Cherokee lands was to both complicate and speed Jackson's efforts to promote his removal program for a solution to the problems of the southeastern Indians. In his message, Jackson dealt with the creation of sympathies toward the condition of the natives. Governmental policy for a period of time had been to civilize the Indians, he said. However he threw aside the impracticable idea of exclusive self government. There could be no independent government inside the bounds of the United States nation. It was incompatible with a strong American nation. The Indians were unready for such an exercise. First, they must be educated. Americans had told the Indians that the idea of self-government was impossible. They lived within the United States. Jackson advisers and speech writers suggested that Jackson tone down the general statements in his speech and address the immediate problem of Georgia and Alabama.

In his actual speech, he told the Indians that they could not form a separate government within the United States. They had no other choice but to move. The whites wanted them out of their state no matter how civilized they were. Such was the land greed and covetous of the whites. It was too late for Federal protection of the Indians in Georgia and Alabama. In fact, this was always the case. It was not hopeless, Jackson had a solution he said; they must move to the west, to lands that the Americans thought of as virtual desert according to the reports of explorers, although Jackson did not say this. [1]

One of the chief policies Jacksonian wanted the Twenty-first Congress to support was Indian removal. He approached the problem from the states rights viewpoint of representatives and senators from the South and other states. He could not, he told Congress, warn them too strongly against all encroachments upon the area of state sovereignty. Jackson was friendly to state rights, but he was a nationalist and was to step upon states rights to protect the nation as he was now to use state rights to promote his Indian solution. The federal government could not permit foreign governments, speaking of the Cherokee and Creek tribal governments, to establish themselves within a state member of the Union.

Despite the civilizing advances of the Indians in southern states, Jackson called them hunters and wanderers on tracts they did not improve and had no rights to. Jackson deviated some from the truth in this. There were many farmers among the Indians he was dealing with and who had made improvements for farming, and certainly the Indians had rights to land they lived on before the settlers came. Jackson did not always stick to the truth. Indian removal was essential for justice and national honor. He also asked the Congress for lands in the west where the southern Indians could have land of their own policed by army units to preserve peace among the Indians and between whites and Indians. After hearing Jackson, the party faithful expressed support while the National Republicans, soon to become Whigs, supported the southern tribes. The opposition criticized the president and urged a flood of petitions opposing removal.

Each house referred the question to its committee on Indian affairs organized by Democrats. Senator Hugh L. White and Representative John Bell introduced bills to the full Senate and House. There was a long debate in the Congress from April the sixth to the final vote on the twenty fourth of April. Democrats, being in the majority, spoke out for removal while the opposition followed the lead of Senator Theodore Frelinghuysen of New Jersey. It was a close and most earnestly contested question in the session. Churchmen were divided. Reverend Isaac McCoy of the Baptist church lobbied for removal while Jeremiah Evarts lobbied for the Indians. [2]

In New York City, Mexican exiles published a Spanish-language newspaper, the *Redaetor*. The exiled General Bravo supposedly wrote an article on Texas annexation and Poinsett, in which he attacked the United States for working for the weakening of Mexico and keeping other countries from entering upon the affairs of Mexico in a constructive manner. The writer denounced the United States for desiring Mexican territory, which was true, and Poinsett as being the author of all the ills from which the Mexicans were suffering from in this world, which was untrue. However, Poinsett had interfered in the country's affairs and earned the hatred of its people.

Bravo did not say that Ward of Great Britain had also played a role in internal matters because that was acceptable by the powers that were in Mexico. They claimed that the American envoy to Mexico, the same Poinsett, was trampling upon the honor and the delicacy of Mexico. He had interfered and his interference had brought, according to their views, Mexico to the state in which it needed the funds the Americans wished to pay the Mexican Union for Texas. Poinsett was their scapegoat. At least Ward did not want Mexican territory. Ward supported the conservatives who were the winning party in Mexico during the Poinsett years there. Butler was to be no better.

The author of the letter claimed that the Americans were at fault for the fact that few Mexicans had populated the Mexican province of Texas. This was nonsense. Actually Spain and Mexico were responsible for the lack of settlers of the Spanish race in Texas. They had plenty of time to settle the province, but did not seem to have done much. There were too few Spaniards and Mexicans who wished to settle the area. They did not have the energy of the Anglo-American settlers. This was where the problem lay. Also the government had done little and the Hispanic Americans were overextended and did not have the population to fully digest what was owned in the sixteenth century.

General Bravo, or whoever wrote the letter, stated that the Mexicans had nothing in common with the North Americans. United States aggrandizement was at the expense of Mexico. North American interests were to suppress the narrow limits of the Mexican economy, in his view. They wished to keep Mexicans in apathy and inaction. He did not say so, but this was different from Ward's British who had capital to invest and a man who could get good trade agreements in the suave Ward and not from the brash Poinsett who could not offer as much and who wanted Texas for his country. That was the crux in Mexican-American relations at this time. [3]

People poured into the frontier region. Their arrival was duly noted in the newspapers of the nation. In one report, Governor James B. Ray of Indiana told the legislators of that state that 65,700 emigrants had increased the population of their state during one year's span. The natural increase in the same period was 5,000 people. At the same time, Missouri gained until its census recorded 112,409 whites and slaves in 1829. According to another news item in Hezeriah Niles' paper, the territory of Michigan was rapidly being settled by "a hardy race of intelligent freeman." The editor received in the previous week "a very neatly printed paper from a place called Ann Arbor, which we never heard of before. The village is located in Washtenaw County, and this paper, the *Western Emigrant* is appointed to publish the laws of the territory."

Travelers continued to make and follow pathways in the west to open up new vistas for both Americans and foreigners. However, in 1829, much land remained to be explored. A well-known traveler in the eastern states arrived at New Orleans. This man, Prince William of Wurtemburg laid plans to go west by the Missouri River, across the mountains, and heading for the Pacific for a complete trip and examination of all of this territory. [4]

While the white man was finding gold in Georgia and the Carolinas, the Choctaws were pleased with their lives to the southwest of the gold country. These Indians found it beneficial to adopt white man ways on their lands. While the white man was interested in Indian lands and were getting closer, the Choctaws were deeply engaged in getting their children educated in the way the white man's children did. Indeed the Five Civilized tribes were more interested in education than the average Southerners, who were soon to be less educated than the Indians they despised. The Choctaws tried to enact good laws for their people to benefit from. Rejecting strong drink, the Choctaws were being brought into the folds of the Christian religion in large numbers.

A Choctaw wrote a letter on the key subject of the time. It was published in the Cherokee *Phenix* and is here given in part. The Indian noted that "it has always been our wish to remain on this side of the Mississippi River; we still wish to remain; we are entirely beyond the control of our chiefs in regard to the disposal of ourselves; we are free to go to stay, and are subject to the will of no aristocrat or nabob." It was and not since had been their resolution to stay in their southern lands "at all hazard. If ever the Choctaw character is renovated, here is the place to do it--if we are ever to experience the blessings of civilization, here is the place," the Indian wrote without the use of a large number of words to say what he wanted to get across to the readers.

At the same time, the governor of Georgia, John Forsyth, presented an idea meant to increase Georgia's representatives in the federal house. The Indians were to be lightly taxed and counted in the 1830 census much as slaves were, but they would not be allowed to participate in the election as Niles divined. Forsyth would probably had the Indians counted for the benefit of white Georgians and then moved west. Not all the Indians were dead set to remain in Georgia. Creek chieftain Benjamin Marshall was just back from the Indian territory that was to be allotted in the west and was very enthusiastic. He told his people of the good hunting and good soil in Arkansas and they responded with enthusiasm and hope. One half of the Creeks would soon move in the opinion of Marshall. [5]

Jackson's dependence upon Kendall and Blair grew out of a mutual agreement about what policies to follow in politics and economics. They were birds of a feather. The two advisers were influential because they were allied with all of Jackson's favorite ideas. The new president could depend upon them. Both men were westerners, Kentucky bred, and very much a part of the natural order of things in the west. They did not allow their slaveholding views get in the way of their provincialism. They were never Southerners and preferred the lower and middle class to the upper class. The Panic of 1819 influenced them and provided themselves an opportunity to become political leaders first in Kentucky and then in the nation. [6]

Upon the death of Justice Bushrod Washington, Jackson nominated Henry Baldwin, an aristocratic supporter of his, to the Supreme Court. The Senate approved with only two dissenting votes. Baldwin was born in New Haven, Connecticut, on January 14, 1780 and graduated from Yale University at seventeen. He studied law under Alexander J. Dallas, a lawyer and reporter of judicial decisions in published volumes. Upon admission to the bar, Baldwin headed for Ohio but stopped in Pittsburgh, gaining through his intelligence and indefatigability political and social prominence in that still frontier town. He served in the U.S. House of Representatives from 1816 to 1822, having been a Federalist and opposed to rural Jeffersonian constituents.

Baldwin had consistent views. He supported unobstructed interstate commerce. He was a Northern states' rights proponent and defended slavery in keeping with Jackson's views. He argued for state sovereignty and a low profile for Federal government, but did not go to extremes. A moderate in other areas, he dissented on occasion from the majority of the Court. [7]

Andrew Jackson was the first westerner to become President. He won the 1828 election with a large popular majority and the electoral votes of the entire western part of the nation, plus most of the South and parts of the northeast. He won Missouri to Pennsylvania and from Louisiana to North Carolina. In 1832, he swept the West again, with the exception of Kentucky that went to Henry Clay.

As a westerner, it could be expected that Jackson would support internal improvements, the chief interest of the western states as they stood at that time. Jackson signed bills that doubled the internal improvement expenditures of the government. However, he opposed the twenty mile long Maysville Road in Clay's Kentucky as a means to strike at Clay, who became his enemy when Clay supported Adams in 1825 and lost the presidency for Jackson in Congress. Since it was a local project, it lost Jackson only a few votes in the election of 1832 when Kentucky went for his opponent Clay, but that was foredoomed anyway. It gained him support in that election, both in the South where internal improvements were seen as a waste of money and in New York and Pennsylvania where these states were financing their own improvements. [8]

On August 7, 1826, at the first local election in Chicago, a half-breed Billy Caldwell was elected justice of the peace. Three-fourths of the votes were mixed blood or pure Indian, but Caldwell probably needed white support to be elected or at least their indulgence. The next year, he bid for United States governmental contracts for Indian housing provisions and to supply Indians with cattle. This same Caldwell actively worked to obtain the removal of is relatives the Potawatomi in 1829, who needed relief that year from misery. For this they would sell a large tract of land south of Chicago to the whites. This fell into the plans of those for Indian removal everywhere. Their agent John Tipton listened and thought it a good idea. He forwarded it to his superiors. Eaton made prompt preparations for a treaty negotiation at Prairie du Chien. [9]

---

[1]Remini, Robert V., *Legacy*, 1988, p. 60-62.

[2]Satz, *American*, pp. 19-21.

[3]*Niles Weekly Register*, January 2, 1830, p. 316.

[4]*Ibid.*, p. 300.

[5]*Ibid.*, November 28, 1829, pp. 213-216.

[6]Latner, Richard B., "A New Look at Jacksonian Politics," *Journal of American History*, LXII No. 3 (March 1975), p. 944.

[7]Seddig, Robert G., "Baldwin, Henry," Hall, Kermit L., *The Oxford Companion to the Supreme Court of the United States*, New York: Oxford University Press, 1992, pp. 59-60.

[8]Van Deusen, Glyndon G., *The Jacksonian Era: 1828-1848*, New York: Harper & Brothers, 1959, pp. 51-54.

[9]Conway, Thomas C., "An Indian Politician and Entrepreneur in the Old Northwest, *Old Northwest*, I, No. 1 (March 1975), 52-53.

Chapter 15

KIT CARSON

Christopher Houston Carson, known as Kit, American trapper, scout, pathfinder, and soldier, was born on December 24, 1809, in Madison County, Kentucky. He was born to Lindsey Carson and his second wife Rebecca Robinson from Greenbier County, Virginia. Lindsey was born in North Carolina. It was a restless family and they found their individual ways to the west in successive moves out there. Lindsey, an industrious farmer and celebrated hunter, moved his family from Madison County to Missouri, then Louisiana territory, on the frontier some 170 miles west of St. Louis, seeking adventure and room to roam and hunt. Kit was one year old at the time. Already there were friends and kindred and more were to follow. They built forts and prepared for the duration, until the call pushed them west. There was to be no more call for Lindsey Carson; he died in September of 1818 from the fall of a limb from a burned tree, while in the process of clearing timber near his cabin. Kit would have to work harder without a father's support. If his father wished him to be a lawyer as has been reported, this idea was lost with fate. When older, he would be set to helping out the family by learning and earning a living. [1]

While his older brothers were out on the trail to Santa Fe or trapping the great west for furs, his mother apprenticed him to William and David Workman to become a saddler like them. He was fifteen and began early in 1825, sweeping out the store and learning to use the awl. It was a good trade for the time and place, since Franklin, Missouri, where he worked was an outfitting point for the Western trails for trade and trapping. But the call of the wild was great. William Workman was set to go out on the trail or underway and the Workman cousin James Workman was just back from New Mexico, where he claimed to have been leader of fifteen men. Kit was not to stay settled for more than a year and by the sixth of October of 1826, he ran away from the saddlery for the adventure of the Santa Fe Trail, followed by his master David in the next spring. He worked in a job on the caravan and soon was in Santa Fe with pay in his pocket. [2]

Young Carson, left without a job by his arrival, went north some miles to Taos, which was soon to become his base of operations. It was already a trapper and trader center with many Americans, which is probably why he went there. Once in Taos, he ran in with a Kincaid, who might have known the Carson family back in Missouri and maybe even Kit himself. It was tough sledding for awhile; he had no marketable skill and as he himself said, was yet too small to set a trap. He did learn the language and was able to serve at odd jobs and from time to time as teamster, cook, and interpreter. Lacking funds, he could not buy an outfit and looked young for his late teens, but he was able bit by bit to make his way. About this time Kincaid passed out of view. After two or so trips, Kit cooked for a living in the winter of 1827-1828 and spent his money on dances. He cooked for Ewing Young. [3]

Back in Missouri, he hired on as an interpreter for trader Colonel Tramele on a forty-day journey through Santa Fe and El Paso to Chihuahua. Once there, he was fortunate enough to meet Robert McKnight and worked as a teamster for a few months for McKnight's cooper mines before returning to Taos. Next, he was with a party fighting the Indians and first proved himself and soon was, with a purchased outfit, leaving Taos in April or August of 1829 with Ewing Youngs's party for trapping in the southwest. This was his big break as we have seen earlier in the account of the Young group. [4]

After his adventures with Young, in September of 1831, the seasoned Kit Carson joined the Thomas Fitzpatrick party of trappers. They went into the northwest Rockies, new territory for Kit and with a more professional bunch of men. Getting a late start to join his partners Fitzpatrick marched his men rapidly upstream. The group Carson was with, trapped to the head of Sweetwater River, down the Green River, and next to Jackson's Hole, before encamping for the winter in Salmon River country in northern Idaho, a fairly rapid pace through land well known by the trappers he was with.

Carson was twenty-two now when winter camp broke up in early 1832. He trapped the Snake, the Bear, and eastward still to the Green. There was another incident in which he played a leading role. Fifty Crow made off with horses during one night and Carson and eleven men sped northward to recover the horses. Tracks were lost in some buffalo herd crossing, but the men managed to track forth and found a good site for overnight. In the distance, they saw fires and creeping up close they discovered the Indians with two small fort-like structures of log and brush. The Indians were celebrating their successes. The Americans waited until the Indians were asleep and slithered forth and freed the horses, and took them back.

Most of the men wanted to leave now, but Carson wanted to punish the Crows. Carson prevailed and the Americans walked upon the camp, waking the Indians, and fired upon them. In a battle, many Indians were killed and an Indian charge failed. More firing followed and the Indians charged again. This forced Carson and his men to retreat to safety. This is but one of the incidents with Indians in Carson's varying life. [5]

One of Lincoln's chief adversaries in the war years was born into an aristocratic Virginia family on January 19,1807. Robert Edward Lee developed into a man of outstanding character and personality and was soon a leader of men in a military career which was to lead him to great fame in the crisis of the Civil War in his fifties. He had most of the advantages that Lincoln did not have, but both reached pinnacles of power and renown together. When Robert was born, his family lived in a great house, but the sire of the house, Henry Lee, had reason to fear bill collectors who sought money from his now bankrupt estate. At age two, the child was temporarily bereft of a father. Light Horse Harry was imprisoned for debt. Henry's wife, Ann Carter Lee, had the income from a trust to support the family but was legally prevented from paying the father's debts with the principal. They moved from the plantation of now limited acres to Alexandria, Virginia, with its then population of 7,000. Robert was brought up in the Episcopal faith. His hero was George Washington and he practiced his self-discipline as instructed by Mrs. Lee.

Young Robert E. Lee applied himself at home and schooling, taking care of his mother and family and learning. No one knows the reason he chose West Point and a military career, but it has been suggested that he did so because his mother could not afford to send him to college and he had no plantation to inherit. His West Point grades were distinguished. His freshman year ended in his appointment as staff sergeant, the highest he could receive in that class. He continued to excel, near the top in academics and engineering. He received the rank of corps adjutant, the highest rank for his general excellence and natural leadership. Lee graduated second in his class, the recognized top cadet, and the first graduate of West Point to never receive any demerits. Afterwards, he cared for his dying mother. After her death, the army commissioned Lee a second lieutenant in the engineering corps, about this time that Lincoln was moving westward. [6]

Lee was to have the special power of an aristocrat. In little Greeneville, Tennessee, workers, artisans, and craftsmen exerted their power too. They elected a mechanics' ticket. Andrew Johnson was one of the winners in 1829 and became an alderman. The little tailor had arrived on a local level and begun the long road to the highest office in the land. Elite citizens were surprised by the outcome. However, he had good relationships and had the respect of all citizens as a master tailor who served them well. Soon Johnson bought real estate. In 1834, the young tailor was elected mayor. The same year, he was chosen a trustee of Rhea Academy. Later, the people elected him to the state legislature of Tennessee. His slashing and sharp style proved a success in his first major campaign. [7]

Henry Lee had been in debtor's jail and when Jackson became president in 1829, there were 75,000 persons annually imprisoned for debt in the country. All states except Ohio and Kentucky imprisoned debtors. For every six prisoners in prisons five were debtors with only one for a crime or so. Most of the debtors in prison were unlike Lee, owning small amounts. One widow woman was in jail for owing sixty-eight cents. Criminals in prison were fed, bedded, and kept warm in winter. Debtors had none of this provided them. The Humane Society fed them and their keepers had to beg for fuel to keep them warm. Fortunately the duration was short. [8]

In the controversy over African American colonization, Baltimore schoolmaster William Watkins, a freeman, spoke out in 1829 and his views became wide-spread. He asked in words that African Americans felt strongly. He counter colonization with the words: "Why should we abandon our firesides and everything associated with the dear name of *home*, undergo the fatigues of a perilous voyage, and expose ourselves, our wives, and our little ones, to the deleterious influences of an inconsequential sun, for the enjoyment of liberty divested of its usual accomplishments, surrounded with circumstances which diminish its intrinsic values..?"

The vast majority of African Americans were not interested in going to Liberia and said so in no uncertain terms. They found an opening in the fact that the societies for colonization were not attacking slavery. If they were not opposed to slavery, why were they claiming to be interested in the welfare of the African American. In fact, they were not, the mass of them wanted to ship the African American to Africa and only the freedmen among them. They feared them and hated them and the movement was taken over by those of these beliefs.

In one colonization meeting, Jacob Greener, an African American stood up and said that their first object should be to educate the children of the freedman. Colonization movements were hurting his people and were propaganda to emphasize their lowly status. Colonizationists needed to eliminate white prejudice. The African Americans organized themselves in a society against colonization and few emigrants to Africa could be found as they mobilized against colonization.

Freemen followed the white agents and whenever an African American enlisted for Liberia, they feed him with ideas against it, resorting most probably to lies in the process. The would-be emigrant then changed his mind. Some of them told the countryside blacks that they would be taken on ship and sold to the West Indies. This brought a reaction of fear and opposition. The war of words went on between the whites and the African Americans. The later had the advantage, for the country minority needed only to know that the whites were for it to be against it The number of emigrants was so low that few colonializing ships sailed with a full load. Not only African Americans but whites also opposed their going. Whites often need the African Americans as laborers and were loath to see them go. Colonization angered white farmers and fishermen as well. They needed their labor. [9]

In Georgia, the state legislature ordered a quarantine of free blacks on ships coming into their harbors. Orders went out to imprison any free black who came ashore and to detain him until the ship was to sail. The British Foreign Office was informed and got legal opinion on the matter. The problem came up in Parliament. The British protested without success. In ensuing years, there were to be problems of this sort with Georgia and other southern Atlantic coast states. There were to be many incidents of this nature. The matter was taken to the courts. Nothing was done; the national government did not wish to coerce the states. It was an explosive issue that was never settled. [10]

William McKinley, Sr., father of a president, was an upright example for his son, also called William. The son took after his father in many aspects, gaining in particular the elder's taciturnity and force of character. The senior McKinley was a strong man with many talents of a hardy nature. Not only could he forge iron, but he could mend fences, paint, plow, care for animals, and build houses and cut and work wood. Occasionally, he invented things. From the age of sixteen, he worked long hours, and was early to rise and early to bed. He read the few books he owned until the pages were thin. Born on November 15, 1807, in New Lisbon, Ohio, where his parents had settled seeking a better life, his life was unsettled, requiring to move around on business trips, so he saw a good deal of the state of Ohio.

In mid-January of 1829, William married Nancy Allison, from a long line of Englishmen and women who came with William Penn to Pennsylvania. They had several children, whom they raised to be upright men and women. Mother McKinley bore with honor her responsibilities as a mother while the father was busy earning the family living looking after his businesses. When a foundry was founded in Niles where he was living with his family, he was for a brief time partner in the plant, producing andirons, stone castings, pipe, and household utensils for sale. He led his family into a desire for reading what little was available. They read Hume, Gibbon, and Dickens among other authors. In addition, they subscribed to monthly magazines and the anti-slavery *Weekly Tribune*. Because of the better schools in Poland, Ohio, the family moved there. [11]

More people entered Texas to settle. Those that were already there began to become quite prosperous. Their hardest struggles were behind them and their harvest was at hand. Most were farmers but the townspeople grew in numbers too and their harvest was before them. This prosperity and growing numbers began to worry Mexican officials. American envoys continued to press for the purchase of Texas by America and this news upset the Mexican people as well as their leaders. Covetous eyes were upon their province they knew and they were naturally suspicious of the existence of slavery in Texas, brought in by the Americans. It was illegal and wrong. So in 1829, the Government forbade slavery and forbade further immigration and importation of slaves. The Texans in their turn were worried. However, the law was a dead letter and men and their families continued to come with their slaves.

Not only were the Mexicans suspicious of land grabbing by the United States but of Indian policy. This was due to the fact that the Anglo-Americans were relatively free of Indian attacks, while the Mexicans had to endure many attacks. They came to believe that the Anglos had a secret understanding with the natives. This was false but the Mexicans felt injured and angry. The Mexican Government issue repressive legislation against the Anglos. This was to play into the hands of that minority of Anglos who wanted independence and union with their former homeland, the United States.

Of course, the warring Comanches were used to western warpaths into Mexico in the west of the Texas plains. They continued their ways during this period and moved little southeastward. Besides, there were tribes in the way of the Comanche if they had wanted wholesale action against the Texans. This would have involved the Comanche with these tribes. As it was the Texans had trouble enough with the hostile tribes between them and the Comanche. [12]

Bedford Brown, American statesman and congressman, was born on June 6, 1795, in Caswell County, North Carolina, to Jethro Brown and Lucy Williamson. The family had to leave South Carolina when the Tories burnt their home for aiding Marion. Bedford went to college for one year. Upon becoming twenty-two, he ran for the legislature of his state where he fathered a controversial resolution thanking President Madison for his conduct in the War of 1812. After five days of debate, the resolution was passed by 76 to 51.

In 1816, he married Mary Lumpkin Glenn, daughter of merchant James Anderson Glenn. Brown's father, prospering from his plantation and tavern, gave the couple a wedding trip to England and Scotland and a plantation. Bedford continued as legislator and obtained the speakership. After defending the caucus system against Charles Fisher's idea of primary contests for presidential electors in the county, Brown left public life. He replaced Barlett Yancey in the state senate. In 1829, he was elected to the national senate, where he supported Jackson. Brown was against nullification and the recognition and annexation of Texas and was for a government that taxed and spent little. [13]

Offspring of Irish parents, Mary Gannon was born in New York City on October 8, 1829. She was almost born into the theater for at age three she played the role of the child in the popular "Daughter of the Regiment." Mary appeared in other performances as the years progressed. At age eight, she was taken to Philadelphia to play the role of Lady Flennap in the Garrick farce "Lilliiput." There were a variety of thespian jobs or acting jobs for the girl and her popularity grew. She danced and played her way into American hearts, much like Shirley Temple of the next century. In her adult years, she had less success. She married a lawyer and went into theatrical decline. Fortune no longer smiled on Mary Gannon Stevenson. She died at age thirty-eight. Her last months were long and painful.

One of the chief performers on the American stage, James E. Murdock had his first role at age seventeen. He was born in 1812, in Philadelphia at a time when the United States became embroiled in a war with the United Kingdom. His father was a bookbinder and James learned the trade before joining an amateur acting association and then becoming a paid actor. His amateur appearance was as Glenalvon in "Douglas" and his first professional performance as Frederic in "Lovers' Vows." This second was on October 13, 1829, at the Arch Street Theatre in his hometown. Soon, he acted the character of Young Noval.

He spent the first part of his career in Philadelphia, before going to New York City in 1838 as Benedick in "Much Ado About Nothing." He served the public in many other roles and then as Henry in the popular "Speed the Plough," having become a stage manager meantime in addition to his acting. About 1842, Murdoch retired to lecture. Like so many, the profession was in his veins and he returned to the American stage to perform as Hamlet in 1845. Eight years later, Murdoch went to California to act. Three years later he was in London. His chief role there was a Young Mirabel.

After a time, Murdoch returned to his country and settled down to agriculture. He had a farm and did some acting in the hinterland. He failed as a soldier due to ill health, but he spent most of the war years helping soldiers in hospitals. After the war, he returned to the stage where he had operated so well in the past. Murdoch had character in real life and expressed character in his parts. He had a terrific voice and expressed the nature of his goodness and firm foundations. He was one of the best actors in America in his century and was well respected for his talent. [14]

---

[1]Sabin, *Kit Carson*, pp. 1-8; Peters, DeWitt C., *The Life and Adventures of Kit Carson, the Nestor of the Rocky Mountains From Facts Narrated by Himself*, 1858, Freeport, NY: Books for Libraries Press, 1970, p. 14.

[2]Sabin, *Kit Carson*, pp. 8, 11-13.

[3]*Ibid.*, pp. 25-26, 31-34; Peters, Life, *pp. 26-27.*

[4]Sabin, *Kit Carson*, pp. 34-37, 40-41ff. Cf. Peters, *Life*, p. 31.

[5]Sabin, *Kit Carson*, pp. 70-72, 76, 208-210.

[6]Dowdey, Clifford, *Lee*, New York: Bonanza Books, 1965, pp. 27-49.

[7]Trefousse, Hans L., *Andrew Johnson: A Biography*, New York: W.W. Norton, 1997, pp. 30-37.

[8]Carlton, Frank T., "Abolition of Imprisonment for Debt in the U.S.," *Yale Review*, XVII (1903/04), 339-340.

[9]Berlin, Ira, *Slaves Without Masters: The Free Negro in the Antebellum South*, New York: Pantheon Books, 1974, pp. 204-207. Quote on p. 204.

[10]Hamer, Philip M., "Great Britain, the United States, and the Negro Seamen Acts, 1822-1848," *Journal of Southern History*, I, No. 1 (February 1935), 12-28.

[11]Morgan, H. Wayne, *William McKinley and His America*, Syracuse, NY: Syracuse University Press, 1963, pp. 3-9.

[12]Winter, Nevin O., *Texas*, pp. 35, 39-40.

[13]Jones, Houston G., "Bedford Brown: States Rights Unionist," *North Carolina Historical Review, XXXII (July 1955), 321-345.*

[14]Brown, Thomas Allston, *History of the American Stage*, New York: Dick & Fritzgerald, 1870, pp. 138, 254, 257.

Chapter 16

RAILROADS

In late 1829, Robert Barnwell Rhett sounded the alarm once again for the people of South Carolina, taking his stand of extreme states rights. This instance was the petitioning of the Charleston Railroad Company to Congress to purchase some of its stock, enabling the company to finance its railroad. To Rhett, this was a big-government and unconstitutional application of funds. He opposed the internal improvement idea, even more because it was his state's material benefit that would corrupt the "abstract, isolated principle of liberty" and "the dignity of consistency between your words and actions." [1]

A meeting was held in early January of 1830 in Charleston to talk over the problem of the railroad. Well attended in its assemblage at City Hall, the meeting was presided over by Thomas Lee, a unanimous choice, and heard a resolution to Congress. Its writer wanted the people to petition the national legislature to recognize the benefit of such a railroad to the city and state and accept congressional actions to purchase the stock and promote it in Congress. The only dissent forced the second part for congressional promotion to a vote. This was overwhelmingly adopted after some discussion. All was needless since the bill to provide funds for this railroad died in the Senate's committee on roads and canals. [2]

Before this rejection and after the Charleston meeting, Rhett and Franklin H. Elmore rallied the stung people of Colleton against funding the line by Congress. Given that, the railroad would benefit the people, it would bring on evils, which would be greater than the favored benefits, if the federal government provided the money for its construction in their view. [3]

As requested by the directors, President William Aiken of the South Carolina Canal and Railroad Company wrote to Daniel Webster to ask him to present a petition to the United States Senate for their aid. It was done after the attempt by Charleston Company's effort. General Robert Y. Hayne was to bring this letter of January 9th of 1830 to Webster along with documents. Colonel Abraham Blanding was at Washington

DC and would answer any questions to aid Webster in this project. Blanding was born in Massachusetts in 1776 and graduated from Brown University in 1796. He moved to South Carolina where he became a successful lawyer. After a time, young Blanding served in the state legislature and as a commissioner of the State Board of Pubic Works under which jurisdiction, the transportation company Aiken was developing came.

Aiken chose Webster because he was known for his support of public power and his philosophy of wider constitutional power, while Hayne and the other congressmen from South Carolina, had opposed federal aid on principle. South Carolina merchants were in need the railroad because exclusive reliance upon South Carolina rivers was uncertain and loss filled. Charleston's harbor was crowded with ships and country warehouses with cotton. Railroads would be more beneficial to the state's economy than deepening the Bar or improving the port of Charleston's facilities. The interior was important for the common defense and domestic opening up of the backcountry. Hayne acted although reluctantly due to his strict construction beliefs. [4]

Soon Webster and Hayne were involved in principle. The famous Webster-Hayne debate began with the debate of land policy. Easterners promoted a scheme to close the opening of new lands in the West, claiming that there already one million acres unsold. Westerners were furious. They said that the easterners wanted the West closed off for emigration because they needed the workers with their low pay to remain in the factories of the northeast. This would benefit one section of the United States at the expense of another. Thomas Hart Benton of Missouri rose and condemned the resolution for closing land. The backers of the resolution should not meddle with western interests. He mentioned the tariff and cotton interests and senators picked up their ears. They decided that they could gain success by allying with the West against their manufacturer enemies in the East. Benton also spoke out for lowering land prices radically. He ended his day and renewed his attack on January 18, 1830.

There was a need for someone to speak out for the South on the issue. That man was Robert Y. Hayne of South Carolina. He was thirty-seven and had been in the Senate since his first election in 1823. Hayne followed the example of Benton "by opposing a public land policy that sought to use the land as a source of revenue and not as a mean of attracting settlers." This revenue would be a fund for corruption. Once said, he launched into a "ranging endorsement of state rights, a philosophy that the Westerners had begun to fear as inimical to future growth, prosperity, and greatness of the nation." Hayne declared that "the very life of our system is the independence of the states and there is no evil more to be deprecated than the consolidation of the Government." He deplored the taxation of the South and wanted no more permanent income for the government like the tariff and land sales income. He would have the federal government exist on a tenuous string and subject to direct small grants. Then Hayne began to get angry and personal.

Webster had come back to the Senate floor in time for this and was persuaded to make a speech in answer. He started talking in defense of the East. He waxed eloquently with great feeling and a powerful voice. He spoke for the sale of land for low prices so that everyone could afford land. However, the land should not be free. Denying any governmental harshness toward the western states and territories, he said that Congress had acted wisely in the acquisition and sale of lands. He was for strong national bounds, a strong Union, a perpetual Union. The Union was essential to national safety and prosperity. Webster spoke against slavery; it had not been allowed in the Old Northwest by ordinance. He turned the debate from land to the defense of his section.

The debate switched to Benton and Hayne. Hayne defended the South and said that Webster had distorted the debate to other subjects. It was Benton and not he who attacked the East. Webster was blaming Hayne. Hayne talked of the benefit of slavery to the nation. He attacked Webster personally and then made a weak defense of nullification. The states should check federal power and nullification quarreled with the Union. Days later the debate continued. Webster gave the speech of his life. The New Englander attacked slavery as an evil, a moral and political evil. Then after defending Massachusetts in a way that made this the best part of his speech, he defended the Constitution. He said that the Constitution was the people, made by and for them, and answerable to them. It was the supreme law and not the states. The last appeal belongs to the judiciary. There was no middle ground. Nullification was direct collision and war. Liberty and Union were inseparable. It packed a wallop and was praised even by Hayne. This was one of the best speeches delivered in America. The speech was a national success and people could talk of nothing else. [5]

Webster's second reply to Hayne was well received by an excited populace and it made him a great reputation as one of the greater leading statesmen of the entire nation. People responded with praise; they came from leaders and followers alike. Madison, Monroe, and Clay all were praising him and he got hundreds of letters from others. It was a fine triumph and might have led to the White House had everything else been equal. Abe Lincoln read the speech in the *Louisville Journal* a couple of weeks before the Lincoln clan left Indiana for Illinois.

Madison later wrote Webster that his speech crushed nullification "and must hasten an abandonment of secession" It was a fine hope but it was an exaggeration. The crisis of nullification was still ahead and it was Jackson who was to crush it. Still patriots used the speech to sway public opinion. Since people wanted to know what Webster said, there was a big demand of copies of the speech, so it was carefully edited and sent out in improved form. More than one hundred thousand copies were distributed in the next year and a half. From this one encounter his name became a household word and he began to be considered a likely presidential contender. It did wonders for Webster. [6]

George M. Dallas had political and personal reasons to dislike the Bank of the United States. Although he had been a lawyer for the bank since its founding and thought himself an authority of its charter, he was miffed in his seeking for power in the bank. Bank president Nicholas Biddle had allied himself with the faction that had opposed Dallas' group. Further, he objected to the power of the private directors and stockholders. This power was excessive in his view. Perhaps he was also jealous, since he did not have all he thought he deserved. In the fall of 1829, he suggested to Biddle and the bank board that Washington, meaning Jackson, should have greater control of its policy. Interesting enough, Dallas' friend and political associate Secretary of the Treasury Ingham would have this power. These were the political and other personal reasons. Dallas was a Jacksonian. Dallas dealt with this maneuver in spite and would have been glad if the bank would be moved to New York.

Ingham used his influence to have the government offer Dallas a government-appointed bank directorship, but Dallas preferred at this point to fight the Bank from the outside. Dallas was not against banks or the Bank as a whole, but he was anti-Biddle. So personally orientated was Dallas that he preferred to have the Bank destroyed rather than see Biddle continued as the president of the Bank of the United States. His view was political. Since Biddle was a political enemy, he would destroy the Bank if he could thereby ruin the head of the Bank. After Jackson attacked the Bank as of doubtful constitutionality, Dallas accepted a directorship in January of 1830. Dallas was a very complex and changing man with a warped personality, generated from within according to the account of his biographer. [7]

There were rumors abroad in Washington DC in February of 1830. Politicians in the city were talking about divisions in Jackson's party. They also said that there were to be changes in office holding and differences in opinion and practices. Controversies swirled around the questions of the tariff and of internal improvements. One South Carolinian in Congress said that Jackson's message to Congress had contained views that he could not countenance. The party would not make him shallow the statement and the country should soon see it.

Editor Niles and his journalists provided at this time, by way of his newspaper, information on Texas. The state (still a part of Mexico) was being populated and the *Register* noted that "if ever Texas shall be acquired, which we do not think very probable," it would have sold land so extensively that there would be a greatly diminished domain and there would be little left for the public domain. When the Mexicans viewed the emigration of settlers from the United States to Texas, they were naturally concerned. On their hand, the Americans lacked confidence in the Mexican authorities and wanted their own way about affairs. The scene was set for trouble, but in early 1830, the settlers were busy with developing their lands and the Mexicans were swept up in internal conflict to the south. Mexican leaders vied with each other for power in central Mexico.

Back in the American nation there was a minor controversy over some memoirs of Jefferson and continued discussions on the tariff issue. Both made good copy for the newspapers and an involved pattern of discussion in the nation. [8]

At this time, the king and queen of Naples were, according to the Baltimore newspapers, visiting Madrid and the king and queen of Spain. In order to pay for the processions, the Naples king had to increase taxes. The higher payments cause discontent in Naples. The people of that country were having economic stress because of a scarcity of flour and corn and the resulting high price of these products necessary for basic life. More money was required for the display and the people were further suppressed. The Americans reading this could well be glad of their nation without damaging displays and with plenty of food at good prices for farmers and people alike. American trade with neighboring Portugal was promoted by the American recognition of Don Miguel and the British were concerned over competition from the Americans. [9]

While in America a commodore talked of the good harbor of Key West and another report of good business at Mobile (with inland trade and the export of cotton through that port) reports about trouble in Latin America took space in the newspapers. In Mexico, Guerrero and Santa Anna retired, if briefly, and General Bustamente took charge of the government. In Venezuela, General Paz came to Caracas for a triumph and prepared to oppose Bolivar. Troops were gathered to fight Bolivar that once noble liberator of much of Spanish America. [10]

Dealing with the Eaton affair, Postmaster General William T. Barry, had his own understanding explained to his daughter on February of 1830, that "Major Eaton is known to be an intimate friend of the president. The extreme jealousy of some of Calhoun's friends induces them to believe that Major Eaton is rather friendlier to Van Buren than to Calhoun. They fear his influence will control the Executive patronage in favor of Van Buren. They want him to leave the cabinet." According to Barry this was what was behind the attack on Mrs. Eaton. Barry himself considered himself to be on good terms with the entire cabinet. Van Buren were not interested in power so much as remaining on the side of Jackson. He said his friends should be in favor of the re-election of Jackson in 1832. Of course power would come to them by that advocacy in the near term. [11]

The most important politician in early Illinois, where Lincoln was to spend most of his life, was Ninian Edwards, territorial governor from 1809 to 1818. Personal feelings and not issues moved early leaders there. They received public offices on grounds of friendship. When Illinois became a state, they declared a truce and apportioned positions by agreement. Shadrach Bond ran for governor without opposition and Edwards became Senator, going to Washington DC. Shortly, in 1819, the controversy over the admission of Missouri sparked a concern and acute debate over slavery. Illinois citizens were divided over the issue. Controversy over slavery lasted for years. In the 1824 elections, anti-slavery forces won a complete victory. Presidential politics were secondary, but there too opinion was divided. Jackson gained strength when his followers claimed that the Adams-Clay alliance was the result of a corrupt bargain. This was so effective that Jackson took Illinois by a very large margin in 1828. When the Lincolns moved to Illinois, they found the divisions at this stage in their development. [12]

On March 1, 1830, the Lincolns, the Hanks, and the Johnston daughters and sons-in-law left Indiana. Abe drove one of the ox-team wagons. They stopped off in what would shortly be Macon County. There he built a cabin and split rails for fences. The Lincolns fenced in ten acres of ground, which they ploughed and planted, raising a crop of corn that year of 1830. Their farms were on the banks of the Sangamon River, several miles out of Decatur. The entire family suffered so much from malaria that they decided they would leave the country. However, they stayed on during a winter of deep snow. [13]

We have here more on that move. Some of the Hanks had moved to the area in the late twenties. They soon sent Thomas Lincoln news of the fertility of Illinois soil being above that of Indiana. He was interested and when a scare of milk sickness swept over Indiana, he decided to move right away. Selling his hundred acres, he set out with some wagons for Illinois on March 1, 1830. With Thomas were his wife and son and her children and their families. They made their way westward in a slow journey which Abraham Lincoln termed to be "painfully slow and tiresome."

In mid-March, the extended Lincoln family reached Decatur in Illinois and camped on the public square in the midst of a dozen log houses making up the town. Early on the next morning, they set out for the farm site in Macon County. The farm was on the north bank of the Sangamon River, where forest and prairie met. Instead of buying the land, Thomas squatted upon it. John Hanks cut the logs that the Lincoln menfolks erected into a new house. They ploughed ten acres of praise and planted corn. They cut down trees and cut rails to make the fences that summer. After the fall harvest, Abraham Lincoln and John Hanks split 3,000 rails for the county sheriff. Next, George Close and Abraham made around 1,000 rails in return for homespun clothing. [14]

Along the way to Illinois, Lincoln had to rescue his dog. According to the story Lincoln told to Herndon in later years, the Lincolns were over the state line when they reached a long loggy corduroy bridge over a wide swamp. Because ice was formed over the bridge, he could not get the oxen to break the ice and go over the bridge. He tried to coax and then threaten, but the oxen would not move. Finally, Abraham had to severely lash the oxen. The oxen moved. Halfway over, he heard his dog howl desperately. Lincoln stopped the oxen, pulled off his shoes, rolled up his pants, and jump into the cold water and ice. Reaching the frightened dog, Lincoln picked him up and lifted him into the wagon. Once on dry land, the dog would not get out, and Abe had to haul him out and put him on the ground. The grateful dog went into antics. [15]

The Illinois farmland was mixed, ranging from poor sand on the banks of the Sangamon to the rich clay on the banks of the Illinois. People who trod the prairie were left with regiments of black sand dust that adhered to their feet and ankles, which wading in the streams could not wash off by mere movement. They raised the crops of wheat and corn and grazed cattle on these lands. Farms were still scattered at this time, and most of the land had yet to be tilled. Farmers had difficulty in breaking up the soil for the first time. The plough had a width of about eighteen inches and two or three inches in depth. The farmer then dropped Indian corn into every third furrow, using a bushel of seed for every ten acres and covered with turf. Only one cultivation was necessary for a result of fifty bushels per acre. A harrow was used for wheat. Melons and potatoes are planted in gardens with natural fertilizers. Despite the newness of the land, the prairie suffered from over grazing. Because of a scarcity of labor, wages were high, increasing prices. [16]

Minister Anthony Butler wrote from Mexico City. General Guerrero was recently expelled from the Mexican presidency. Butler saw a thick political cloud in Mexican times. He was expecting another revolution in Mexico. The party in power were conservatives, in this case the rule of the wealthy and aristocrats. They were already faced with revolt in eight Mexican states. Congress had annulled the elections of many states. Indeed troops were amassed for the expected struggle. The Conservatives were arresting as their enemy Alpuche, former president of the Chamber of Deputies, for the false charge of high treason because of his defensive efforts for Guerrero and his Government, just before they fell. Shortly, Butler was busy trying to buy Texas from Mexico, which did not suit the Conservatives of Mexico at all. [17]

Of primary importance in early spring was a discussion and debate on the removal and protection of the Cherokees. There was an interest in New England for the protection of the southern Indians. Jackson had addressed this in his speeches for their consumption. Meetings were held over all parts of Massachusetts for the good treatment of the natives. Noah Worcester wrote Daniel Webster from Brighton on March 12, 1830, connecting this with Webster's famous speech nationalism and against extreme state rights with the case of the Cherokees and Georgia. He felt that Webster had sapped the principles of Georgia. People in the state of Massachusetts hoped that Webster would speak out on the Indian question. With his eyes on national politics and the presidency, Webster did not take the hoped for stand. He did not participate in the debate and only voted once for the record when he voted in favor of an amendment guaranteeing protection of the Cherokees spending removal. The amendment was soundly beaten in Congress. [18]

Jackson's Indian Removal bill became contested. At the head of the opposition, Senator Theodore Frelinghuysen of New Jersey spoke for three days. Deeply religious with a strong caring for the Indians, the Christian senator labeled the bill to be guilty of hypocrisy and attacked the Democrats in Congress who supported the president on the bill. Frelinghuysen's Indians were given total removal or if that failed, they would be subject to the "tender mercies" of the states. The Indians he said in counter to this had the rights of property and treaties. Should Jackson threaten or harass them, because that would lead to violence. It was the responsibility of the nation to protect them from the states. Congress must act to protect the Indians.

Frelinghuysen told his fellow senators that the Indians had been faced with white greed. They believed it when the whites called them brothers and they forced to sign over millions of acres. We had them cornered, he said, and still we forced them once again to move to the edge of their lands and still the whites cried out for more, still more. John Forsyth had a ready reply. The Indians in New York, New England, Virginia and so forth were left to the tender mercies of these states, while the Jackson Indian bill would protect the Cherokees, Choctaws, Chickasaw, and Creeks using government forces. The North and East were allowed to get away with what the South were denied. Mississippi's Robert Adams stated that all Indians should be subject to the laws of the states. This avoided chaos.

Maine's Peleg Sprague spoke out against the bill by reminding the body that it was responsible to carry out the terms of the previous Indian treaties. This bill was unconstitutional, Ascher Robbins of Rhode Island stated. David Barton of Missouri and others senators asked for an amendment providing for open negotiations with the native

Americans to prevent underhanded deals and rewards, threats, and intimidation in negotiations. The Senate rejected this last provision. They wanted these things which helped them in the battle against the Indians for land grants from the natives. Frelinghuysen wanted a delay to decide if other lands would be sufficient for the Indians in the west. Following strict party lines of 18 to 19, the Senate and then the House passed the bill.

It was a closer call in the House. The Democrats were divided in the House being subjected to Quakers and others in their districts who might vote against them in subsequent elections. Henry R. Storrs of New York attacked Jackson. Wilson Lumpkin of Georgia claimed those against the bill with partisan politics. Removal would protect the Indians and Andrew Jackson entertained the kindness feeling toward the Indian, more so than any other man did. Actually, Jackson hated the Indians. William Ellsworth of Connecticut claimed it would cost millions for this shameful act. The vote was 98 to 98 for a substitute bill with Speaker c of Virginia, a loyal party man, voted against the substitute making 98 for and 99 against. Jackson intervened and the Senate passed bill was voted 102 to 97. [19]

Internal matters in France intervened and the claims issue was delayed. On March 18, 1830, and new elections were set for the last of June and the first of July. Because the ministers were concerned about the forthcoming elections, they could not concentrate upon foreign matters such as the American claims against the French. At this point in time, the issue of the tariff came into consideration. The American Senate was considering the proposition for repeal of all duties on wines, silks, and other French products.

On April 6, 1830, Rives wrote Van Buren that it would be wise not to give away this bargaining chip which might be used in the claims issue before the French government. Of value were the difficulties of French vine growers. They had lost part of their market when the northern Europeans because the French had imposed duties on foreign irons and linens. The winegrowers of France were asking for relief and the Americans were already forming a taste for French wines. Rives also suggested the ending of discriminatory tariffs on American cotton at a time when there was a demand for this product in France. The elections went against the Polignac government. [20]

Several things of interest and importance were remarked on in Niles' newspaper of the twentieth of March of 1830. While the Astor cases were being decided upon in the courts of New York State (the Astor having won one), the widow of Stephen Decatur, Susan Decatur, had a bill of recompensation to provide for her and others, in the national Congress. Also at this time there was a report on army desertions. Fourteen percent of the soldiers in the American army in one given year (on average) deserted, half of these in their first year of enlistment and most of that number deserting in the first six months. This was a high rate. Recently, a sergeant and twelve men had left the army together for Canada without leave. There they found work as laborers on the Rideau canal. [21]

---

[1] White, L.A., 1931, p. 18. Quote on p. 18.
[2] *Niles Weekly Register*, January 23, 1830, p. 368, December 4. 1930. p. 245.

[3]White, p. 19.

[4]Webster, Daniel, *Correspondence*, III (1977), 4-5, 9.

[5]Remini, Robert V., *Daniel Webster: The Man and His Time*, New York: W.W. Norton, 1997, pp. 316-331.

[6]Brown, Norman D., *Daniel Webster and the Politics of Availability*, 1969, pp. 6-7; Beveridge, Albert J., *Abraham Lincoln, 1809-1858*, 2 vols., Boston: Houghton Mifflin, 1928, I, 102.

[7]Belohlavek, *Dallas*, pp. 30-31.

[8]*Niles Weekly Register*, February 6, 1830, pp. 393-395.

[9]*Ibid.*, February 13, 1830, pp. 411-412.

[10]*Ibid.*, February 20, 1830, pp. 429-430.

[11]Fowler, D.G., 1943, p. 11. Quote on p. 11.

[12]Thompson, Charles Manfred, *The Illinois Whigs Before 1846*, University of Illinois Press, 1915; Rep. Johnson Reprint, 1967, pp. 9-36. See Wait on the Adams-Jackson struggle in the previous book on the Age of Lincoln series,due out soon.

[13]Basler, R.P, IV, 48, 63.

[14]Pratt, Harry E., *Lincoln, 1809-1839*, Springfield, Ill: Abraham Lincoln Association, 1941, pp. xxi-xxii, 8.

[15]Hertz, Emmanuel, *The Hidden Lincoln*, 1938, p. 227.

[16]Shirreff, Patrick.

[17]Anthony Butler to Martin Van Buren, March 9, 1830, Butler, Anthony, Papers, Center of American History, University of Texas at Austin.

[18]Webster, *Correspondence*, III, 32-33.

[19]Remini, *Legacy*, pp. 62-66.

[20]McLemore, pp. 64-67.

[21]*Niles Weekly Register*, March 20, 1830, pp. 67-68.

Chapter 17

JACKSON DEMOCRATS

Weed became the editor of the Anti-Masonic New York newspaper, named the *Albany Evening Journal* and appearing first on March 22, 1830. He wrote editorials attacking the Regency and Jackson and supporting Wirt. He deliberately turned from attacks upon Masonry to further conservatism in New York politics. His efforts in the election of 1832 failed. The Whig party was founded in these years and Weed was in on the bottom floor. Weed worked in 1834 for the election of Seward for governor. The Democrats won however and the greatly disappointed Weed thought of moving to Michigan.

In the early spring of 1830, considerable politicking took place in preparation for the next election in the United States over two years later. Democratic members of the Pennsylvania legislature met in caucus to support Jackson for a second term in office. They unanimously voted to express their happiness with Jackson's work and the prosperity of the country in his administration. They noted that it was their opinion that Jackson would run for president the next time around. There were soon reports of the caucus which were negative. It was claimed that attendance was low, that there was a division in the ranks, and that Van Buren and Calhoun wings clashed. Friends of Jackson called these negative reports ridiculous and lacking in foundation.

New Yorker legislators also formed a caucus meeting and, almost without reception, supported Jackson. They called for a convention to be held at Herkimer in September. It would have delegates from each assembly districts. Members expressed happiness with Jackson's reelection to the presidency. [1]

Reports publishing by Hezekiah Niles showed that between the adoption of the constitution and October the first of 1829, there had been expended over four million dollars for public internal improvements in the United States. This compared with a ten-year total of fourteen million dollars for pensions covering these last years. The government expended this much more on pensions for a shorter period than for the development of roads, river improvements, and canals.

The largest amount of the total of four million dollars was spent for the Cumberland to Ohio road. Close to half of the money was appropriated for this road. They expended over $1.6 million on this pike. In the long period government officials provided $390 thousand for improvements in Ohio and over $307 thousand for roads and canals in Delaware. Both states had early routes in this field. Virginia received $150 thousand, Indiana received $108 thousand, Massachusetts got $104 thousand, with lesser amounts in Maine, Connecticut, Rhode Island, New York, Pennsylvania, Maryland, North Carolina, Tennessee, Mississippi, Illinois, Alabama, Missouri, Arkansas, Michigan, and Florida. The general government appropriated $90 in Kentucky.

Large amounts were provided for the continuance of the Cumberland road and its repairs. Other roads were built. These were the roads from Nashville to Natchez, the road from Wheeling to the Mississippi, the road from Mississippi to Ohio, the roads from Georgia to New Orleans, the road from Nashville to New Orleans, and the road through the Creek nation. Other expenditures were military roads; roads in Tennessee, Louisiana, and Georgia; surveys, maps, and charts on the Mississippi and Ohio rivers; opening of the old Natchez road; and the five thousand dollar break-water at the mouth of the Delaware bay. [2]

The Jacksonian Democrats controlled the legislature of New Jersey and elected a majority of Democrats to Congress, but they lost the presidential electors in the state in 1828 and 1836, winning in 1824 and 1832. In early 1830, there appeared in Newark a group of employers and employees using the term "workingmen" in their operations. A man going under the designation "A Mechanic" spoke out in sympathy for workers, finding fault with the town's school board. There were other things in the town he did not like.

Mechanics in town met and made a platform and nominations for town offices. They favored universal free education, help for the poor, and new methods for voting regulations. On the presidency, an issue of importance, they refused to put forth a choice. A Jacksonian group there disagreed with the mechanics' choice of town officials in nomination.

At a town meeting on April 12, 1830, the workingmen won elections for their candidates and support for their platform. Constables were limited in number, a ballot replaced voice votes, and school money was better distributed in Newark. The success of the workingmen kept them active for the rest of the year. Later, the workingmen moved into the state as opposed to city elections, receiving an appeal from the Whigs who said that their candidates were good mechanics and workingmen also. Jacksonian Democrats then joined with the mechanics party. The politicians wanted in on a good thing. The Whigs were left out. The combined group won many electoral victories that year of 1830. Whigs lost crucial elections.

With victory, the workingmen dissolved as a political group and the Whigs triumphed in congressional elections. The workingmen did not have the staying power and things changed. Democratic support came generally from farmers and not the workingmen who were sporadic in their political activities in 1830 and in subsequent years in New Jersey. Then too they probable realized that the Democrats were not a labor party at the time and voted on other issues besides the labor issue. This explains their general support of Whigs in the next election after their big victory. The labor radicals could not stand alone, lacking in numbers or they would have kept power and a laboring movement. However, for a time the labor interest was a cohesive force in New Jersey politics for the first time in the United States of America. [3]

Before the Indian Removal Act of 1830 was passed, the Choctaw mixed-blood leader Greenwood Le Flore decided to take advantage of the opportunity to gain favorable treatment for himself and his tribe. He had long been urged to emigrate westward from Choctaw lands in Mississippi and Alabama. Having listened to efforts for years to gain his support, Le Flore took the opportunity to submit a removal treaty to President Jackson in April, urged on by Methodist missionary Alexander Talley, who feared that it the state abrogated tribal law, it would lead to Choctaw demoralization and the wholesale introduction of liquor. Jackson reacted promptly. This could be, he thought, the basis of a formal agreement.

The president asked the advice of the Senate and said the amount the land could then be sold for by the federal government to the individual settlers. Still, most senators thought the terms were too extravagant and sent it back to Jackson, without taking any such action such as the amendment Jackson suggested. With the ball back in his court, Jackson sent Secretary Eaton and his close friend John Coffee to Mississippi to negotiate a formal treaty. Coffee had been a general in the War of 1812, who had fought under Jackson and who had destroyed Tallushatchee and fought in other Jacksonian battles. [4]

General Bustamante was president of Mexico when the immigration law of 1830 was passed. He had a friend in Manuel de Mier y Teran and appointed him special commissioner of colonization to enforce the law and deal with the colonists. The Texans expected the worst in Teran since he was associated with their hated enemy Bustamante. However, the new official and Stephen F. Austin had known each other back in Mexico City and became close friends in Texas. Teran had written Austin that they were the only two men who understood Texan affairs, and they alone were able to regulate them. He proved to be a very lenient manager for the colonists. It was natural when a loyal Austin suggested that the colonists should exhibit patience and peace.

Things were not to become so peaceful. The Texan could not guarantee that. Anahuac on Trinity Bay, was a major port in the Mexican state. Colonel Juan Davis Bradburn was a Kentuckian in the Mexican army. Bradburn was appointed to command the fort and the Serbian from Southeastern Europe was made customs collector. Bradburn was to be the center of trouble later in the history of Texas. [5]

Meanwhile, American novelist James Fenimore Cooper was visiting in Venice. He got the idea for *The Bravo* there and used a reading in Venetian history to flesh out the plot. Still in Europe, he got information for the book's scope and message from the July Revolution in France and the resulting Belgian revolution against the Dutch and Polish resurrection against the Russians. Deeply sympathetic to the people seeking democracy and freedom, he was glad to see his friend achieve success in enthroning a citizen- king.

In Rome in the preceding year, Cooper had made friends with Polish patriot and poet Adam Mickiewicz. The American worked to raise funds for the Polish in Paris by serving on a committee and in the United States with appeals. His European book centered on an heiress and her unloved and unloving fiancé and a happy young nobleman. Other characters are a tenderhearted jailer's daughter and an assassin for excitement. The Council's murder of a protesting old fisherman whose grandson was impressed to service in a terrible life rowing in state galleys forms the subject. [6]

Charlotte Cushman was one of the great actresses of her generation with acclaim at home after their recognition in London proved much praised. She was born in Boston of Puritan ancestry and well educated. Her birth date was in November of 1814. Because she was a good singer, she decided to make that her career. With instruction from the masters, Cushman appeared in a concert in Boston on March 25, 1830. Mrs. Joseph Wood was in Boston for a program featuring her singing and she noted Charlotte who was one of her singers. The professional regarded the amateur as having a fine contralto and advised the fledging to sing on the stage. Her first important performance was a Countess Almaviva in "The Marriage of Figaro" at Tremont Theatre in the city. This was on April 8, 1835. She was twenty.

Soon, Cushman sailed for New Orleans, but upon performing had voice problems by trying for soprano parts of the program. This strained her voice and she abandoned singing roles for straight acting. She was Lady Macbeth in New York's Bowery Theatre and then was a leading actress at Park. She went to Philadelphia and starred. At the opening of the National Theatre, she then went to England. The critics there acknowledged her as one of the finest artists in her generation. She played in roles with Macready, the famous Shakespearean actor of England. That was a great opportunity and resulted in recognition and great praise.

Charlotte was in Europe for three or four years, before returning to New York City's Broadway Theatre as Mrs. Haller. After this, she was an actress in Europe and America in various parts. Still later, she raised money to care for the Union wounded in the Civil War. The crowds flocked to the plays she acted in and the way was open for the future to consider Cushman to be one of the greats of her generation. She never married. [7]

The son of a poor man, a man who had made it on his own, a powerful debater in Congress, a nullifier who had started as a strong nationalist like Calhoun, George McDuffie prepared a report on the Bank. It was unusual in a man of his beliefs to favor the bank cause, but this McDuffie did and very assertively at that. He was entrusted with the report because he was chairman of the ways and means committee. [8]

He presented three questions. Did the Congress have the constitutional power to charter the bank? Was it expedient to establish such a bank? Was it expedient to establish a national bank, founded upon the credit of the government and revenues? McDuffie wrote to the point, Congress did have the right to charter the bank. The representative was so certain that he wrote that the government's right was no longer subject to controversy. The founders of the constitution in Washington's administration also shared this idea. Jefferson had differed during in his terms in office and the matter caused a division between the political parties. There were those in Jefferson's cabinet who favored a national bank. Trouble changed minds and the Madison government decided to re-establish the Bank of the United States to solve these problems. When the war ended, the bank charter for the second bank was dropped only to be reestablished in later years. It was expedient to prolong the bank because of the prosperity the bank helped maintain. The Bank of the United States was necessary for the country's future, bringing strength to the government, the nation, and its economy. [9]

Still deceived as to Jackson's true hostility toward his Bank of the United States, Nicholas Biddle wrote William B. Lewis on May 8, 1830, thanking him for his favor and going into detail on his feelings, believing that Jackson could not be but impressed by the bank's good work. He wrote that since he had talked with Lewis, he felt that Jackson would be favorable once he understood that the Bank was doing great things for the government. Jackson did not see this and remained hostile despite the blindness of Biddle who still thought that Jackson would support the Bank when he knew all of this good work. His friendly feelings for Jackson were not appreciated nor was his non-political stance. Jackson wanted to use the Bank for political purposes and did not want a neutral bank above partisanship. Jackson was for partisans and being a politician of time would never have stood for the bi-partisanship of a Truman or Eisenhower. It was the president's view or nothing.

Biddle refused to recognize that the Whigs and Jackson friends were telling the truth when they said that Jackson was hostile to the Bank. He believed what he wanted to believe, that is that he was safe being above politics and that Jackson would follow sound thinking men in the country who supported the Bank. Biddle knew that the Bank was a credit to the nation and its economy and thought that Jackson knew that also. He also thought that Van Buren was friendly to the Bank, but this was not the case either. The banker refused to see the truth. And Lewis deliberately mislead Biddle by telling him the lie that the president would accept a national bank. He said that Jackson would support the Bank of the United States Van Buren himself was hesitant about attacking the Bank and this mislead Biddle.

On June 14, 1830, Clay wrote from Ashland to Biddle, warning him of the plan to destroy the Bank. It was the third intimation of danger that the banker received following a long press campaign against the Bank and a long spat of rumors. Clay wrote that he had received information from an intelligent citizen of Virginia that "the plan was laid at Richmond during a visit to that place by the secretary of state least autumn, to make the destruction of the Bank the basis of the next presidential election. The message of the president, and other indications, are the supposed consequences of that plan."

During that summer, Jackson was in Nashville and Josiah Nichol, head of the bank there, tried to convince Jackson of the good work the bank was doing in Tennessee. Nichol reported to Biddle that Jackson's only complaint was that foreigners owned so much of the bank's stock. He was well satisfied that Jackson was convinced of the non-political stand of the bank. Jackson wanted to control the situation and do away with a strong bank, so Nichol was also misleading Biddle. Jackson kept his views from Biddle and delayed action only because the government and public opinion was not ready for an anti-Bank move. Jackson reportedly believed that Biddle was a great banker, but this was not necessary a true statement, even if Jackson did say it. It took the next year for Biddle to wake up. He wrote on May 4, 1831, that Jackson was intent upon destroying the Bank. The president would use all of the power he had to do this. [10]

Writing as an economist and financier in December of 1830, Albert Gallatin published an essay supporting the idea of the Bank of the United States as a good power in the nation. It had, he wrote, done many valuable acts to benefit the national economy. The bank was very useful and served the interests of the nation's people. Mr. Biddle circulated Gallatin's pamphlet seeking to influence public opinion. Later, Gallatin wrote a pamphlet stressing the value of free trade. He came to the opinion that a tariff of 25% would be enough to take care of governmental expenses. He called for tariff reform to reduce the tariff to that figure. He wrote of free trade theory. Gallatin was later to go to New York City and become a bank president. He worked to advance education for all of the people. People must be educated to vote right and intelligently. He promoted a new university. [11]

In Jackson's day, the exports were mostly that of cotton and the economy subject to the production and demand of that product. The flow of capital was from capital rich Great Britain to capital scarce American. It varied in accord to expected returns. When returns looked good, money flowed into the United States. America was a varying market. American affected Great Britain and was affected by her. Expansion was strong from a trough in incorporations of 1820-22, about that time for building, public land sales from 1823, immigrations in 1823, and in transport from 1825. Peaks were reached in 1832, 1834, 1835,1836, and 1837. The Jackson years as a rule were prosperous years. The country was growing.

Exports were strong primarily in cotton from 1829. Imports provided things Americans could use. Capital flowed in England. The export market was related to American demands for foreign capital. Wheat, corn, and hogs were exported also, especially to the southern states. Southerners kept accounts in London counting houses. Most foreign capital though went to purchasing state and local bond issues used for roads and railroads. [12]

---

[1]*Niles Weekly Register*, April 24, 1830, pp. 169-170.

[2]*Ibid.*, April 10, 1830, p. 123.

[3]Nadwornz, Milton J., "New Jersey Workingmen and the Jacksonians," *New Jersey History*, 67 July 1949, pp. 186-189, 198.

[4]Satz, *American*, pp. 66-68; Wait, Eugene M., *America and the War of 1812*, Commack, NY: Kroshka Books, 1999, p. 197.

[5]McAlister, G.A., *Alamo*, p. 54.

[6]Grossman, *Cooper*, pp. 75-77.

[7]Brown, *History*, p. 89.

[8]*Niles Weekly Register*, May 1, 1830, pp. 183ff; *Dictionary of American Biography*, VI (2) 34-36.

[9]*Niles Weekly Register*, May 1, 1830, pp. 184-185.

[10]Biddle, pp. 99-108, 126.

[11]Adams, Henry, *The Life of Albert Gallatin*, 1879, Rep. New York: Peter Smith, 1943, pp. 638-640, 648.

[12]Williamson, J.G., "International Trade and United States Economic Development: 1827-1843," pp. 372-378.

Chapter 18

JAIL

On May 15, 1830, while Garrison was in jail for his beliefs and hard language, the English, in distant London across the Atlantic, were making history. They met in Exeter Hall to hold their annual convention of the Anti-Slavery Society. And aged William Wilberforce sat with other leaders on the platform while his follower Thomas Fowell Buxton resolved to abolish imperial slavery and the earliest possible moment. The moderates in their society supported the resolution, which less patient and more militant abolitionists amended to make stronger and provide for immediate action. The radicals then went throughout their country to organize and preach with lectures, pamphlets, handbills, and posters. They were to have an overwhelming success by August 19, 1833, when slaves were freed in West Indies. Garrison saw an affinity and decided to use the radical's methods. In England, the abolitionists had a powerful parliament, while in the United States, Congress had certain limits. And in the United States there was a Southern interest, which was strong and overwhelmed the abolitionist until the Southerners overreacted and seceded form the Union. Southerners tended to dominate the nation from 1789 to 1860. [1]

On May 23, 1830, a son was born to the John Tellers. They named him Henry Moore Teller. This son was later to go west and become a mining lawyer. He was to be a senator and Secretary of the Interior and fight for the cause of silver and cheap money. His father, John Teller was a farmer who owned a heavily wooded section of land in Allegheny County, a frontier type area which emigrations and development had passed by. Henry was to work on the farm and go to school with Sundays set aside for church and talking politics. The mail came once a week to the village store and the people would gather there on Saturday afternoons and receive their mail. John was a Democrat and a temperance man who lived according to a strict code and subscribed to the cause at hand. He soon became an abolitionist. His interest in the needy was great and he saw to it that his sons rose in life through education. Henry was his big success story of his life. Like a true man, his children were important to him and he worked for their betterment. [2]

The people of Maryland were unhappy with the defeat of their Baltimore and Ohio Railroad bill in Congress, while the people of Kentucky were joyful with the passage of their Maysville road within the state. When Jackson received the Maysville road bill in the White House, he wasted no time in vetoing the bill. In addition, the president rejected by veto the Washington, Rockville, and Frederick Turnpike road bill. He stated his friendliness to internal improvements. He noted the wide areas of opinion in the nation on the issue. After writing of his views and on constitutionality, he decided that the bills were unconstitutional. His exposition was long and wordy. [3]

There were a large number of Americans who stood steadfastly against the Jackson Indian Removal Bill. One of these was William Wirt, the attorney general in the Monroe cabinet. He was noted as a lawyer and an author of a book on Virginia life and had prosecuted Aaron Burr. On May 28, 1830, Congress passed the bill by a narrow margin, to Wirt's disgust. He opposed Jacksonian Indian policy so much after that that he became counsel to the Cherokees.

In order to achieve the implementation of the Indian Removal Act, President Jackson called for the Cherokees, Creeks, Chickasaw, and Choctaws to meet with him in Nashville, Tennessee. When, he received news of the call, John Ross held a general council of Cherokees in July. Jeremiah Evarts, who had been their advocate, advised the Cherokees to send the Ridges, father and son, and the principal chief to see Jackson and learned what was on his mind and guard against the purchase of individual Cherokees. The Cherokees did not follow Evarts' advice and did not send a deputation to Nashville. Jackson rightfully blamed Wirt for this decision. John Ridge prevailed upon the Creeks to also boycott the Nashville meeting.

At the council, Major Ridge spoke and the council passed a resolution authorizing Ross to take their case to the courts, because Jackson had decided not to pay the annuity in one lump sum to the Cherokee treasury but to divide it up on a per capita basis to prevent the Cherokee leadership from using the money. Some of the Indians would have to travel 180 miles for fifty cents. However the Cherokees were able to depend upon northern sympathizers for their legal fees. The public spirited Wirt and other lawyers were eager for the fray. Wirt and his fellows found a case they could use in the Georgia courts and appeal to the American Supreme Court by a writ of error. [4]

Minister McLane in London, faced with a stalemate so far in Anglo-American relations, used other means to obtain a commercial agreement. Van Buren intimate C.C. Cambreleng submitted a report against the tariff and in favor of free trade. McLane circulated this report widely in England. The attitude was warming in Great Britain at this time and McLane told the New York merchant and congressman Cambreleng that we shall recover the direct trade. On the twenty-sixth of May, Jackson sent a positive message to Congress that he would receive dispatches from McLane. At this point, on the 29th, there was a step forward when Senator Samuel Smith, a Baltimore merchant in the Senate, sponsored a measure which passed on that day. This resolution authorized Jackson "to issue a proclamation of reciprocity which he had satisfactory evidence that the British would resume trade based upon the Act of 1825."

During the succeeding summer, McLane worked for the success of the trade issue. In July, he was able to informed Aberdeen that Congress had just passed a law, which reduced the duties on West Indian produce. He said that Jackson and Congress showed themselves willing to compromise and McLane insisted that Parliament do the same. On August 17, 1830, Aberdeen, the British foreign minister was able to inform the American minister that American trade would be restored on the basis of the Act of 1825. Months later, the Wellington-Aberdeen coalition fell. Lord Palmerston would become foreign secretary. He had conservative commercial policies and a questionable friendship for the United States. The American vessels could now trade directly with Canadians and West Indian folk. [5]

In Maine about this time, there was an aspiring young lawyer by the name of Hannibal Hamlin, who was a follower of Jackson's, a born leader in his community, but so far of minor importance. Hamlin was destined to become a senator and the first vice-president of Lincoln's administration. Born into a middle class family whose father was a doctor, Hannibal grew up to be a skilled athlete who was fair minded about his victories. At one time or the other Hamlin wanted to be a soldier and an actor, but instead he received more education and became a lawyer, a political leader whose father divined politics to be his son's forte. His father's death prevented Hannibal from getting more education than an academy schooling. Instead, he took care of the family farm and read law as a means of becoming a lawyer.

When still a boy, Hannibal had read the *Eastern Argus* when it was delivered because his father was busy with the reading of the Adams Republicans paper in the state. The broad-minded father subscribed to both the Adams and Jacksonian newspapers. From reading this Democratic paper, Hannibal became a Jacksonian Democrat, while his father had been an Adams Republican. His fate was set. Once grown, he and Horatio King purchased the *Oxford Jeffersonian* in May of 1830. They learned how to set type and press the paper and spoke out for the common man's president and his party in the elections of 1830. Within months, it was evident that he would not get rich or anywhere near rich publishing the paper so he sold out to King, his portion.

Hamlin's militia company nominated him for the state legislature where once elected, he became the leader of new members. A staunch Democrat, a staunch Jacksonian Democrat, Hamlin was swept into office like was usual in the Democratic state, basic views of democracy and equal opportunities kept him fresh in state politics with a strong following among the people. He supported Jackson's stand on currency, considering hard or metal currency to be the best currency deserving of a premium in the market place. [6]

One Dr. Ephraim McDowell was a noted physician. Born in Rockbridge County, Virginia, on November 11, 1771, he was the son of Samuel McDowell and his wife Mary McClung. He received a medical degree from the University of Maryland in 1825 and had earlier gone to lectures for medical students at the University of Edinburgh in Scotland from 1793 to 1794. Marrying Sarah Shiby in 1802, they went to Kentucky.

They had six children. A pioneer in abdominal surgery, he performed the first ovariotomy in the United States in 1809. He performed twelve more with only one death by 1824 and repeatedly performed radical operative cures for monstrangulated hernias, at least 32 operations for bladder stones with a single death, and used lateral perineal incision. Often, he worked for charity patients. Helping found the Episcopal Church of Danville, Kentucky, and Centre College in Danville, he died there on June 25, 1830, and was buried in Danville. [7]

There was a more famous person than McDowell coming to America about the time of the surgeon's death. On May 25, 1830, Mexican liberal Lorenzo de Zavala, with his life threatened by the ruling party, left Mexico City for exile in the United States in the company of Colonel Jose Antonio Mejia. His companion was secretary of the Mexican legation to Washington. The two men departed for New Orleans, where they were to be plagued by mosquitoes. Fernando VII of Spain had a newspaper in that city entitled *El Espanol*. The editor took notice of Zavala's arrival with insults, but other newspapers praised him. New Orleans's architecture did not appeal to him, but he took a great delight in its commercial and shipping power at the crossroads of the great river and its tributaries and the Gulf.

Zavala had arrived on June 10th, and lodged in luxury at the French inns of Madame, one of the best in the city. It cost three dollars a day for the good food and beds. He found the city gloomy and unhealthy. Indeed, the city's location was suitable for nothing except for commerce. For the latter, Zavala thought its location was ideal. New Orleans was lower than the river and was protected by sand levees. The ships were able to load and unload using short planks because of the deepness of the river next to the levees. He liked the navigable waters of inland rivers, which stretched into the interior and along the coast to Florida. New Orleans had about seventy thousand people at the time, a people subjected to yellow fever, intermittent fever, and other diseases. [8]

---

[1]Thomas, *Liberator*, pp. 121-123.

[2]Ellis, Elmer, *Henry Moore Teller: Defender of the West*, Caldwell, Idaho: Caxton, 1941, *passim*.

[3]*Niles Weekly Register*, June 5, 1830, pp. 269-275.

[4]Wilkins, 1986, pp. 214-215.

[5]Belohlavek, *Eagle*, pp. 57-58.

[6]Hunt, Draper, *Hannibal Hamlin of Maine: Lincoln's First Vice-President*, Syracuse: Syracuse University Press, 1969, pp. 4-11, 15-18.

[7]*Who Was Who*, Historical, p. 416.

[8]Zavala, Lorenzo de, *Journey to the United States of North America*, Trans. Woolsey, Wallace, Austin, Tx: Shoal Creek, 1980, pp. 7-12.

Chapter 19

JACKSON'S TRIP HOME

Headed home for a vacation, Jackson arrived in Cincinnati by steamboat on June 28, 1830, and was well received. A large crowd ran along the bank of the Ohio River to greet the incoming president in their spontaneous manner. Virtually unplanned, the celebration did have some made-up banners, but mostly it was natural. There were flags, shouts, and joyful words. Lower classes of workers, laborers, and craftsmen seem particularly happy at their president's arrival.

On June 29, the traveling Mexican democrat Lorenzo de Zavala and General Don Jose Antonio Mejia, then in Cincinnati, met with Jackson in his modestly furnished house, borrowed for his stay. The president was in an armchair with some 25 or 30 persons, whom Zavala took for workmen and craftsman. Cordially received, the Mexicans talked with the old general, who asked of the fate of General Vicente Guerrero, who had been president of Mexico. Jackson was sad at his ouster. Doubtless the people's cause that Guerrero was promoting would end in a complete triumph. [1]

Jackson reached Nashville and his home. It was a relaxed visit among friends and other friendly citizens. Topping off the visit was a dinner with them in a grove between Nashville and his plantation called the Hermitage. Some four hundred people were assembled and seated at a table the length of one hundred yards for a fine repast in a simple setting. They ate good food without luxury. The meeting was easy and outgoing. He talked freely with these his friends and neighbors and the many enjoyed brief greetings and talks with the president.

In the same season, Henry Clay was honored with dinners and meetings. At Columbus, Ohio, he partook of a meeting and public dinner in which extensive toasts was made. Clay found himself among friends who welcomed the chance of expressing themselves and listening to Clay. The congressman from Kentucky toasted Columbus and the people toasted Clay as a first rate workman and protector. Men made toasts also to internal improvements. R.C. Cowles stated that western republicans despite the presidential veto would sustain the roads and canals. [2]

In the summer of 1830, travelers were enjoying riding on the Baltimore and Ohio Railroad. Some people thought that interest would subside after the adventurous had their ride on the line. Their curiosity would then had been satisfied and they would not concern themselves further. The repeated trips of the many proved this idea wrong. People enjoyed the trip and increasingly saw its value. Traveling at a usual rate of ten miles per hour, the train provided a good choice for traffic. Men and women from other parts of the Union were highly gratified and people from the west saw its benefits for them. Westerners wanted it to reach their lands. They were enthusiastic over the railroad.

Travelers watched the scenery out of their windows. They also saw the roadway, bridges, and cuts since it was a double track. Their marvel was over the turns outs and crossing places which improved the railway. Granite rails were then being used.

While people were enjoying the trip over already completed lines, construction continued. The granite rails were economically equal to wood and wore much better. Workers made progress on the triple-arched viaduct at Ellicott's' mill. Below them was the right of way of the turnpike. A passage was cut at Tarpeian Rock to provide a clear way toward Patapsco. Workers extended the line toward the forty-mile mark. When the viaduct was finished there followed a celebration presided over by Philip E. Thomas, president of the line. [3]

At this time, in Vermont, Benjamin F. Bailey ran for Congress. His campaign manager was that versatile Vermonter, George Perkins Marsh, who later spent so much time in Italy as a diplomat. Marsh was born on March 15, 1801, in Woodstock to Charles Marsh and his wife Susan Perkins Marsh. Charles was a lawyer and a large landowner. They were Calvinists, conservatives, and gentlemen. At a young age, George preferred to stay indoors and play with girls. He early studied Latin and Greek under the tutoring of his half-brother Charles Marsh Jr. Introduced to books, he almost went blind. When he had recovered somewhat from this, he took to the outdoors. He grew to love nature. After four years of being unable to read, he received his first formal education.

In 1816, his father sent him away to Phillips Academy at Andover, Massachusetts. After a few months there he went away to Dartmouth for more narrow and humdrum education. He was ahead of his class and had little socializing with others. Once again, he had trouble with his eyes, but after a time he studied law and became a lawyer in Burlington, Vermont. He made a partnership with Bailey and followed Governor Cornelius P. Van Ness, whom came to support Jackson in 1828. Now in Vermont, Jackson was unpopular, and the Jacksonians in the state had to share that position. When Bailey died in May of 1832, Marsh found a partner in Wyllys Lyman, his brother-in-law. In 1828, he had married a lady of even temper, cheerfulness, and high spirit named Harriet Buell, who died five years later, leaving behind two children. The eldest son died eleven days after Harriet. After a time, he married the young Caroline Crane. Following this marriage, he became more social and also took up the study of the Goths and immediately got them confused with the Anglo-Saxons of his ancestry. [4]

In June, the Jacksonian secretary of war wrote Greenwood Le Flore about a possible united government of Cherokees, Creeks, and Chickasaw in the western Indian preserve.

He recognized their degree of civilization and thought that they might eventually be given one or more delegates in Congress for them to be able to represent their political views there and influence legislation. They could not fail to become a great people and eventually might even obtain territorial government.

There was one serious problem, the Government might not be able to find land for the Chickasaw. If suitable land was not found then they could not be moved. He suggested that the Choctaws might give them land on their northern border. The Choctaws did have some fifteen or seventeen million acres of land and should be able to provide land for the Chickasaw tribe.

"The Chickasaws so long accustomed to self-control, would dislike to have merged their national name and character. They would prefer their ancient customs and own self-government; but upon the federative plan I have spoken of, both nations would presently become the same people, and dwell under the same principles of government. The strength of each nation would be greatly increased." They could preserve their traditions but this was only possible through a government, rational and inspiring. If the Indians followed his suggestions there would be a great future promise for Indian happiness. [5]

Among the Cherokees, Chief Ross made a speech on July 11th, the whites had mistreated telling of the ways his tribe. He gave the grievances at length, of violated white honor. He ended his perforation with an appeal to God. "Confiding in the superintending care of a kind Providence we should not despair even should we for a season be plunged into the cells of Georgia prisons. Means for our deliverance may yet be found. Let us not forget the circumstance in Holy Writ of the safe passage of the children of Israel through the crystal walls of the Red Sea and the fate of their wicked pursuers; let out faith in the unsearchable mysteries of an omnipotent and all-wise Being be unshaken; for in the appearance of impossibilities there is still hope." [6]

When Jackson secured a bill to effect transfer of Indian lands to the United States, he was ready for a visit home to Tennessee. He, John H. Eaton, and John Coffee, reached Eaton's home in Franklin on August 11th to try and get a meeting with Indian delegates. However, there was internal strife among the Choctaw Nation and it was possible for them to send delegates to the president. Only Chickasaw delegates appeared. Eaton and Coffee went to Mississippi to talk to the Choctaw Indians, after negotiating a provisional treaty with the Chickasaw.

The shrewd half-breed Greenwood La Flore, although chief of only one of the three Chickasaw districts, had an influence throughout that nation. An intelligent and forceful man, he had called a meeting of some headmen friendly to him and told them there must be one chief of the entire tribe. He wanted the position. He said that it was a good move to be undertaken in a crisis. They voted to make La Flore that chief. He claimed title and quickly announced for emigration. When La Flore gave a treaty for this purpose to Jackson's envoy Major D.W. Haley, the other chiefs and many of their braves protested. However, the Senate rejected the treaty and La Flore had to begin all over again.

La Flore tried to get Chief Mushulatubbe to resign, but the district leader refused and the conflict revolved around the two men. Opposition continued to mount, and the full bloods remembered that La Flore had tried to Christianize them. Some of them burnt some books and one or two churches. A conflict frizzled and finally La Flore rather unexpectedly had his way about the removal to the West. They signed a treaty to this effect on May 28, 1830. Most of the warriors opposed the treaty but they had no leader who could organize them to fight the Dancing Rabbit Creek Treaty as it was called. [7]

Jackson's political opponents seized upon the Indian Removal Act of 1830 to attack the president. It was fourth only to the tariff, internal improvements, and bank issues. Henry Clay, seeking the presidency, acted to rally support for his ideas and protest against Jacksonian policy for the 1832 election. He encouraged the holding of public meetings to lobby nation-wide. A flood of petitions reached Congress from religious and humanitarian groups to urge the repeal of the Removal Act. Clay and his friends urged the Cherokees to appeal to the people and the Supreme Court to enlist their sympathy. To help them Jeremiah Evarts composed a popular appeal and William Wirt was enlisted to plead the Cherokee case before the high court.

Clay, Webster, Spencer, Frelinghuysen in particular championed the Cherokee case. Although Clay had a low opinion of Indian character and thought that the natives were justly doomed to extinction, he believed that the United States had complete sovereignty over the Indians and their territory. Also he thought that the United States had to respect Indian treaty rights. He was at odds with most Jacksonian thoughts on the issue. Daniel Webster had long contended that the Indians had clear title to their lands, but he was eager to invest in land taken from the Indians in the Old Northwest.

Congressman Ambrose Spencer differed in words and action also. He appealed to feelings of humanity toward a noble and injured people, but eight years earlier had tried to extend state law over the Indians in his state, New York. The policy and action of Frelinghuysen coincided. His sympathy for the Indian was deep and like the other three, he believed the Cherokee and Creek had rights to independence. Although not without political ambitions, he felt that he was doing God's work in this world.

William Wirt was persuaded to undertake the legal defense of the Indians in order to embarrass the president politically although he had previously accepted the arguments of Thomas McKenney. He could not pass by the chance to take action against the president. From this moment, he argued that the Indians had a legal right to remain in Georgia and other states. He joined Chief Justice John Marshall's sympathy for the Indians and planned a test case. Evarts collected statements in a book and arranged anti-removal article in the *North American Review*. At this point Jackson made the mistake of relieving McKenney of his position after the success in Congress. McKenney joined Clay at his friends and spoke out against the removal policy of the president. [8]

Jackson was anti-black as well as anti-Indian. He was after all a slaveholder. Another important reason for Jackson's hostility to abolitionists was a fear of secession by southern states. Southerners such as Robert Walker of Mississippi believed that it were the abolitionists who were the non-unionists, because their success would lead to disunion. Northern Democrats feared this and actively worked to defeat the anti-slavery forces in the nation. Garrett D. Wall of New Jersey stated on February 29, 1836, that slavery was such a pillar of the nation, of the Union, that to remove the foundation in slavery would destroy the entire edifice. He was a Democrat and a former governor.

In their support of slavery, the Democrats had sympathy and personal political ties to Southerners. They also had an allegiance to Andrew Jackson, a slaveholder, and vigorous buyer and seller of slaves. He could and did offer a reward for an escaped slave, plus extra money if the captor or any person was liberal with the poor creature's flogging up to 300 blows, which was enough to bring death for the weaker among the enslaved. Boston authorities prevented African American students from attending the festivities upon a Jackson visit in the summer of 1833 so that they could not offend the president with the free African Americans of that city. Englishman Edward S. Abdy recorded that all of the African Americans that he met were anti-Jacksonians. Many Democratic leaders were slaveholders or had been owners of slaves. Jackson and other leaders of the party were hostile to abolitionism. Almost all of the nation's Democrats were pro-slavery. The president condemned the anti-slavery agitators as monsters, who should be killed. Labor leader Ely Moore stated that abolitionism was allied to fanaticism and would spread conflagration and death in the nation. Jackson surely agreed with such a view as a slaveholder.

Senator John M. Niles of Connecticut held the abolitionists up to scorn because they had petitioned on the behalf of Indians and would use the national surplus to dispatch missionaries to Asia. They were meddling with matters outside their understanding and business. Orestes A. Brownson from Massachusetts felt that abolitionism was the ultimate evil. New Yorker James K. Paulding wrote that they were enemies of law, religion, and rights. They did not love liberty or justice, George Henry Evans believed, but were merely interested in converting the blacks to their sect. These were lies as were the following. Democrats felt that slavery was a matter of property rights and states rights.

The African Americans were inferior and would create a problem if freed. The white man must maintain superiority. Slaves were free from care and unlike whites and freed blacks, would be cared for in their old age. Slavery elevated African Americans from their fellows in Africa. They were better off than the white workers of the North or the white peasants of Europe. These were the views of Northern Democrats. They also blamed England and France for abolitionism and claimed the goals of these two nations were to arrest progress in the United States. [9]

The Tappan brothers were the sons of a modest businessman and an orthodox mother. Five of them did well financially and socially, rising to a status superior to that of their sire. Lewis and Arthur were to become abolitionists in their middle age, a growth perhaps of their Calvinistic upbringing and their mother's oft expressed concern for their salvation during their childhood and adulthood alike. Lewis was a Federalist and wrote newspaper articles attacking Madison's War of 1812. His chief idea was to push for an immediate settlement. Not an ultra-Federalist, Lewis wanted the Federals to adopt Jeffersonian's political techniques and be positive instead of negative. After the war, he turned to philanthropy instead of a continued presence in politics. This philanthropic bent was a direct antecedent for his later abolitionism. He emphasized education as the solution to social ills. Religiously, Lewis became a Unitarian, but only after a careful study. Arthur also became a philanthropist, giving away much of his profits to worthy causes, and needy relatives. He pressured Lewis to return to orthodoxy.

Then on a mid-summer day in 1830, a young man came into the Tappan establishment. Dressed like a dandy and with an expression of rectitude, he introduced himself as William Lloyd Garrison and told Lewis he wanted to see the senior partner. Led to the office of Arthur Tappan, he turned his great charm on the merchant and gained an one hundred-dollar donation to join with the gifts of others to publish his newspapers on the first day of the following year. The slavery issue had long interested the brothers. Earlier they had played a supporting role in the American Colonization Society. Because of the African colonies had a rum trade, Arthur had withdrawn from the organization. [10]

The Jacksonian found Supreme Court Justice Joseph Story to be a burr under their saddle. Since, they disagreed with his Whig philosophy, they felt that he was dangerous. Louis McLane found him to be a miserable and frivolous bookworm without understanding. Rumors reached Story that Jackson himself thought him to be a most dangerous opponent. Story had started out to be a Jeffersonian and as such was appointed to the Court in 1811. Lawyers sometime change following judicial appointments. One year later, Jefferson thought Story to be a pseudo-Republican. The justice proved an able man and the Jacksonians must have wished him on their side.

Webster found Story to be an especially valuable adviser and drew upon him in questions of law on numerous occasions. Joseph became known in the fields of the judiciary, education, and legal publicity, but behind the scenes, he was an influential politician who played a major role in the early success of Charles Sumner among others. He lectured at Harvard Law School and wrote three major legal books. European jurists especially read these books. A sharp and good mind and much work aided his many areas of expertise. Although his word carried weight in the Whig party, he was never much of a party man. However, he was a conservative and was comfortable among Whigs. His role was as party statesman. [11]

The administration of James Monroe had pledged itself to a republican Latin America, but Spain had not yet pledged itself to accept that fact and not to try to reconquer the parts of their empire in America. Ideologically and commercially, the United States felt her interest was to convince the Spanish that military conquest was folly. There was already reparation claims against the Spanish government for over one million dollars and the Portuguese government for $150,000. These amounts were incurred by Spanish ships in damages done to United States shipping in the revolutionary wars earlier in the century. The Jacksonians wished a favorable commercial treaty with Spain. During Jackson's first term, the Americans averaged slightly over one million dollars in imports and appropriately $400,000 in exports to Spain.

Cuban trade was more prominent than trade with the home country. The North-Americans imported more than $8 million annually in Cuban sugar, coffee, and tobacco.

We exported over $5 million to Cuba in agricultural produce and other items. Only Spain had a greater trade with their captive Cuba than the United States. Jackson's administration had four consuls in Puerto Rico. Cuban trade was eight percent of United States exports. Almost half of the ships who came into Cuba's ports were United States vessels, so that there was an even greater indirect trade, despite discriminatory tonnage duties and tariff rates.

Woodbury was a wise selection to resolve the difficulties with Spain. He possessed great ties in commerce and marriage, understood the Spanish situation, and served as the chairman of the Senate Committee on Congress. The same connection which would have serve America so well was the stumbling block because his wife and children were not eager to cross the Atlantic and did not wish to stay abroad for at least four years. Governor Cornelius P. Van Ness of Vermont did take up the challenge. Jackson instructed Van Ness to obtain a treaty of reciprocity, and to resolve the claims question, which Madrid was still delaying. It was suggested that he remind the Spanish of American friendship with their king. Not only did the United States navy stop a combined Mexican-Colombian expedition that threatened Cuba, but it would stand ready to repeat any such invasion of Cuba in the fifties. It was to be stated that Jackson would act as a mediator to facilitate Spain's recognition of the Hispanic American republics.

In July of 1830, the French overthrew Charles X and the Spanish king Fernando was a little shocked because he relied upon the French king for support. The Spanish king also faced with internecine feuding over the Spanish succession. Van Ness reported in January of 1831 that the Spanish government would not come to an agreement. Later, in that year he criticized the Spanish and hinted at action. Early in 1832, the Spanish reopened talks and Van Ness was partially successful. He got a conditional reduction of tonnage duties for Americans and Spanish continental ports. [12]

In the summer, emigrants from Europe continued to land and settle in the United States. Irishmen were especially set on coming to America. In a given week in July there were two vessels of immigrants from Ireland mixed with a few from elsewhere landed followed by many more. Not all of them stayed. *Niles Weekly Register* noted one rather unusual case. There were seventy British immigrants just arrived at New York. They took a look at the dull business of the time and were alarmed at the heat of the weather, so they turned around and returned to Great Britain. Most immigrants came through New York City. One week alone saw over a thousand people coming through the city. Others came through Baltimore at a rate of over five hundred a month. Gold fields in the southern states from Virginia to Georgia did not draw them, since those finds were limited. Still southern states were busy with the various finds. Slaves working in the gold fields concealed some of it in their hair. Slave owners shaved the "wool" and discovered the gold. [13]

---

[1]Zavala, *Journey*, pp. 49-50.
[2]*Niles Weekly Register*, August 7, 1830, pp. 16-17.
[3]*Ibid.*, August 28, 1830, p. 12, September 4, 1830, p. 17.

[4]Lowenthal, David, *George Perkins Marsh: Versatile Vermonter*, New York: Columbia University Press, 1958, pp. 3-67; Wait, Eugene M., *The March of the Teutons*, New York: Carlton Press, 1972, *passim*.

[5]Foreman, Grant, *Indian Removal: The Emigration of the Five Civilized Tribes of Indians*, Norman, Okla: University of Oklahoma Press, pp. 194-195. Quote on p. 195.

[6]Cunningham, Hugh T., "A History of the Cherokee Indians, III," *Chronicles of Oklahoma*, VIII (1930), 407. Quote on p. 407.

[7]Foreman, *Indian Removal*, pp. 22-30.

[8]Satz, *American*, pp. 39-43.

[9]Henig, Gerald S., "The Jacksonian Attitude Toward Abolitionism in the 1830's," Tennessee Historical Quarterly, *XXVIII (1969), 42-56.*

[10]Wyatt-Brown, Bertram, *Lewis Tappan and the Evangelical War Against Slavery*, Cleveland, Ohio: Press of Case Western Reserve University, 1969, pp. 1-36ff, 78-80, 85-87.

[11]Newmyer, R. Kent, "A Note on the Whig Politics of Justice Story,' *Mississippi Valley Historical Review*, XLVIII (December 1961, 480-491.

[12]Belohlavek, *Eagle*, pp. 75-78.

[13]*Niles Weekly Register*, August 7, 1830, p. 419.

Chapter 20

ILLINOIS ON JACKSON

A fter a bitter debate in Congress, the congressmen voted for the Indian Removal Bill on May 28, 1830. This act set the policy of the national government on Indian matters. It pronounced a policy of Indian removal and gave Jackson authority to secure exchanges of land. The president and Eaton had planned to vacation in Tennessee, so they decided to confer there with delegates from the four tribes who had promised to move west as wished by the Americans. The two executives, accompanied by John Coffee went to Eaton's home in Franklin. They arrived on August 11, 1830.

Shortly, Coffee and Eaton went on to Dancing Rabbit Creek in the Choctaw Nation to meet with its leaders. The American warned the Indians that the federal government could not protect them from the laws of Mississippi, despite any federal treaties. Should they resist the state's anti-Indian laws, a multitude of armed white men would force them to submit. There was only one thing the Indians could do. They must move to western lands. The Indians were divided in their counsels. After some controversy, many Choctaw left. To the remainder, John Pitchlynn, an Indian, suggested that merchant George S. Gainer, whom they honored for his honesty, character, and ability, conduct a party of Choctaw to the west to look over the lands and decide whether they were satisfactory or not. Gainer would then manage the removal if the western lands were suitable. In order to clinch the deal, Coffee and Eaton arranged that the chiefs and leading men be given land. They passed out medals and gratuities. The Choctaw ceded all the land they held east of the Mississippi. The Treaty of Dancing Rabbit Creek was signed. It gave the Indians three years to move west. Most Choctaw opposed the treaty, but they lacked the necessary leadership to defeat those who were convinced by land and money to give up the lands east of the great river. [1]

In New York State, there was a series of conventions for the purpose of making nominations. The Anti-Masonic convention, the first of three, nominated Francis Granger for the governorship and Samuel Stevens for the lieutenant governor. Granger, of Ontario, New York, was chosen unanimously on the first ballot, and Stevens of New

York City received almost all of the votes on the first ballot and was then chosen unanimously. This was a show of stolidity needed for such a comparatively small party wishing to sweep the state. [2]

Granger was born in Connecticut into a good family. When he was growing up his father, Gideon, was selected by Jefferson as his postmaster general and was carried on as such by Madison. Francis was graduated at Yale and then followed his father to New York. Marrying well, he was later elected to the state assembly in 1825 and served there as a follower of Governor Clinton. A popular man himself, he ran for lieutenant governor and governor at various times including 1830. [3]

The other two conventions were the Republican one at Herkimer and the working man convention at Salina. At this time there were to be others in Delaware, Kentucky, Indiana, and Missouri. Henry M. Ridgely of Delaware was nominated as congressman. He had already been in the national senate. In Kentucky, the Jackson people did not fare too well and in Indiana they lost power in the legislature, Clay having a majority of the state legislature. The followers of Clay made important strides in St. Louis in elections over Jacksonians, who had done well there two years earlier.

Meanwhile, Clay had traveled toward home, being in great demand at stops along the way. He had declined an invitation at Columbus, Ohio, until it was pressed upon him further. Speaking there, he accepted other invitations. At Cincinnati, he received a great welcome, entering in great style and as a conquering general would have been treated. At Lawrenceburg, Indiana, an immense crowd greeted him. General Dill received him there and after a dinner with some four hundred people, Clay spoke for nearly two hours. Clay was entertained at Burlington, Kentucky. He made a well-received speech. His way was smooth and without problems. Clay was clearly in the ascendancy in this summer of 1830, two years before the next presidential election. [4]

Before returning to the national capital, Andrew Jackson met with a delegation from the Chickasaw people in Franklin, Tennessee, on August 27, 1830. Eaton and Coffee were there. One Indian presented a brief address in which they stated their agreement to the white terms. Jackson had sent a message to them four days earlier in which the president stated his pleasures at the prospect of greeting them. He noted their loyalty in the War of 1812 and expressed the problem facing them.

He had learned their plight and their wish to go to new lands beyond the Mississippi. When the laws of Mississippi were extended over them, they had become alarmed. When they agreed to a treaty and sent it to Washington, the U.S. Senate rejected it. Next, Jackson noted, they had asked to see him. President Jackson agreed and was empowered to pay the expenses of their removal to the Indian territories beyond the frontier.

Jackson reassured them. White laws had not harmed the whites and they lived comfortably under them. There was no reason why the Indians could not live contentedly under them. Should they be moved westward, they would find a place where they could live peaceable without intrusion or inter-tribal wars. They would have the protection of the federal government. They chose to move rather than live under the white man's law and they were soon moved, leaving their lands to the greed of the white citizens of Mississippi. [5]

There was no organized party in Illinois at this time, but politics evolved around personalities. There were pro-Jackson men and anti-Jackson men, but since most of the voters were pro-Jackson, no anti-Jackson men could be elected to the governorship or Congress. There was no discernible division, only the lines of principles of government. The parties of the east were not a part of frontier Illinois. Emigrants from those areas were surprised that little attention was paid in the state to party affiliations and the eastern political development was not present in the state. The people of Illinois did not feel the need to have political parties.

An election for the governorship was slated in August of 1830. There were two pro-Jackson candidates. The first, with the lead, was John Reynolds, a judge of the state supreme court for awhile. Thomas Ford was to write of the man, that he was good-natured and easily pliable. His early education was classical and he had peculiar talents. However he spoke like a barely literate man, which was a presentable education for his times. Before running for governor, he had been a farmer, a lawyer, a soldier, a judge, and a legislator. He could and did talk to the backwoods people as one of their own. His education did not protrude upon his appeal to them as an official and person. They accepted him as one of their own and he gained their votes. This was much of a sham, but he did have remarkable good sense and shrewdness for his chosen place in life with a fertile imagination, a ready eloquence, and mirth and pleasant natures when he mingled with the people of common origins. His heart was kind and he was willing to do favors. He did not hold a grudge but banished resentment from his mind.

His opponent was a preacher who preached to the better sort and won their votes, and drank with the lesser ones and won their votes. Candidates would generally provide free liquor to the voters several weeks before elections in a success at virtually buying their votes. Most men drank and many got drunk to celebrate their politics. Both men bought out groceries as they were then called, which were grog shops in fact. This was a fact of electioneering in frontier Illinois. They paid the owners of the groceries and had them dispense whisky free of charge to the voters, which were all men at the time.

Ford wrote that William Kinney, the other candidate as noted, was a whole hog Jackson man as opposed to Reynold's nominal Jackson beliefs, but this did not help Kinney much in the election since he was defeated. Kinney, according to Ford, was possessed of a vigorous understanding. He was an original genius and warm and true to friends, but a bitter enemy unlike Reynolds. He was witty, merry, and jovial and had the esteem of those who knew him. Because the minority anti-Jackson men hated him more than Reynolds, they helped sway the election by voting for Reynolds. This probably clinched the election for Reynolds in 1830. [6]

Garrison's editor Benjamin Lundy was a friend of Lucretia and James Mott's of Philadelphia and when the young journalist was on the way to Boston from Baltimore, Lundy suggested that he visit the Motts. Garrison told the Motts of his libel suit imprisonment. The journalist did not bow down nor was he penitent in the least. He told them that the suit only proved that a pro-slavery faction was growing in power and in ability to silence critics by recourse to the courts. African American friends had told Garrison that they did not wish to return to Africa. They had never seen the land. America was home and they desired to stay there and share in American prosperity. Colonization only strengthened public fears that the black and white could not live side by side and denied education to the African Americans. Young Garrison convinced Lucretia and her husband that colonization was not the answer and promised to support Garrisonian immediate emancipation.

Lucretia arranged for Garrison to talk to the Franklin Institute to a largely Quaker crowd. However, during the first lecture, Garrison read his speech and mumbled. She told him he must speak without a planned talk, and talk about the subject where the Spirit led him. That was what she did. Taking her advice, William Lloyd Garrison developed into an able speaker. She also helped free Garrison from what the male abolitionist called sectarian prejudices. Although she thought he was often too strident in tone, she would frequently argue with him and was influenced at times by the fiery crusader. She suitably impressed him and called her a sweet tempered Quaker lady with extraordinary intellect for a woman. [7]

In mid-September of 1830, five to six thousand Choctaws met the negotiators at Dancing Rabbit Creek in Noxubee County, Mississippi, where they were fed by the army during the parley. Eaton expelled the missionaries and then proceeded to distribute generous supplies of calico, quilts, soap, razors, and other items to the Choctaws. He and Coffee were busy in the process of warning the Choctaws that the only alternative to removal was subjection to the state laws and end of tribal life. The officials promised land grants and other privileges to tribal leaders, annuities to support education and tribal government, reimbursement for property and livestock left behind, transportation, and subsistence for one year. The Choctaw chiefs, captains, and headsmen signed the treaty on the 27th and 28th. They were soon underway for new homes in Oklahoma in three stages. The first were leaving in the fall of 1831, the second in the fall of 1832, and the last in the fall of 1833.

There was immediate dissension and an outbreak of intertribal conflict in Mississippi. Generally, the mixed bloods supported emigration and the full bloods wanted to remain in tribal lands. One district voted to replace La Flore as chieftain. Others wished the signers of the treaty to be deposed. Many thought Eaton and Coffee had deceived them about the alternatives. Mushulatubba had signed the treaty, but now he argued that the rights of the Choctaws to their lands were paramount.

Eaton acted to bind the Choctaws to the treaty by intimidation and interference in tribal government. He threatened the result of bloodshed would be imprisonment and dispatched a cavalry company to keep the peace. The Indian agent was to tell the Choctaws that settlement in the west would leave them at liberty to choose their own chiefs. Meanwhile, Eaton would not recognize any new chiefs or leaders. Next, Eaton granted special privileges to tribal leaders finding a private academy in Georgia for the two sons of Chief David Folsom. Meanwhile, it took the Senate five months for ratification. Jackson and his officials did not wait to prepare for the process of removal. General Edmund Pendleton Gaines took a party of Choctaws to the selected lands and they returned pleased with its suitability for farming and wood gathering. This helped George S. Gaines reconcile the majority of the Choctaws toward removal. The Gaines were brothers. [8]

Under the charge that the Bank was interfering in the elections, Nicholas Biddle took occasion to warn the alleged offenders that this was not acceptable. The States Rights Party of Charleston made this charge against the head of the Bank in Charleston and President Biddle, and Biddle was quick to write the banker in Charleston that the Bank's officers were to refrain from taking a part in politics. It was the object of the bank to tend to its own concerns and to belong to the entire country, avoiding public matters. They would be subservient to no Government but bound to the interests of all. Bankers served members of all parties and did not favor one over the other. The people of South Carolina were concerned that they would be ruled or were being ruled by northern traders, officials of the federal judiciary, custom officers, and the United States Bank. Biddle was concerned that he would be involved in the quicksand of politics. [9]

For awhile, there were great hopes for the American claims against the French. Now that the July Revolution had intervened in Paris, the Americans could hope that with LaFayette, who was head of the French militia and had influence. One could expect that he would assert his influence and the American claims against France would be resolved. They expected also that the more liberal French government would be favorable to the Jackson government. Rives wrote to Van Buren with great praise for the revolutionaries, but he noted that the liberal party would be more opposed to the claim than the royalists had been, because of their attachment to the public purse. Should they overcome the principle, they would limit the claims as for as was possible.

Count Louis M. Mole was named to the foreign affairs post. He had held political posts under Napoleon, but for the first time was in a diplomatic position. The foreign minister was ready to admit French responsibility, but stated that it was a complex question needing much study. In order to come to a decision, he appointed a commission from the two French houses. Since the French ministers were telling the French government that the interest in the claims were confined to a few on the American seacoast, Rives told Van Buren that it should be the object of America to stress the wide interests of Americans that the claims be settled. Jackson responded in his state of the union address in strong terms that there must be urgent prosecution of the claims. Old and vexatious problems must be resolved if a firm and cordial friendship was to be maintained. This influenced the new French king to tell Rives that he would do everything in his power to resolve the issue soon.

There was presented in the spring of 1831, a commission report. The majority presented a claim responsibility of from ten to fifteen million and the minority presented a claim of thirty million. In the midst of this favorable success of American diplomacy, the new foreign minister Count Horace Francois Sebastiani thought the American claims were greatly exaggerated. Rives worked on that matter, but the French persisted in offering lower claim amounts than the Americans would accept, but at least at the time, the nations' representatives were talking about amounts. Rives came down to a compromise of forty million francs, down from ninety-two million francs. Basing his final decision upon a dispatch of Gallatin to Adams that the claims do not exceed five million francs, two million of which could not be obtained. The amount of French claims upon the United States was pegged at almost 4.7 million francs, which were trimmed down to 1.5 million francs.

After a discussion of details, the exchange in favor of the United States of claims was reached. In addition, the duties on French wines were reduced. In return for this, France would abandon her pretensions on the eighth article of the treaty of cession of Louisiana and a reduction on the duty on American cotton. The Franco-American treaty was signed on July 4, 1831. It passed the United States Senate and then the American House of Representatives. The latter had to pass the necessary tariff provisions, which it readily did. Unfortunately, the chambers of the French houses of parliament delayed the French execution of the treaty, which raised the ire of both Jackson and Henry Clay. There was talk of a Franco-American war by Americans of all political stripes. Further delay followed, but finally there was mediation though Great Britain and war was averted and a settlement was made. [10]

New Yorker Philip Hone reflected on French events on September 28th. Everyone believed that the new king owed his throne to LaFayette. Had the friend of America promoted a republic it would be LaFayette's popularity and influence were so great in France that he could carry it off. Hone was a conservative and favored a king for France. He thought that the French people would cut one another's throats in a republic and he had the French Revolution in the previous century as an example. Pleased with a kingdom and the patriotic ruler of it, he felt that the French had settled down under a liberal form of government and had the liberties Americans enjoyed under a different kind of political organization. [11]

In Macon County, Lincoln helped Charles Hanks break the prairie with a joint team and took a role in politics. He made his first political speech in Illinois during the campaign of 1830 at Decatur. In front of Renshaw's store, the men gathered to hear candidates for the Illinois legislature. After the candidates spoke, Lincoln advocated the improvement of the Sangamon Rivers in order that it would-be useful for navigation. Because of a six months residence requirement, Lincoln was not yet eligible to vote in the August 2, 1830, election. [12]

No sooner was the treaty signed for the Choctaw Nation than settlers began to move into lands reserved for the Indians. It had not yet been ratified, but the mere news of the Indian signing was enough to encourage the whites to take lands from the natives. They felt it was their right. The Indians and whites alike lived in confusion over the matter. The whites did not care for clarification. They were not interested in native rights, only their own. The Choctaw were uncertain, especially disheartened because the crop was poor. Some wanted to go, while others wanted to become a part of the white man's world and laws of the state. Jealous, distrustful, and suspicious, that made up their lives in this bad period for the Indian. Some left for the western country where they would be free.

With the treaty's ratification, federal white authorities made preparations for an expedition to search out the western lands and make decisions about Choctaw settlement there. George S. Gaines closed his business and led the expedition. An independent exploration party went west and soon returned with the advice that the land was good and crossed by streams with mill sites. There was room for the Indians and the soil was good for corn, cotton, and wheat with plenty of deer, bear, and turkey to hunt. There were also buffalo.

On their way back, they met Gaines and his party going west. Gaines also saw plenty of game and fine weather. Later, the weather became icy. The Indians with his party were pleased at what they saw, but they became fearful of the Plains Indians and thought that they might be attacked in numbers superior to their sixty-man party. However, they were not attacked and decided to go no further west. Then after a four-month absence, they returned home to tell of their delight in what they saw.

Meanwhile, Le Flore was busy getting Indians to move to the West. He wrote the war department that he found "it impossible to prevent my people from emigrating immediately in considerable bodies. Many of them, in consequence of the disturbances in the spring, and the excessive dry summer, are without provision; and must seek them in the forest, go into the white settlements, or emigrate at the risqué of suffering in their new home. I have advised the latter as the most prudent course." Many Indians proceeded under his advice and in search of a better life and subsistence. They were generally poor. [13]

---

[1]Foreman, *Indian*, pp. 21-22, 26-30.

[2]*Niles Weekly Register*, August 21, 1830, p. 447.

[3]*Dictionary of American Biography*, IV (1), 482-483.

[4]*Niles Weekly Register*, August 21, 1830, p. 447.

[5]*Ibid.*, September 18, 1830, pp. 67-68.

[6]Ford, Thomas, *A History of Illinois: From Its Commencement as a State in 1818 to 1847*, Chicago: S.C. Griggs, 1854, Urbana: University of Illinois Press, 1995, pp. 67-69. Quote on p. 69.

[7]Bacon, Margaret Hope, *Valiant Friend: the Life of Lucretia Mott*, New York: Walker, 1980, pp. 53-54.

[8]Satz, *American*, pp. 69-72.

[9]*Niles Weekly Register*, February 25, 1832, p. 478.

[10]McLemore, pp. 69-91, 95-96ff.

[11]Hone, Philip, *The Diary of Philip Hone, 1825-1851*, Nevins, Allan ed, 2 vols., New York: Dodd, Mead, 1927, I, 27-28.

[12]Pratt, *Lincoln*, pp. 8-9.

[13]Foreman, *Indian Removal*, pp. 31-41. Quote on pp. 38-39.

Chapter 21

ELECTION TIME

On October 4, 1830, the Maryland elections was held with favorable results for the Whigs and Henry Clay. The people of that state elected an anti-Jacksonian governor and council by a large majority. In the lower house, Jackson was undone. Only sixteen of the members were Jackson men against sixty-four for the Whigs. In Ohio, Clay supporters won the governorship and control of the state senate by a narrow margin. Clay did better in the lower house. Webster found Maryland's results electrifying, believing it a decisive and gratifying triumph never before seen in the cause of public virtue and patriotism. [1]

Fall elections brought forth a few surprises. In Massachusetts John Quincy Adams was nominated to be representative in the federal house to replace the retiring Joseph Richardson, a man in his fifties who was trained in the ministry. For almost a dozen years the outgoing representative served in several representative posts. He was four years in the House of Representatives.

In Vermont, elections had not been conclusive. There was no majority and the legislators had to vote. Election results found the national republican group's standard bearer, Samuel C. Crafts with 13,476 votes; the Anti-Masonic group's William A. Palmer with 10,923 votes; and Ezra Meach, a Jacksonite with 6,285 votes. Thirty-seven votes were scattered. The legislators selected Samuel Crafts.

Jackson won a majority in New Jersey when forty Jackson legislators won and twenty-two anti-Jackson electors were elected to the two state legislator houses. Jackson had a better majority in 1828. The president did well in Pennsylvania as he had before. In nearby Delaware anti-Jacksonians had won thoroughly. The margin was 24 to 6. Elections took place in other states also. Enthusiasm for Jackson abated somewhat but he was still a popular president in the houses. He still dominated in the south and west with exceptions such as Ohio where Jackson's friends won a minority only of the representation of the state in Congress and Clay came out on top. [2]

At this time, Jackson learned of his vice-president's hostility to him and his acts in the Florida affair. Major Lewis brought the news to Jackson. The president learned of a letter written with full information and he immediately demanded to see the letter. Jackson was mad, furious, and wrote Calhoun for an explanation. The reply of Calhoun admitted the charge without being outright about it and damned clearly the revelation of a cabinet secret by Crawford from whom the information came. This hostility by Jackson was to clinch the defeat of Calhoun in his presidential aspirations. [3]

Among those listening to Garrison's first lectures on slavery was Alcott, who found the speech to be "full of truth and power." Bronson wrote a piece on the subject for a Boston newspaper, but it was not published. The second lecture was about the cruelty of many slaveholders. He thought Garrison lectured well. For his own views, Bronson Alcott wrote in his journal that there was "sometimes a want of discrimination, perhaps, between the slave-holder who keeps his slaves from motives of expediency and the one whose principles are in favor of slavery." The educator met with others three weeks later to form an anti-slavery society. [4]

America was at peace, but war clouds showed up on Europe's horizon. Russia, Austria, and Prussia were most unhappy with the revolution in France and with France's publican king. The triple alliance of the three nations was enmeshed in autocracy and now France was reforming and had overthrown their autocrat. It was more than the triple alliance could bear. It was expected that Great Britain would support France, which was preparing for war. There was insurrection enough in the British Isles with men on the rampage, burning houses and breaking threshing machines. In London mobs and police clashed, but no one was killed or wounded, only knocked down, bruised, or maimed. [5]

The maneuvering of the Pennsylvanian Jacksonians led by Dallas and Ingham was beginning to undermine their alliance with Jackson. They were noted by their partisanship for Calhoun and when the president and Calhoun began to fall out, the Family as Dallas and the group were known because of their marriage into power and wealth, began to decline. Van Buren's rise also led to the decline of the group. Jackson began withholding patronage and Governor George Wolf took his cue to do the same.

The greed and ambition of the Family group eroded the discipline of the rank and file and malcontents split the organization apart leaving to James Buchanan better organizational abilities to form a stronger Pennsylvania political group. Dallas and Ingham had not distanced themselves from Calhoun soon enough to avoid a falling out. The party was distracted because of the personal ambitions of its members, Dallas wrote. Seeking the election of Judge William Wilkins to the Senate, they were successful only after twenty-one ballots. The victory was too costly and the group was in trouble. Power moved toward Buchanan. [6]

Writing from Raleigh on December 1, 1830, to James K. Polk, was classmate William D. Moseley, serving in the state senate. He wrote that he had a beautiful wife and three children, still young. He gave his wife the breast pin Polk had given him upon departing which became his wife's most cherish jewel. She was an ardent Jacksonian, but William had voted against Jackson. Moseley admired Jackson's skills as a general, but he did not think him safe as president. Jackson's veto of the United States Bank recharter bill changed his mind however. Afterwards, he was a Jackson man. [7]

Jackson was a believer in direct actions and so he had earlier severely lectured an old army friend because he had circulated offensive stories about Mrs. Eaton that he could not prove. Next, he had proved false the charges by the minister of the church he attended in Washington DC, but he had been unable to get the preacher to correct or change his beliefs about Peggy Eaton. When the minister refused to be swayed by the facts and continued his conduct, Jackson went to a different church. The situation in the cabinet was harder to deal with. Jackson might have had failings as president, but he was a real man.

Closer to home, the wife of the president's nephew and private secretary Andrew J. Donelson turned against Mrs. Eaton. Mrs. Donelson endured the secretary of war's wife for awhile, but she found her to be very crude and blacklisted her. Jackson used pressure on Mrs. Donelson to support him in the Eaton case, but she went home to Tennessee to visit in the summer of 1830 and would not return to the national capital.

The problem of the treatment that Mrs. Eaton received from members of the cabinet and their families surfaced again in December of 1830. The families of Calhoun, Ingham, Branch, and Barrien refused to recognize Mrs. Eaton socially. Jackson was exasperated, but did not stay his hand long. When he learned the families were attempting to persuade other people to follow their example in ignoring Peggy, the president called the secretaries over to the White House and lectured them. He told the officials in the conference that he would not part with Major Eaton. He threatened the cabinet secretaries that "those who could not harmonize with him had better withdraw, for harmony he must and would have. The men promised that they would not and could not undertake to control their families. Jackson did not like this impasse, but he did not know what to do next until Van Buren came up with an idea.

Van Buren was in a unique position in the matter. Being a widower with no daughters to head up a household and a shrewd fellow, Van Buren made the best of a promising situation. Although he did not take part in the controversy, Martin paid courteous attention to the blacklisted lady. Jackson was grateful to Van Buren once again. He was thoroughly entrenched with the president already by the support he had give through the years and had purposely made friends with Jackson's personal advisers, the Kitchen cabinet. Because of certain upcoming tough issues, he was content to withdraw from the regular cabinet and serve the president behind the scenes. This was the birth of the withdrawal of Van Buren from the cabinet, this Eaton matter and his response. His goal was to further demolish any influence his rival Calhoun had with the president for a future of becoming president.

Van Buren came to Jackson and reminded him of the friction in the cabinet and suggested that resignations were in order. Since he and Eaton were immediate causes of the friction, they should resign. With their resignations, Jackson could obtain the resignations of other members and Jackson could reconstitute the entire cabinet. If everyone was out, no one could legitimately complain. Jackson saw the chief advantages in such an action. He could get rid of Calhoun's friends in the government and, thankful for Van Buren's high altruism, Jackson thought the idea was a good one. The president persuaded Eaton to resign on April 7, 1831, and four days later Martin Van Buren sent in his resignation. The rest followed.

Hoping that Eaton could replace Hugh L. White of Tennessee in the Senate, Jackson offered the secretaryship to White, but the latter declined. Lewis Cass took the position. The able lawyer and subordinate of Jackson at the Battle of New Orleans, Edward Livingston from New York, succeeded Van Buren as secretary of state. Van Buren's friend Louis McLane of Delaware became treasury secretary. Another Van Buren man, Levi Woodbury of New Hampshire, was naval secretary and Barry was again made Postmaster General. Roger Taney was appointed attorney general on June 21, 1831.

Clay and Calhoun were most observant about Van Buren's movements. Clay wrote Francis Brook on the first of May of 1831 that the Van Buren letter of resignation was "perfectly characteristic the man--a labored effort to conceal the true motives, and to assign assumed ones, for his resignation, under the evident hope of profiting by the latter. The delicate step, I apprehend, has been taken, because foreseeing the gathering storm, he wished early to secure safe refuge. Whether that will be on his farm, or at London, we shall see."

Calhoun wrote Maxcy on the sixteenth that Van Buren's object was to increase "his control in the movements of government and at the same time to diminish his responsibility. It was a great point for him to remove Ingham and Branch, while his own presence could be dispensed with at Washington. He has so surrounded the president with his creatures that his affairs can be safely administered in his absence." Indeed Van Buren had secured for himself the presidential succession. [8]

Before the resignations, *Telegraph* editor Duff Green was working to get Calhoun elected in 1832 in the place of Jackson. He had a plot to earn for Van Buren the condemnation of the public so great that Jackson could not save him. He tried to get J.M. Duncanson in on the scheme. He wanted the respected Washington citizen to take editorship of the *Argus* and upon cue attack Van Buren and undermine Jackson to get Calhoun selected and elected. Duncanson was not interested. Green planned to turn the people against Jackson by press attacks. Duncanson informed Jackson of the scheme and learned that Jackson already had suspicions about Green. He immediately had Francis P. Blair found the *Globe* on his behalf and gave him the government business that Green had had. By his means Jackson secured for himself a secure press and undercut Green's attempt to use the press to destroy him. [9]

Three days before the end of 1830, John Pintard was involved in the news from Europe and expressed his views about the Russian threat to the new French government. Wall Street was set astir with the rumors that the Russians were marching with the support of Austria to invade France. The French reacted by preparing for war. It looked like it would be a general war in Europe. Great Britain might form a defense treaty with France it was thought. Pintard believed that France could hold its own against the Russians with the French national guard as the core of the French army. Phillippe was enormously popular and those for Charles X were few and scattered so that was little danger of Frenchmen supporting a Russian invasion. The only problem was from the French clergy and this was no obstacle to a French defense. [10]

Far from rich France was modest Illinois. When the Lincolns moved on to Illinois, they found another rapidly growing state. The population of Illinois was then 161,055 inhabitants or less than half that of Indiana, but more than double that of the previous state census five years earlier. They went westward as there was no change in climate with severe winter weather in January and early February, but the winters were fairly long, suited to wheat fields. In northern Illinois, the Irish potato flourished and in southern Illinois the sweet potato was grown. Among fruit trees grown were apple, pear, peach, persimmons, and pawpaw. The land the Lincolns found was a predominantly level ground with woods and prairies, suitable for agriculture. Some of the land had to drained however. [11]

On December 16, 1830, Lincoln and John W. Reed were asked to appraise an Estray more recently taken up by Jonathan B. Brown. In the appraisal statement, the two men found her to be four years old on the next spring., The mare was a bright bay fourteen hands high. There was a small blaze and a snip in her face. The right hind foot with a white strip down the hoof and white hairs around the edge of the hoof was a mark of the horse The mane and tail was black. Reed and Lincoln found no brand on her. They appraised the mare's value to be thirty dollars. Earlier in that year, Lincoln signed a petition to change the precinct place from Permenlus Smallwood to Decatur's courthouse. Because he did not have a six month's residence, he was not yet a qualified voter, but the time was passed by November and it is assumed he voted in November for officials. He signed and drew up for friends other documents during his early years in Illinois.

In his early years citizens hired Lincoln to raft their families and goods down river. One of these was Dr. David P. Nelson, who lived near New Salem. When he moved to Texas, Abe took his family and goods down the Sangamon River to Beardstown. In March 1831, he floated the produce of merchant Denton Offutt down to New Orleans to sell. Back in New Salem, Lincoln clerked in Offutt's store. [12]

The first winter the Lincolns spent in Illinois was marked by heavy snow especially during the holidays. On Christmas Eve of 1830, central Illinois began to get a small snowfall. People awoke to find a foot of snow on the ground and were overjoyed. Then a bitter cold settled over the countryside and snow fell for several days. Finally, there was four to five feet deep at ground level. The children made up sleds and sleighs and the doctors with their fast horses pulled them down the streets of Springfield until they tired of the sport. There was also suffering in the countryside especially. They could not go to the mills for flour and had to live for awhile on homemade corn grits. Their hogs froze to death in the woods with the game animals and meat was unavailable. Wood was hard to get. The Lincoln family survived along with the rest. [13]

Meanwhile, the situation deteriorated for the Cherokee in Georgia. The people of that state knew that Jackson planned an act that would displace all Indians and move them westward. The president had said so. They were emboldened to take matters in their own hands and decided not to wait. Georgia's legislature annexed Cherokee lands and nullified Cherokee laws there. They proscribed the Indian government and forbade leaders from urging resistance on their tribesmen. Indians could not mine gold legally, nor could they testify against white men in state courts. In Washington, Edward Everett claimed that this would lead to white plundering, arson, assault, and murder of Cherokees. Indeed there was plunder since disappointed white miners squatted on Cherokee lands and rustled Indian cattle. The law did not protect the Indians and the whites went unpunished. Everett was excessive in his statement, but had the Indians not been removed later, he might have seen his statement come fully true. [14]

Houston returned to Washington DC in 1830 to find Thomas L. McKenney advertising for proposals to furnish rations for the emigrating Indians. When the secretary of war said that no contracts would be awarded to any of the thirteen bidders, Houston returned to his home among the Cherokee Indians already beyond the frontier. At the time he arrived at the mouth of the White River where mosquitoes plagued him, Sam wrote Eaton to apply for the position of sutler being vacated by General John Nicks at Fort Gibson. Next, he loaded a keel boat with supplies from New York and Nashville to be prepared for the position of storekeeper. The load included nine barrels of whiskey, brandy, gin, rum, and wine and various other goods.

On June 13, 1830, Houston wrote Eaton that he was now satisfied from personal inquiry that Nicks had done nothing that would justify his removal. Therefore, he withdrew from an application for military storekeeper. He could not, as a man of honor accept a post not vacated with good cause. Houston closed that "the claim of $50,000, due the Cherokees, under the last treaty is in a fair way to be swindled from them. It is paid to the holders of those certificates, paid in the name of Jolly and Black Fox, it will be a fraud, by the government of the United States upon the Cherokees. The Indian in the census are rated at some seventeen or eighteen hundred, when in fact, they exceed four thousand in number." Houston then decided to use his supplies to stock a store of his own.

For the second half of 1830, Houston wrote letters under the name of Tah-lan-tuskee which were published in the Arkansas *Gazette*. In Washington, he had brought forth memorials from the Indians for their bad treatment by agents. Several agents were removed at his urging and he made many enemies. Sam Houston went into this controversy in his letters in the newspaper, which was Arkansas' leading periodical. He purchased a tract of land containing salt springs, above Fort Gibson and soon sold a one-third interest in one of these tract; one third of a section of land. Because he received a highly profitable return, getting thirty dollars per acre, very high for the time. Soon, he took an Indian wife, the widow Dianna Rogers Gentry, who after he left the Indians for Texas, found a new husband in Samuel D. McGrady. Houston did not consider her his legal wife although his brother did, but white-Indian marriages were often short and temporary in the nineteenth century. [15]

Stephen F. Austin chose to guide his colonists on a neutral pathway between the two Mexican parties then in conflict in Mexico, although he and most Texans preferred the federalists who wanted a liberal republic like that of the United States. Those Mexicans favored a weak central government and strong independent states. There opponents were the centralists favoring a strong national government and weak states. Many Texans resisted the efforts of the successful centralist faction in 1830 to establish a conservative even monarchical country. [16]

---

[1]Webster, *Correspondence*, III, 85-86.

[2]*Niles Weekly Register*, October 23, 1830, pp. 137-139, October 30, 1830, p. 154; *Who Was Who*, I, 512.

[3]Bowers, *Party*, pp. 103-106, 110-112.

[4]Alcott, *Journal*, pp. 25-26. Quotes on p. 25.

[5]*Niles Weekly Register*, January 1, 1831, p. 321.

[6]Belohlavek, *Dallas*, pp. 31-33.

[7]William D. Moseley to James K. Polk, December 1, 1830.

[8]Swisher, *Taney*, pp. 135-141. Quotes on pp. 138-9, 139.

[9]Benton, *Forty Years*, pp. 128-130.

[10]Pintard, *Letters*, III, 206-207.

[11]Peck, John Mason, *A Guide for Emigrants*, Boston: Lincoln & Edmunds, 1831, Rep. New York: Arno Press, 1975, pp. 3, 11-12, 38, 90-91.

[12]Basler, Roy P., ed, *The Collected Works of Abraham Lincoln*, 9 vols., New Brunswick, NJ: Rutgers University Press, 1953, I, 2-4.

[13]Angle, Paul M., *"Have I Have Lived": A History of Lincoln's Springfield, 1821-1865*, New Brunswick, NJ: Rutgers University Press, 1935, pp. 33-34.

[14]Wilkins, pp. 209-211, 225.

[15]Foreman, Grant, "Some New Light on Houston's Life Among the Cherokee Indians," *Chronicles of Oklahoma*, IX No. 2 (June 1931), 140-152.

[16]Henson, Margaret Swett, "Tory Sentiment in Anglo-Texan Public Opinion, 1832-1836," *Southwestern Historical Quarterly*, XC NO. 1 (July 1986), 1-34.

Chapter 22

NULLIFICATION

Southerners were increasingly dissatisfied with the federal government and with the Union. South Carolinians were opposed to the Bank of the United States, internal improvements, and the tariff since none of these benefited them and were paid for in part by South Carolinians. The people along the coast of the South were especially opposed to the tariff being unwilling to pay for the prosperity of the northern states. Wanting a weak federal government and caring not for what would help other people, they did want strong state governments, so they raised the issue of constitutionality and John C. Calhoun led the way. He wrote that the power of Congress to pass protective tariffs might "make one section tributary to another, and he used by the administration and artful and corrupt politicians to buy up partisans and retain power.

There was a considerable amount of press reaction to the issue in exaggerated terms and great party feeling. The Charleston *Mercury* spoke of the economic decline of the city and state supposedly caused by the tariff. The *National Intelligencer* said that the tariff attack was a mere cover-up by Jackson men to create a separate nation for Jackson. Southerners were not being treasonous as suggested by the Adams newspaper. There were almost no disunion talks in the South. In fact, in 1828, the *Charleston Courier* denounced the idea of disunion. When the editor of the *Charleston City Gazette* suggested disunion, he was attacked widely.

Next came the idea of nullification, an idea brought up by James Hamilton, Jr., at a Walterboro gathering on October 12, 1828. He relied on the Virginia and Kentucky Resolutions of '98, on which Hamilton placed his citadel. Nullification, he said, might be applied by the state through legislatures or conventions. This might not result in disunion, unless the opponents they faced so willed it. Thus he put the onus on the North. The general government might submit to this mode of address by allowing the South Carolinians to cease paying tariff duties, to appeal to the convention of the states called to decide upon its constitutionality, or force the South Carolinians to pay with the use of force. The remedy he chose was the second. Should three fourths of the states declare for the tariff's constitutionality, South Carolina would then decide whether to go along with the decision or not. However, he thought the convention would reject the tariff. [1]

The passage of the Mallory bill with its high tariff brought increasing protest in South Carolina. Voices called for the exercise of sovereignty to free the people of the higher price paid for goods due to the tariff. Despite all that George McDuffie could do, he had been unable of lower tariffs in his congressional battles and the people of South Carolina sought protest as the solution to the problem.

Writers in the state led by Francis W. Pickens sought to promote nullification and argue always the disunion connotations. A few wrote of peaceful secession, while others separated nullification and succession. Nullification or voiding of federal laws by decisions of the state was simple. Unionists in the state deplored nullification in any form. When Unionists seemed to gain the upper hand in mid 1830, South Carolinian nullifiers redoubled their efforts. They wanted to redress the wrongs being done them by the tariff, but they differ as to how they should act. They loved the state above the nation. There was a strong demand for nullifying the tariff.

Nullifiers were greatly encouraged when men from the north spoke in favor of their doctrine. They became bolder. To them, it was the duty of South Carolina leaders to press hard and take advantage of the times to carry the day and establish nullification as a legitimate rule. The first victory would be to dictate the amount of duties for South Carolinians and any other state. Unionists did not believe in nullification however much they thought the protective tariff was wrong. They preferred other remedies. Pure constitutionists, they thought the system was right and should not be tampered with. The judiciary should decide cases of friction between the states and the federal government. Unionists thought that nullification would mean rule by a minority. Indeed it would have been the case. [2]

African Americans were at a severe disadvantage in American society in the North as well as in the South. It operated out of fear and a dislike for those who were different. Whites did not want the races to be assimilated, and there was a frequently expressed fear of and opposition to white-black unions. Northern hatred of the blacks and racism was common and believed unchangeable, because in the view of northerners it was an ordination of God. Even the abolitionists accepted racism. Shortly after he founded his newspaper, Garrison wrote that the black was "branded by the hand of nature with a perpetual mark of disgrace." Northerners bared African Americans from jury boxes, election polls, white men's schools, and railroad cars. African Americans were limited to certain occupations and certain pews in the churches. Segregation even prevailed in the graveyards of the North.

Many Northerners believed that the solution for the problem of the black in America was slavery at home or African American colonization abroad. They did not believe that the freedman among blacks had a place in the United States. Behind these beliefs was a fear that the alternative was either race war or miscegenation. There was no middle ground. The two races must completely separate and leave America or they must merged.

Destruction would follow the existence of the free African American in the United States in the poverty and disgrace they had in the North.

Although they viewed the slave as contented and cowardly, they feared the future when the freedom and hope would revive that which was dormant. Blacks would not be satisfied with little, but would demand more and more. The basis to this fear was that he would want white women. Slaves would want to marry the master's daughter. Further, the blacks would seek revenge. Abolitionists would uplift the African Americans and give them opportunity so they must be opposed. Even African Americans with second class citizenship would be too much for the anti-abolitionists. [3]

The abolitionist Theodore Dwight Weld, born in Connecticut on November 23, 1803, was the son of a stern Congregationalist minister in his home of Hampton. About 1810, the prankster boy had turned to religion and on one school day, a new African American student came to the school to learn. Their teacher forced little Jerry to sit apart. When called upon to recite, the little boy responded. Afterwards, the teacher humiliated him. Weld asked that his seat be put near to the black. The teacher replied, "why are you a niggar too!" The other children chorused, "Theodore Weld is a nigger." From this point forward the boys persecuted Theodore, especially since he began to excel in school.

At age fifteen, Weld entered Andover Academy to prepare for college with an aim of the ministry. It was there that the young man had eye troubles, which forced him to leave the academy, and regain his eyesight in a dark room at home. Then for over two years, he traveled Connecticut, New York, and the upper South to lecture on the art and science of memory. In 1824, the elder Weld moved to New York State where he was a minister-at-large in the Presbyterian church. Theodore helped his parent move and stay in the area. He spent most of his time in the Utica circle of Erastus Clark, his uncle. Then against his will, Weld was influenced by Charles Grandison Finney and joined him on the revival path. His particular specialty was temperance lecturing. Weld said that alcohol killed more bodies and damned more souls than anything else. [4]

There were strong personal ties between planters and their cotton factors. They were close friends with enduring business relationships. Also they were social equals. Factors would loan large sums of money to tide the planter over with no formal security. However, the planters were rich in lands and slaves and both planters and factors were men of their word. There was a foundation of need since the plantation owner was unable to oversee the sale of their cotton because of the distance of the markets. A specialist was required. The factors also operated as bankers for the purchase of land and slaves and to carry the planter over to his harvest. The planters lived on credit.

Factors often got the money to lend from foreign import houses and Northern manufacturers. It was a costly operation because of high interest rates and higher prices for goods and supplies which planters purchased from merchants. For example, the planter paid twenty cents a pound for bacon that was sold for twelve cents a pound if bought in cash. Even when cotton was baled, the factors might hold it in reserve for better prices and advance the planter money needed for provisions and other expenditures. Advances could be in goods, bills of exchange, or cash. The factors often drew up contracts on future cotton crops whereby the planter could use his services to factor a certain number of bales and pay the factor a sum if production of cotton fell short. The usual commission was two and a half percent. [5]

While New England was flooded with converts to Unitarianism, Lincoln's westerners resisted the ideas of that Church and Unitarian missionaries and preachers had a hard time in the West. Methodist missionaries reached the frontier early and in numbers twice as many people were Methodist than the numbers of their nearest rivals. When one Presbyterian preacher sought souls in the Ohio Valley, he learned that a Methodist minister had been in each cabin throughout the west ahead of him. However, Presbyterians were the religion of choice by the next more numerous of westerners. In the countryside there were many Baptist farmer-preachers and in the cities there were Roman Catholics in numbers.

Other religions tagged the Unitarians "infidels." This meant that westerners were suspicious of Unitarians since they were roundly denounced to be heretics. The charge meant technically that the Unitarians did not believe that the Bible was the exact word of God, but in terms of emotion, the frontiersmen considered Unitarians were ungodly. The masses opposed Unitarian reforms and were led by orthodox ministers and aided by the orthodox congregations and their elders. [6]

On November 12, 1830, Joseph Henry recommended the works of Ferdinand Rudolph Hassler for use in Albany Academy. From his expertise in science and education, he was able to inform the trustees of the fine recognition of the author in the world of science. He found the textbooks of Hassler's to be far superior to those of others on the subject of mathematics and were used at West Point. However, he criticized Hassler's arithmetic text because it lacked sufficient examples. The book was not generally useful for some pupils. He recommended the use of Hassler's Arithmetic for older students and that when each student began to study Trigonometry and higher Algebra, he should be required to buy a copy of Hessler's Mathematical Tables.

Henry had the Academy procure scientific apparatus paid for with a donated $362 to buy thirty-two items. These included a telescope, a large cylindrical electrical machine, a hydraulic ram, a hydrostatic machine, whirling table, reaction mill, paradoxical balance, a fountain, geometrical apparatus, electrical battery, cryophorus, parabola mirrors, war hammer, weighing machine, hygrometer, safety lamp, thermometer, and scales and weights. There were others such as a specific gravity apparatus and steam apparatus. Meanwhile, he was working on electromagnetism. Benjamin Stilliman, Sr., of Yale published Henry's article on the subject in his scientific journal. The editor provided him with fifty copies to give to his friends. Henry made a large magnet for Stilliman for his use in demonstrating its power. [7]

Back in 1824, Seward and his wife Francis went on a family outing to Niagara Falls. On the return trip, they were passing through Rochester. When their carriage lost a wheel they met some men including Thurlow Weed who helped them. Journalist Weed was born on November 15, 1797, in Greene County, New York. His father was an itinerant farmer who had been in debtor's prison. With little formal schooling, Weed began to work at age eight. A blacksmith paid him six cents a day to be his assistant. Weed move up in the world when he became a printer's apprentice about age eleven. Time passed and Anti-Masons supported the journalist in his Rochester newspaper. When Weed discovered Seward agreed with him in political matters, a strong friendship was sealed. In 1828 and 1829, Seward tried to join the National Republicans and Anti-Masons of Cayuga County in a common cause. Cayuga Anti-Masons nominated Seward for Congress, but the National Republicans jeered him and Seward withdrew. Each of these two parties had their candidates and the Jackson-Van Buren candidate won out over the other two. If they had a combined candidate in Seward, they might have won.

Thurlow Weed moved to Albany where he ran the *Albany Evening Journal* and was a legislator. In 1830, Seward was nominated to the New York State senate with Weed's initiative and maneuvers. He won big over the Jackson-Van Buren candidate. Seward went to Albany where he met Millard Fillmore, Francis Granger, and Albert Tracy. There was also his friend Weed. Seward wrote home that Weed's exciting principle was personal friendship or opposition and not self-interest. Further he was very generous and kind with an open heart and great sincerity. They were confidential buddies. In his turn, Weed would later write that Seward had a stern integrity and earnest patriotism. Seward was a man of great loyalties. [8]

John Springs III was born in 1782 in Mecklenburg County, North Carolina, to Richard and Jean Baxter Springs of Dutch origins. The name was originally Springsteens. They had received a land grant in New Netherlands (later New York). They settled there and some moved to Delaware after the British took over. The Delaware Springsteens shortened the name to Springs. When he was fifty years old or so, John Springs I moved his family to Mecklenburg County where he bought extensive portions of land in 1776. He had two sons, John II and Richard, who were revolutionary Whigs in North Carolina. Richard Springs moved to South Carolina. John II was the third's grandfather. John III was married to a first cousin, a common enough practice for the rich to keep the money in the family. The marriage took place on January 9, 1806; Mary and John took up housekeeping and farmed. He began to accumulate money and an upcountry cotton plantation was theirs.

He was able to cash in on the cotton bonanza and according to his biographer was with a minority in feeding his slaves well. He toured to buy more slaves. One batch of 41 turned a quick profit. Buying them for the low price of $10,200, he sold them for $15,425 to South Carolina's Senator William Smith, who took off time from Washington to buy the slaves for his Alabama plantation. In 1825, Springs was able to buy his father's plantation for just over $4,000. Slaves were much more expensive than farmland.

He had had a store since 1812 on his plantation in partnership with his wife's brother, Adam Springs. Later he went into partner with his older brother Eli Springs in Charlotte. Eli died in 1833 and John paid his brother's heirs for Eli's part and gave his second son Leroy Springs the store. Leroy had been working in a merchant's concern in

New York City for the experience. He gave his eldest son Richard Austin Springs a plantation and then money so he could enter into a partnership in a Yorkville firm for merchandise. He built a gristmill with William Elliott White, a fellow cotton planter and a near neighbor. He entered into business with other sons and relatives. [9]

From cramped quarters in Boston's Merchant's Hall, William Lloyd Garrison issued the first number of the *Liberator* on January 1, 1831. There were a mere four hundred copies to carry his challenge to slavery. He wrote that he would be "as harsh as truth, and as uncompromising as justice." Since no man would moderately save his wife from ravishment or a woman moderately save her baby from fire, he would not be moderate in writing against slavery. Garrison let it be known that he would not equivocate, excuse, or retreat.

Garrison's life in the early months of his anti-slavery newspaper was of a hand-to-mouth existence. There was food, chiefly water, and stale bread for him and his partner Isaac Knapp. They did all of the work for the first weeks, and hired a black apprentice to help from February of 1831 on. The hours were long, but visitors often interrupted work. Some came out of curiosity. Others who had dropped by were interested and wished to help in the cause. Visitors would listen to Garrison's monologue. Garrison gathered friends, but generally his strong stand in the *Liberator* drew the hostile, who also increased in numbers. Apathy was the general result in those early years.

At the end of 1831, he had only fifty white subscribers and if it were not for white philanthropists and black freemen with their contributions, the sheet would not have survived that long. A chief weapon against slavery was Garrison's exchange program with large numbers of periodicals. The favorable comments of he press helped promote the newspaper, but the attacks of most promoted his ideas. Southern righteous anger made the *Liberator* famous. A limited number read the newspaper, but large numbers read about it in other journals. His invective stirred up enmity, which was to spread with the Nat Turner rebellion in August. Garrison welcomed any publicity. [10]

Upon launching his anti-slavery *The Liberator* with its issue of January 1, 1831, William Lloyd Garrison targeted his readership in New England, where the soil seemed ready. He also expected to do well in other free states, but thought the South would be less revolutionary in anti-slavery sentiment. Indeed in his contempt directed at the southern states and in his militancy, Garrison effectively wrote off the South. Anti-slavery southerners were lost by a fear of black slave rebellions and withered on the vine. Garrison especially appealed to the emotions rather than the mind, and lost many people as a result while gaining others. Perhaps, the anti-slavery advocacy among the southern people would have been lost anyway, but abolitionist and black rebels frightened anti-slavery southerners as well as slave owners and the evolution of anti-slavery sentiment in the South was reversed.

In his thunderous words, Garrison lost every chance to appeal to the South. When he wrote in that first issue to "let southern oppressors tremble--let their secret abettors tremble--let their northern apologists tremble--let all the enemies of the persecuted blacks tremble," he could hardly expect a sympathetic hearing in the South. Garrison was a fiery advocate of freedom for the slaves and his propaganda for freedom, he struck a cord with many, so he gained on one side what he lost of the other. He expected assistance from churches and parties, but he got little of this. However, his advocacy reached many and prepared the way for the growth of anti-slavery sentiment in free states, despite abundant hostility when he demanded immediate enfranchisement for the slaves. Garrison would have them freed and allowed to vote. This was unacceptable to the multitude, but it appealed to others.

He was for immediate freedom and full rights for the slave. He would accept no moderation or delay and although he inspired some he had nothing to bargain with for the many. He was definitely not timid and indeed right. Never one for retreat, he never did. When told that his hard line would hurt the cause, he did not believe this. He considered himself right and he lived up to his strong words.

On that same front page, he presented an editorial from the Washington *Spectator* against slavery in the federal district and its mart for selling people. It concerned a petition to end slavery there. Following this, Garrison found exception to American hypocritical oppression at home in the form of slavery. A parade celebrating recent revolution in France for freedom had met a procession of African American slaves handcuffed in pairs traveling the other way. Garrison lauded Daniel O'Connell of Ireland for calling American hypocrites, who talked freedom and kept slaves. There was a great need of an O'Connell in the United States, Garrison wrote. The shocking scenes of the capital must cease if America was to obtain mercy from God. Americans had claimed a couple of generations earlier that all men were free and equal and that this was a God-ordained truth. Garrison was of course right, but that did not do but little in advancing his cause of anti-slavery. [11]

At the beginning there was considerable affection between Garrison and African Americans in 1829, while he was helping Lundy in Boston. Then when he launched his militant newspaper in 1831, this was a solid tie because he was all for them, their white knight in the battle for freedom, and would not moderate his advocacy for their cause to gain Southern support. They needed to know that they had a powerful advocate in the harsh world. He told free African Americans, who struggled under the pressure of wind and tide that he would make atonement for the wrongs suffered by them from the whites. When he understood their position on colonization, he turned against sending them to Liberia. For three years they subscribed and made gifts to the paper. Their gifts enable the triumphant Garrison to make an important trip to England in their behalf. [12]

[1]Boucher, Chauncey Samuel, *The Nullification Controversy in South Carolina*, Chicago: University of Chicago Press, 1916, pp. 1ff.

[2]*Ibid.*, pp. 46-62, 65-77.

[3]Richards, *Gentlemen*, pp. 32-33, 44-46.

[4]Abzug, Robert H., *Passionate Liberator: Theodore Dwight Weld and the Dilemma of Reform*, New York: Oxford University Press, 1980, pp. 17-19, 24-25, 29-30, 47-50, 57.

[5]Buck, Norman Sydney, *The Development of the Organization of Anglo-American Trade, 1800-1850*, New Haven, Conn: Yale University Press, 1925, Rep: Archon Books, 1969, pp. 68-78.

[6]Habich, Robert D., *Transcendentalism and the Western Messenger: A History of the Magazine and Its Contributors, 1835-1841*, Rutherford: Fairleigh Dickinson University Press, 1985, pp. 26-28.

[7]Henry, I, 297-324, 338-339, 343-345ff.

[8]Taylor, John M., *William Henry Seward: Lincoln's Right Hand*, New York: HarperCollins, 1991, pp. 23-25.

[9]Ford, Lacy K. Jr., "The Two Entrepreneurs in the Old South: John Springs III and Hiram Hutchison of the South Carolina Upcountry," *South Carolina Historical Magazine*, XCV No. 3 (July 1994), 202-205.

[10]Thomas, *Liberator*, pp. 127-134, 138.

[11]*The Liberator*, January 1, 1831, p. 1.

[12]Quarles, Benjamin, *Black Abolitionists*, New York: Oxford University Press, 1969, pp. 18-20.

Chapter 23

NEW ORLEANS

At this time, Carl David Arfwedson visited New Orleans. He noted the location in a semicircle along the banks of the Mississippi. It was inland one hundred and five miles from its Balize mouth and one thousand miles south of its junction with the Ohio River. New Orleans streets followed the curve of the stream and are dissected by streets from the Mississippi eastward. He found only one street paved, but the people were talking about paving more streets. Paving was necessary to prevent sinking after rains. The dust was bad in dry weather. The Old French town, and the rest of the town formed two cities in one. Wide streets were planted with trees, forming boundaries. Both parts were different. The early buildings and houses were of wood and the later were of brick. The Creoles were satisfied and did not want trouble, relaxing and happy. The Americans were enterprising and active. Cotton was their source of wealth. They were moving into the city and were increasingly prosperous, filled with schemes and speculations. The chief topic was cotton prices. It was a city of many languages, races, and nationalities. [1]

About seventy percent of western merchants, with much of the goods going by way of New Orleans, were Whigs during the Jackson years. These businessmen considered Henry Clay to be their hero because of his stands on banking, internal improvements, tariffs to build new roads and canals, his opposition to Jacksonian politicians who rubbed the frontier merchants the wrong way. When the Whig party failed in the fifties, these merchants were to join the Republican party in equal numbers.

Meanwhile, they favored strong banks that would facilitate trade. The fluctuating values of state banks notes provided a problem for merchants. State bank notes were often discounted when needed to pay eastern wholesale merchants and wagoners. Roads were primitive and rivers dangerous and made for high freight rates. When the states spent money on improved waterways, the merchants saved great sums over and above improvements costs in savings to commerce. Snags in the Ohio and Mississippi rivers for a five-year saw a loss of $381,000, a steep decline. Successful Jacksonian opposition to the Whig program concerned the merchants and Democratic attacks were vociferous.

In St. Louis, the *Republican* was the leading opposition newspaper, but soon after Jackson's first inauguration, Charles Keemle started his Democratic *St. Louis Beacon*. He used a heavy-handed approach to politics and alienated one of his best advertisers in G.K. M'Gunnegle. Hill and M'Gunnegle was a commission firm with Ohio River and New Orleans connections which sold goods they advertised in Keemle's newspaper. M'Gunnegle got tired of its rhetoric, stopped his subscriptions in the summer of 1830 and then ceased advertising. Keemle complained in the pages of his paper about this treatment. Other merchants followed Hilland M'Gunnegle, but all the merchants later returned and Keemle was 100 new subscriptions ahead. [2]

In 1830, when Stephen F. Austin considered settling Germans in Texas, there had been considerable interest on the subject of Texas in Germany. At a time when Texas was still Spanish, Spanish consul Morphi at New Orleans proposed to the Spanish government, which was fighting the French, that German and Polish soldiers be sent to Texas to live and settle. The idea was to use them as a force to prevent Napoleonic hopes of taking the province. The general's aggressions must be clipped. The hold on Spanish America was weak and Napoleon was a threat to the Spanish colonies as well as Spain itself under the control of King Joseph Bonoparte. Morphi wanted to detach these soldiers from the armies of the French emperor.

Morphi had inducements. He suggested granting the soldiers seven leagues of land upon the Gulf of Mexico near American Louisiana. They would be exempted from taxation, allowed free trade, and have their own local government. For his part, the consul wanted only that they be mechanics and artisans and of good character. This idea was stillborn. The Spanish government felt that it would be a Trojan horse and that such settlers would obey Napoleon in Texas when the time came and deliver the province over to the French. The Regency rejected all such ideas of settlements in Texas, although it might form a barrier to an invasion of the province by foreigners.

Later, there were to be other ideas of settling Irishmen, Germans, and Swiss on Texas lands. These were to be farmers, sheepmen, and silkworm culturists. Then in 1821, J. Val. Hecke published a book about his travels in North America and suggested Prussia buy Texas from Spain on money advanced from German merchants. They would form an official trading company and the Prussian government would provide soldiers to protect the new Prussian colony. Each of ten thousand soldiers should receive title to a hundred acres. Hecke suggested the growing of wheat and the finding of gold in Texas mountains. The products of Texas could be shipped through Galveston to Prussia and Latin America. It would be a prosperous colony for the Prussians.

Five years later, Joseph Vehlein delivered a power of attorney to Dr. John Lucius Woodbury to arrange for a land grant in Texas to settle German and Swiss Catholics on. There was no success on their part and Vehlein founded a colonization company in 1830 with David G. Burnet and Lorenzo de Zavala. This was the Galveston Bay and Texas Land Company. It had the backing of Boston and New York capitalists for large-scale settlement of people from the United States and Europe. At this same time Austin wanted to settle Swiss and German emigrants because of his admiration for their steadiness and industry. Austin did not think much of the American land speculators. He wanted to settle and not make great profits. Austin was against slavery and thought rightfully they would inhibit slavery in Texas, which they would have in great numbers. Germans in Texas were not slave-buyers.

A Creole of Guadalajara named Tadeo Ortiz de Ayala, who wanted to safeguard Mexico and its provinces, proposed to the Mexican minister of foreign affairs, Lucas Alaman, establishing colonies from Germany or Switzerland in Texas. Manuel de Mier y Teran, Commissioner for Colonization, wrote Alaman that this was a good idea. The first Germans came to Texas late in 1833 with Dr. J.C. Beales of New York City. Germans back home in central Europe had begun talking about settling in Texas and the door was opening. Beales failed but the settlers in his ship took up residence in Texas, including the Germans. [3]

Nehemiah Caulkins was a member of the Baptist Church in Waterford, Connecticut, and had a high reputation in that town, vouched for by several citizens for his truth and veracity. He was a pious man and man of integrity. During eleven winters between 1824 and 1830, he spent time in North Carolina on plantations. It was not a social visit because Caulkins was a carpenter who did work on the plantations. He gave a good account of what he saw and learnt while enjoying the better climate of the vicinity of Wilmington. Four of the periods were at the plantation of John Swan. Swan had had about seventy slaves. Some were married and some merely lived together with no ceremony. The owners were indifferent to the situations, since slave marriages were not required in the slave codes. However, the slaves themselves thought much of being married by ministers.

Caulkins told this about the overseer of Swan's. This overseer had been a Methodist minister. He left that employment when his wife died. He was so angry at her death that he swore he would never preach another sermon for the Lord. The overseer was a cruel man. At the close of three years, Swan owed him $400. In payment, he gave the overseer twenty acres of land and a slave woman. The man built a log hut and lived with the woman, having several children by her.

He told a number of incidents. Some are given below: It was customary in the South to let hogs run in the woods. "On one occasion, a slave caught a pig about two months old, which he carried to his quarters." When the overseer saw this, he went to the field and called the slave to him. The slave ran and the overseer shot him. Slaves carried the wounded man to the plantation hospital. A doctor attended to the slave who recovered with some of the duck shot still in his body. The doctor had done an incomplete job on the slave.

When Swan was absent, a slave named Harry ran off into the woods to escape the overseer. He took items with him, which would enable him to prepare his food. In the woods for three months, he robbed the rice fields. Other slaves visited him at night and on Sundays. When Swan finally returned, he sent slaves for Harry. The slave was seized and put into the stocks. He was there for a week at night. During the mornings, he was flogged and during the days, he worked in the fields fastened to a log he had to drag around with him while working.

Swan did not give the slaves much clothing, only one outfit a year at Christmas. There was no change of clothing that could be done. However, the slaves found work to do at nights and on Sundays to pay for more clothes. A favorite way of earning money was to cut wood and with the owners permission to sell this wood in Wilmington. They were poorly fed and did not receive any meat except a little on rare occasions. The rice that they received was rejected rice, that rice that could not be sold in the market. Sometimes they got fish. Medical care was poor and there was no dental care. Flogging for even the least of things was very common, for women and men alike. [4]

Meanwhile, the slaves were resisting their condition by such things as feigning illness and mutilating themselves by cutting off fingers and hands so that they could escape the unceasing drudgery of required labor. Some slaves went so far as to commit suicide rather than to submit to slavery, seeking release from a world of work and woe. These were drastic measures but in drastic situations. Mothers destroyed their babies at birth rather than to allow them to live in such a world of lash and the auction block. More drastic measures were done in the face of cruelty and trouble such as murdering masters. Other measures of resistance included slowing up their work in the fields, stealing masters' property and destroying property from burning barns to burning crops and farm implements.

They were rightfully afraid of speaking out, but they could keep their own thoughts and found refuge in such songs as those of liberation. Favorite songs were about Moses freeing his people from Egypt and they took joy in the refrain: "Let my people go." They could pray for deliverance from oppression on earth. Finally they could escape or hide in the swamps and woods to live free or freer lives. Tens of thousands of slaves made their way northward. Also, there were the rare revolts and some murders of masters.

These things kept their masters in fear and agitation and were soon to impel them to blame the abolitionists for all this. The scored them for exciting their slaves in ideas of freedom, as if this did not come naturally to the slaves, who after all were human beings who could and did think like the whites or anybody else. Some were docile and satisfied, but most had the idea of natural liberty in their hearts and souls. The slaves were also to hear their masters speak of such things soon more about the dreaded abolitionists, although abolitionist writings rarely reached them. The slaves that heard such things talked about them to the others. In all it was a placid situation, but there was fire beneath the surface. [5]

Far from this world, in the world of fiction, the Bannisters acted in a variety of roles. Nathaniel H. Bannister, born in Baltimore, made his first stage appearance in 1830. He acted the part of Young Norval at the Front Street Theatre. His first New York performance was the next year when he expounded his talents at the Chatham Theatre, home of many performances over the years. He moved on to the Bowery. On June 19, 1832, he played Glenalvon in "Douglas" at the Arch Street Theatre for his first

Philadelphia experience in his career. He married Amelia Green, who evidently had been married twice before. At least she was known by two married names before her union with Nathaniel. Born in Chester, New Hampshire, she was in Pittsburgh, when she played the role of Mrs. Blandford in "Speed the Plough." Her first New York appearance was as Adelgitha in the play of that name. After their marriage, Nathaniel wrote the equestrian drama of "Putnam" in 1844. He died in 1847. [6]

George Wolf, congressman and governor from Pennsylvania, was born on August 12, 1777, in Northampton County, the son of George and Mary Margaret Wolf. His father emigrated from Alsace, Germany, where he was a farmer. George was educated in a local classical school, but did not go on to a higher education. He worked on his father's farm and was principal of the local academy for a time. While a registrar's clerk in Easton, Wolf read law in the offices of the rising young who became a noted judge, John Ross by name. He married and entered politics as a Jeffersonian. In 1801, he was named postmaster of Easton and was court clerk of an orphans' court. Later he became a legislator, but when he ran for the state senate, he suffered a defeat. He served in Congress as a representative from December 9, 1824 to his resignation in 1829. He had supported the tariff and other measures to aid industry. Next Wolf served as governor with an election while he was still in the Congress.

He was governor at a hard time in the state's history. The primary problem he faced was the near-bankruptcy of the state because of excessive construction of internal improvements. He instituted economy in state government and reorganized the financial structure. To help restore the state, he levied new taxes. He initiated a revision of the state laws. It had been unrevised for a century. His chief achievement was his restoration of finances, but he was most lauded by his free public school act of 1834. He had promote this and worked hard to sell the idea to the public in speeches and messages to the legislature. Although a supporter of Jackson, he deplored the Jackson attack upon the Bank. He worked for its charter renewal. Because of this, he was defeated in his try for a third term in 1835. Surprisingly Jackson and Van Buren did not hold his support of the Bank against him and Jackson appointed him comptroller of the treasury and Van Buren to the job of customs collector at Philadelphia. He died in the latter post on March 11, 1840. [7]

---

[1]Eaton, Clement, *The Leaven of Democracy*, 1963, pp. 343-345.

[2]Atherton, Lewis E., *The Frontier Merchant in Mid-America*, Columbia, Mo: University of Missouri Press, 1971, pp. 33-36.

[3]Biesele, Rudolph Leopold, *The History of the German Settlement in Texas 1831-1861*, 1930, Austin, Tx: Eakin Press, 1987, pp. 21-28.

[4]Weld, Theodore Dwight, *American Slavery As It Is: Testimony of a Thousand Witnesses*, New York: American Anti-Slavery Society, 1939, Rep. New York: Arno Press, 1968, pp. 10-17.

[5]Mandel, Bernard, *Labor: Free and Slave: Workingmen and the Anti-Slavery Movement in the United States*, New York: Associated Authors, 1955, pp. 23-24.

[6]Brown, *History*, p. 18.

[7]*Dictionary of American Biography*, X (2), 446-447.

Chapter 24

NEW YEARS 1831

O n the fourth day of the new year 1831, the Illinois legislature nominated Andrew Jackson to be president of the nation to succeed himself. Illinois legislators voted overwhelmingly for Jackson. They voted 14 to three in the senate and 28 to six in the lower house. Noting that they had entire confidence in Jackson's unbending integrity, patriotism, and political experience, they followed republican members of the legislators of Pennsylvania, New York, New Hampshire, North Carolina, and Alabama. At this time, the legislators of Delaware, reacting to the nomination of Jackson, did nominate Henry Clay as presidential candidate. Early 1831 drew the lines for the campaign of the following year.

Although Jackson had vetoed one internal improvement bill passed by Congress, internal development was finding much support in industrial states. In Pennsylvania the state legislature passed several bills appropriating two million, one hundred and twenty-six dollars for building canals and railroads within the state including railroads from Philadelphia to the western turnpikes by way of Columbia. In the city of Paterson, the people subscribed money for the building of a railroad to the Hudson River. They required some $250,000, but soon after the books were closed, it was found five times that, and some $1,291,750 had been provided for the project.

The Congress in its session of 1830-1831 had passed various improvement bills allowing for money to be spent on roads and railroads. Some $175 thousand was appropriated by the national congress for continuation work on the Cumberland Road going through the Middle West. They passed a bill of one million dollars for a Chesapeake-Ohio Canal. Ohio was given land to pay for canals in that state. [1]

The reviewer in the *North American Review* expected an easy renewal of the Bank charter and wrote that the matter should be brought before the people on its own merits. He stated that Jackson could not be charged with having presented the Bank issue prematurely for the decision of the people. Also since the Bank was founded to serve the government and public, it could not rightfully shun public discussion. The Bank had nothing to fear from a public investigation. He felt the Bank would pass such an inquiry with flying colors. The Bank followed the same practices, which the best banks in the nation had adhered to. The Bank was a good institution and had performed well in terms of public finance, domestic commerce, and exchange. [2]

Chief Justice Marshall gave the majority opinion of the Supreme Court on the Cherokee case. The Cherokee had sought an injunction to prevent the state of Georgia from executing certain state laws, which would annihilate the tribe as a political society and take from the Cherokee lands, which belonged to them by solemn treaty, still in force. The case would excite sympathies for the Indians. The Cherokee had been a nation which was once numerous and powerful and independent. They had extensive lands and now wished to preserve the residue of the land for their enjoyment and livelihood.

The Supreme Court had jurisdiction because the Cherokee was a separate entity, a foreign state. Soon he was to deny that jurisdiction when he said that the United States was a guardian for the Cherokees. That made the Cherokee dependents. Although the constitution said that the government had the right to treat with foreign nations and Indian tribes, the injunction was denied. The Cherokee had rights, it was true, but the Court was not the place to redress the wrongs done them. The Court could not prevent the future.

He took the middle position and stated that they were not subject to state laws also. The Cherokees though they had a great victory. They thought the federal government would be forced to protect Indian rights and property. Almost a quarter of a year earlier, the Georgian legislature passed a law to prevent white men from entering Indian lands. The object was to prevent missionaries from stirring up the natives. Missionaries Samuel A. Worchester and Dr. Elizur Butler defied the state law. They and nine others were arrested. Only these two men refused to get pardons for their promises to stay out of the reserve and as martyrs were put in jail. They sued and the Supreme Court ruled on March 3, 1832, that this law was unconstitutional and Georgia had to release the missionaries, which they did next year.

Meanwhile, Cherokee Indian Major Ridge, the able and wealthy Cherokee leader, viewed the Court's ruling and decided it left the Indians to their fate, which it did. Since he was in the capital, he went to see President Jackson. He asked him whether he would force the state of Georgia to release the missionaries. Jackson was just as frank and he said he would not. So seeing the light, Ridge went home to Georgia to tell his tribesmen that their only choice, their only hope was to abandon their lands and go across the Mississippi to make a new home. He told the bad news to his people and a Treaty party formed around him. This was a minor party. Most Cherokees formed the National party for staying where they were. This was under Principal Chief John Ross. [3]

There were other foreign nations to interest the people of the United States. The American people had an interest in foreign affairs and throughout the years of 1830 and 1831, they read of events in the rest of the world. They had noted the revolutions of Europe with hope and common feelings and wished for a similar revolt in England to help the heavily taxed and oppressed people of that country too. Belgium became free. A reactionary monarch in France was overthrown. Italy, Spain, Portugal, and Poland had attempts in favor of freedom. There were other revolts in Germany.

Hope resigned for Europe, but Hezekiah Niles viewed the Hispanic countries of South America with despair. He noted the information flowing into Baltimore of happenings there. In the south there were insurrections and revolutions one after the other. He would feel no interest in these affairs until the people there obtained power. However that was almost hopeless. He thought them once rich and flourishing countries, even under Spanish despotism. Now they were the victims of unprincipled chiefs who pretended to love liberty.

Americans read of a dinner to commemorate the late revolution and honor the French including Lafayette. Englishmen and Americans attended the celebration. Unfortunately, the food was less than good but numerous toasts were given and the dinner went off well, with no trouble. The chairman, Buckingham, toasted the French revolutionaries of 1830 and the kings of England and France and the president of the United States. All three were the most popular rulers of the most independent nations in the world. This was just the beginning of long windiness at the repast. [4]

On February 16, 1831, Joseph B. Hinton wrote Jackson, both being in Washington DC, that "crowds of persons and letters doubtlessly are daily pressing upon you, and were it not that I am confident that the countenance and converse of a friend was welcome and grateful to our feelings, I would refrain from increasing the number. Among your *friends*, I know I desire to be ranked, not only because you had my vote and what influence I could exert, as early as 1824, but because I labored to impress it upon the senate of my own state, and through that body upon the nation at large, for the repose and harmony of this country."

He goes on to speak of the need for Jackson's re-election. Joseph wrote that on the fifteen, he tried to see the president, but was turned away at the door. It was, he believed, a settled fact that Judge John McLean would run against him. McLean had church interests in his favor. Joseph expected John Calhoun to be the next secretary of state. On this point, Hinton was out of touch with reality. Hinton was a minor fish in the vast sea and he overstated any interest Jackson had in him. Should Americans continue true to the revolutionary principles, they would soon overdo the absolute powers in the world. He thought that the Reform Church would join the Jackson cause and he could have victory in North Carolina where McLean was popular to no avail. Calhoun was falling in favor in the state and Van Buren was rising.

Hinton wanted something of Jackson. Few did not. The North Carolinian, in another letter more than a month later, wrote of the federal revenues at North Carolina ports being larger than expenditures in the state by the federal government. In the first letter, he was optimistic but in the second, he was pessimistic, seeking to gain the extra expenditures for his state, probably for internal improvements. Jackson, if he read the letter, must have thought he was a donkey. [5]

Abe was crossing the frozen Sangamon River when he broke through the ice and got his feet wet. His feet got frozen on the two-mile walk to the house of William Warnick.

Mrs. Warnick came to Lincoln's rescue, used snow to take out the frostbite, and then rubbed them with grease. By this treatment, she saved Lincoln's feet. [6]

Denton Offutt was an Illinois businessman, with some goods to sell in New Orleans. He came to the house of John Hanks with a job offer. Having heard that Hanks was quite a flatboatman in Kentucky, he wanted Hanks to run his flatboat to New Orleans soon after the snow melted. With this in hand, he went to see Abe and John D. Johnston and then introduce them to Offutt. The three young men all agreed to take the boat downriver for 50 cents a day and $60 additional. By that time, floods covered the country. John Hanks and Abe went down the Sangamon River in a canoe to Jamestown and walked five miles westward to Springfield. They found Offutt who was unable to get a boat. They then contracted to cut timbers and use them to build a flatboat. It took four weeks. Afterwards, they loaded up and headed down river. When they landed in New Orleans, they saw black slaves being chained, maltreated, whipped, and scourged. Lincoln did not say much, but what he saw sadden him. His strongest feelings against slavery were forged by what he saw. [7]

The Creeks of the South were having trouble. On April 8, 1831, a number wrote the secretary of war that murders had already taken place. Some whites killed Indians and some Indians killed whites. The whites went unpunished, while the Indian murderers were punished. They wrote that they were weak and their testimony in court was rejected under Alabama Law, which decreed that an Indian could not testify against a white man in the courts of law. The Creeks neither expected justice nor received justice. They wrote that they "may expect murders to be more frequent. They bring spirits among us for the purpose of practicing frauds; they daily rob us of our property; they bring white officers among us, and take our property from us for debts that we were never contracted. We are made subject to laws we have no means of comprehending; we never know when we are doing right." They could not agree to remove to the West because "our aged fathers and mothers beseech us to remain upon the land that gave us birth, where the bones of their kindred are buried, so that when they die, they may mingle their ashes together." They were destitute and starving and they appealed to Cass for assistance. [8]

Freidrich Ernst came to America in 1829, with the idea of settling in New York. However, when he read Duden's book, he decided upon Missouri instead. Gottfried Duden had just published a book against overpopulation as the creator of human ills. He preached emigration as a solution. Ernst was influenced and decided against an overpopulated city and sought open space. Others were affected too and soon the move to emigrate spread wide in Germany with results, which we shall see. Duden had just spent four years in Missouri and so it was to that state that Ernst went.

Ernst talked to Charles Fordtran who came along with him. They went by ship to New Orleans, where a fellow-passenger gave them a pamphlet on Texas. The two young men decided Texas was the best place to go. They took ship to Harrisburg and went to San Felipe de Austin, fifty miles into the interior. Austin granted him a league of land in Indian country on April 15, 1831. They went there and found the natives friendly. Fordtran surveyed the land for one-fourth of the grant. German families followed Ernst there and he wrote Schwarz in Oldenburg, who published the letter in a newspaper. Land was cheap and good, he said, and prosperity was to be had by all with the fruitful crop yields.

Many Germans came to Texas and joined Ernst in the community of Industry. It was not easy at first since they were far from human inhabitation, but the land could be developed. They hunted and planted orchards and vegetable gardens. They grew crops. Ernst plotted some of his land and sold town lots for Germans. He sold them for a very reasonable price, saying that he was not in the development business for getting rich. Like Austin, Ernst had character. So the town was founded in 1838. It grew slowly since many came there to go on to other places. At first Industry was all German, but in time other peoples settled there until one eighth of the population was non-German in 1860. [9]

[1]*Niles Weekly Register*, February 19, 1831, pp. 448-449; March 19, 1831, p. 50; March 26, 1831.

[2]"Bank of the United States," *North American Review*, January 1831, pp. 21-23.

[3]"The Cherokee Case," *North American Review*, July 1831, pp. 137-142; Remini, *Legacy*, pp. 68-69, 72-73.

[4]*Niles Weekly Register*, February 12, 1831, pp. 429, 431-432.

[5]McPherson, Elizabeth Gregory, "Unpublished Letters of North Carolinians to Andrew Jackson," *The North Carolina Historical Review*, XIV (January-October 1937), p. 369. Quote on p. 369.

[6]Pratt, *Lincoln*, p. 9.

[7]Hertz, *Hidden*, pp. 348-349; Basler, IV, 63-64.

[8]Foreman, *Indian Removal*, pp. 107-108.

[9]Biesele, *History*, pp. 3, 43-47.

Chapter 25

TOCQUEVILLE

While the state legislature of New York passed a resolution to start a movement among the states to refund to the states portions of surplus national revenue according to population, the state legislature of Pennsylvania went on the record to promote a renewal of the charter of the United States Bank. Two resolutions were passed by the Pennsylvania legislature. The first resolution maintained, in its own words, that since "the Bank of the United States has tended to maintain a sound and uniform currency; to facilitate the financial operations of the government; to regulate foreign and domestic exchange, and has been conducive to commercial prosperity, that the legislature of Pennsylvania recommend a renewal of its charter."

Renewal of the bank charter would require "such regulations and restrictions as to the power of the respective states as Congress may deem right and proper." The second resolution was more moderate in its use of words, but it equally desired a bank. It was resolved that "the constitution of the bank of the United States and near half a century's experience, sanctions a bank of the United States, as necessary and proper to regulate the value of money and prevent paper currency of unequal and depreciated value." Since the bank had its home in the state, it received great acceptance in the state's legislature. New Yorkers opposed the Bank as did President Jackson, in their case because it was headquartered in rival Philadelphia. [1]

Ambrose Spencer wrote Daniel Webster from New York State on April 19, 1831, that he talked to leading Anti-Masons in the state and learned that they would not support Henry Clay for the presidency. Clay could not renounce his Masonic principles without ruin and dishonor. Either way, Caly could not be nominated, much less elected. The anti-Masonic movement was growing stronger in New York State and its leaders and followers were very conscious of their strength. Spencer himself sought a neutral stand wishing to be vice-president. He was a Mason of the 3rd degree, but had not attended a lodge for more than thirty years. He wished to see Clay become president, not because he was the fittest man for the office, which he was, but because the anti-Jacksonians could rally around him. [2]

Connecticut born Ambrose graduated from Harvard and studied law at Sharon under John Canfield, whose daughter he married. He was admitted to the bar and became clerk of the city of Hudson, New York. In 1793, he was elected as a Federalist to the Assembly and in 1795, to the state senate. He switched to the Republican party in 1798 and vitally ruled New York State for two decades. Spencer and De Witt Clinton established the spoils system in New York. During this period, he served as attorney general and then was appointed to the state supreme court bench in 1804, becoming chief justice in 1819. Later, he served two years as mayor of Albany and was elected to Congress in 1829. He was a most prominent man in his years in public office and excelled as a jurist and a chief justice. [3]

Two Southerners founded New Salem village. South Carolinian born James Rutledge and his wife's nephew John M. Camron of Georgia moved to Illinois in 1813. The educated Rutledge was quiet and dignified. He and Camron were religious. Indeed, the strong millwright nephew was an ordained Cumberland Presbyterian minister. Twelve or thirteen year later, they moved to Concord Green, some seven miles north of the village site. These two men purchased land from the government, but their planned mill could not be built there because of the creek's lack of a sufficient flow of water. They moved southward and constructed new homes on a bluff and with permission from the state legislature to build a dam, they did so with the addition of a sawmill and gristmill to process lumber and flour. It was a success and they opened the store on the hill. Shortly, some one built a saloon. The pair hired a surveyor to plan and lay out the town in October of 1829. [4]

By the spring of 1831, Garrison decided upon a verbal and literary attack not on the slaveholders of the South, but on the half-committed of the North as he saw them. Determined to root out the colonizationists and turn them into abolitionists, to destroy the meager achievements in benefiting the black, and to galvanize the indifferent, Garrison tried to defeat them in debates. They were not interested. He was irked and angrily called them "good society folks "who would not stoop to a word fight like the rabble. They had a pride, which would have a mighty fall. However, he would fight them and wrote a pamphlet to discredit the Americans Colonization Society. There was no rebuttal of any effectiveness from them.

To the aggravated Garrison, the greatest obstacle to his movement was complacent Northerners. He would have everyone in the North join his ranks in anti-slavery. In time, he was to identify the lack of Christian ideals for the evil of slavery. The colonizationists were the enemy at hand. Garrison was influenced by William Watkins who asked by the Negro should be forced to leave his Christian home for a pagan and certain death in Africa. He read Walker's *Appeal* and learned of the failures in colonization. Why should Americans be duped, Garrison asked, into believing that blacks were unfit for American civilization. True enough, there were thousands of African Americans in the crime and squalor of Northern slums, but these could be raised to the levels of the African

Americans Walker and Watkins by education, both secular and Christian. Garrison claimed that colonizationists hated blacks, which some did, and were involved in a conspiracy against the human rights of black Americans. Free blacks in the North supported him. They flattered and consulted him, while he lectured them to follow the example of and find refugee in Jesus. African Americans should not follow the paths of hatred and violence. [5]

Shortly after Lincoln came to New Salem and was clerking, his boss Offutt betted William Clary that Abe could beat in wrestling any man in the county. Clary was sure of his candidate and took the bet. He called in the best in the county, Jack Armstrong. The people in New Salem neighborhood and many from the surrounding countryside came to watch. Although Jack was a stout man, strong as an ox, and very muscular, he was no match for Lincoln. Abe was getting the best of him, so he broke his hold to grab Abe by the leg and throw him. However, Lincoln seized him by the throat and pushed him away at arm's length. There would have been a good general fight had not James Rutledge come in to pacify those who favored Lincoln's chances and felt that Armstrong had played foul. Afterwards, Jack and his friends became warm friends and supporters of Lincoln. Later, Lincoln was to use his legal talents to clear Jack's son of a murder charges. [6]

After the series of cabinet resignations in April of 1831, the people of the United States were perturbed and uncertain. Of particular question was the resignation of the secretary of state, Martin Van Buren, who was known as an able official and politician. Only those behind the scenes could understand the reason and impact of the actions by Van Buren and other popular cabinet ministers. The editors of the *Niles Weekly Register* summed it up in a sentence: "that the retirement of Mr. Van Buren from the office of secretary of state, is not yet generally understood." In dealing with Van Buren's position, the New York *Courier*, noted quite wisely, that "well indeed may Mr. Van Buren be called 'the great magician,' for *he raises his wand, and the whole cabinet vanishes.*" [7]

Alexis Charles Henri Clerel de Tocqueville, the great writer on American democracy in Jacksonian America, was born into nobility on July 29, 1805, and into a family marred by the French Revolution, whose grandfather, the Marquis de Rosambro was executed in the Terror. Only the fall of Robespierre saved his father and mother from execution. The Tocquevilles found obscurity during the days of Napoleon and young Alexis had a placid childhood, but the traditions and history of France were passed on to him early in life. When Napoleon fell the second time, there was a position as prefect of the department of Oise for Alexis's father, followed by other positions. At first the boy spent much time with his mother, but later with his father. Next, he received a formal education of a little Greek, more Latin and mathematics, and much history and French composition. He was not especially interested in books, but excelled in the art of rhetoric and French writing. His failing in the classics later handicapped the young Alexis. In religion, he read some skeptical or agnostic works, which shook his Catholic faith irreparably.

Next, he had three years of law, traveled for a time, and in 1827 entered a career in the magistracy as an apprentice magistrate in the government court at Versailles.

Associating with the ranks of peers and lawyers, Alexis showed a great degree of eloquence among them, but Alexis was unhappy with his work. The young Tocqueville felt awkward and ill at ease on his feet. The pedantry and intricacies of the law stifled him.

Wishing to become more than a jurist, to become a statesman, he is interested himself in politics. Unlike his family, he was sympathetic with the liberal movement and troubled by the reactionary obstinacy of Charles X. Soon he was unable to talk politics with his conservative family. His idealism was established with the liberal influence of the time. He was independent and thought for himself. His ties were with the champions of the liberalism of his day. Alexis thought to serve his country by finding a reasonable program for France for the good of humanity. He was indeed an aristocrat in the liberal fold.

Before long, he made the fortunate contact with Gustave Auguste de la Bonniniere de Beaumont (1802-1866), who became his lifelong friend. Both were idealistic liberals seeking answers to political life. Beaumont was born at Beaumont-la-Chartre (Sarthe) in February of 1802 after the Concordat with Rome and before Napoleon's election as first consul for life. He and his siblings were brought up on a small tree-shaded farm on a hillside. Their father was mayor of the commune. It was a rural tranquil life, but events still had an influence there. The people were torn between loyalty to the old families and the clergy and the influence of liberals, Benjamin Constant and Lafayette.

The pair was influenced by English political history, and particularly by the work of J.B. Say on political economy. Professor Guizot also influenced them. They learned of the idea of gradual, inevitable progress and of the idea of democracy as a part of that progress. At this time, unrest raised its head under the reactionary Polignac administration. Tocqueville was restless also and he interviewed one or two politicians only to be disillusioned by their dishonesty. He was surprised that they had no plan; that the affairs of state were not going in accord with a preconceived plan. Politicians had no program to present the young idealist. He and Beaumont could do nothing but watch for the catastrophe sure to come. At this point, Charles X in a try for absolute power was overthrown and departed for the safety of England.

Despite his liberalism, Tocqueville regretted the July Revolution and despised Louis Philippe. When he took the oath to the July monarchy, he lost friends and family. Unsatisfied with situations in France, Tocqueville longed for some escape. He and Beaumont submitted a request to go to the United States to study the new American prison reforms at a time when the government was eager about all sorts of reforms. This would be the first step towards influence and fame. Both men decided to go to the United States and upon their return to publish a book on America. It required three months of effort to get their leaves and for the families to finance the two young men's trip.

On their way across the ocean, Tocqueville and Beaumont cultivated the English and Americans to improve their English and to learn more about America, economics, and politics. They had the help of a former member of parliament, who thought the French mission was a good idea. The two men spoke only English on the voyage. An American girl on board gave them their daily English lessons. Also, they set themselves to translate an English language work on the prisons of America and read a complete history of the United States. The distinguished New York merchant Peter Schermerhorn told Tocqueville "that there were no parties in America as was with us; the nation is no longer divided into two by contrary principles, serving as barriers. The state of affairs came to an end with the extinction of the Federalists and the non-Federalists and non-Federalists. Now no one knows only those who support and those who attack the measures of the administration, in order to obtain jobs and win public opinion over to their side." Schermerhorn spoke too soon.

There were the negative aspects to life in America. Businessman Schermerhorn saw the chief blot in the avid desire of its people to get rich by any means whatsoever. Further, the great number of business failures did not sufficiently injure the men most responsible for the failures. On national unity, he foresaw the inevitability of divisions between the states, but not for the near future.

On May 9, 1831, with the dawn, the passengers on the ship were able to see Long Island. They were getting closer to the shore and the travelers rejoiced. Soon, however, they were faced by a wind from the west and the captain directed the tacking to prevent the ship from being blown out to sea. Because of the difficulty of sailing and shortage of food, the passengers suggested they drop anchor in the outer harbor of Newport. A fishing dory took them into Newport. The Frenchmen wondered about the town and noted its cleanliness and the ugliness of their women. They noticed also that no one could tell the nationality of its people. The town had 16,000 people living there. Beaumont recorded the presence of four or five banks in Newport and was impressed with American commerce.

The Frenchmen boarded a steamship on the way from Providence to New York. The vessel was large and fast, and the wind-bound sailing vessel which they had come across in. They were impressed with its interior with three great saloons, two being for men and one for women given the larger number of men traveling. So different from their sail trip, the steamship could contain four or eight hundred people for eating and sleeping. The sea and wind was contrary, but they made the sixty leagues between Newport and New York City.

Also, the country houses in the environs of New York City impressed the young men. The big and carefully worked houses were set in a slope of lawn down to the Sound. They were not expensive as Beaumont later found out. He noted that they had nothing like these environs in France. The steamship made its way to the foot of Manhattan at Courtlandt Street on the morning of the eleventh of May. They caught up on their sleep.

The young men were welcomed. On May 18th, the *New York Daily Advertiser* published the facts of their arrival. To the newspaper, it was "gratifying to learn that the French government are engaged in extensive examinations on the important subject of prison discipline. Commissioners, it is stated, have already gone to the different countries of Europe, and two have arrived here in the packet ship *Havre*, who are to visit our principal prisons and penitentiaries, and report on their return to France. They are Messrs. De Beaumont and Tocqueville. As humanity is deeply interested in the improvement of the prisons of France and of all Europe, we hope our philanthropists will afford the gentlemen all desirable facilities."

Serurier in Washington had written the two Frenchmen the day before that their mission "will flatter the natural pride of a young nation which sees travelers from the old societies of Europe coming to learn something from it." It was a compliment that the French wished to study how American did anything. The French in this matter, thought they could learn something from the Americans and they were flattered. Travelers from the Old World had been criticizing Americans in their books. This compliment was a switch.

There were in the United States two new prison systems. One could be found in New York's Auburn in 1822 and the other was at Philadelphia's Eastern State Penitentiary in 1824. Boston's Prison Discipline Society had reviewed the prison reform movement and in Philadelphia, the Quakers considered the problem. Sing Sing was being constructed upriver from New York City on the Auburn style. The problem was the high level of visibility and the two travelers benefited from this. Indeed, the invitations and visitors came to the Frenchmen. Peter Schermerhorn came to introduce them to New York society. Their bankers in New York took them in. As much as the Americans were interesting, Beaumont found the French consul boring. He could not tell them much about the society in which he lived. They met the governor and the mayor and lesser officials, and were offered their services to find out about America.

Shortly after their arrival, they were introduced to American equality. Tocqueville noted that the authorities seemed extraordinarily approachable and that the greatest equality existed among those who occupied different positions in society. They were favorably impressed about this, but not about the architecture of New York City and its lack of prominent buildings and of great domes and bell towers. Although streets were very badly paved, they had sidewalks. The people were filled with a national conceit. They were without class; everyone being or seeming to be of the middle class with those values and breeding or lack of the breeding of Europe's upper class.

On the strength of family life and the morals of the people, Tocqueville wrote that chiefly it was the religious spirit, which dominated society, which accounted for that. Nowhere in the Christian world were religious ideas more in honor in practice. Further, because the people were busy, there was no time for seduction. There were no garrison towns with the excess of unmarried men.

Fulfilling their main reason for coming to America, they made their round of institutions in a series of ceremonies and planned later to make a working tour. They visited the House of Refuge for delinquent minors. This establishment was already known in Europe and a like institution was being constructed at Melun. At the Bloomingdale hospital for the insane they met a fifteen-year old charming girl whose religious ideas had unbalanced her mind, which were quite frequent. Next they went to the deaf and mute establishment and then to the poorhouse, where they were dinned and feted by all of the first officials of New York City. The poor house resembled a palace. Their final tour stop was Blackwell's Island, a penitentiary prison for three or four hundred prisoners who were busy building an annex. On the next day, they went to Sing Sing, about 25 miles from New York on the left bank of the Hudson.

Reform in the United States and the creation of prisons as punishment and imprisonment was a reaction against death penalties, mutilation, and whipping posts. The kindly and intelligent Quakers were the leaders in these reforms. Prison had been in the early period places where everybody was herded indiscriminately in large, unventilated and unclean rooms. They were unhealthy and had degenerated into schools of crime and vice. The prison problem became acute.

The Quaker reform was to reform criminals. Quaker placed criminals into single solitary cells where they would have time to mediate and repent of their misdeeds and would be protected from bad influences from other imprisoned criminals. It was called a penitentiary because it was a house of penitence and reform. Because of overcrowding the trial had not succeeded and even where the penitentiary had space solitary confinement often brought a break in the mind and spirit of the man confined from loneliness and idleness ending in insanity and death. In the next phase work and instruction were added to the original principle.

At Auburn in western New York, the officials developed the use of work outside of the cells with a rule of silence to fit the original idea and enforced with the use of the whip. They used cell blocks, which were now used only for sleeping and placed back in rows and tiers so the inmate could not talk to one another. Mullet-story buildings were used. In Pennsylvania, they provided work in the cell and an exercise area for each cell. Meanwhile at Sing Sing the prisoners had work on the construction of their own prisons unmoved and almost unguarded and slept in tents at night.

The two Frenchmen came to Sing Sing to be impressed by the sight of convicts working in the open with unarmed guards of thirty men watching after 900 condemned men. The system was based on moral force and the isolation of silence. They noted the system and in his report Tocqueville was to write that "one cannot see the prison the prison of Sing Sing and the system of labor, which is there, established without being struck by astonishment and fear. Although the discipline is perfect, one feels that it rests of fragile foundations: it is due to a *tour de force* which is reborn unceasingly and which has to be reproduced each day, under penalty of compromising the whole system of discipline." They spent two weeks in studying the operation and results of the institution.

Beaumont and Tocqueville had gone to Sunday worship to observe the moral education of criminals and Gusteve soon found himself watching the faces of the convicts intent upon the moral precepts of Christianity. He noted the religious attitude of the men and the fact that dogma was not taught by various religions taking part, but that morality was. It mattered not to the convicts the dogmas of the preachers. These were not taught to appeal to the varying faiths of the convicts. The two Frenchmen learned more of the toleration of different religions, which was a part and parcel of the American system. There was a notable influence upon all Americans, this toleration. Even in the prison walls they learned of what made American ticked. [8]

---

[1]*Niles Weekly Register*, March 26 1831, pp. 69-70. Quotes on p. 69.

[2]Webster, *Correspondence*, III, 111.

[3]*Dictionary of American Biography*, IX (1) 443-445.

[4]Thomas, Benjamin P., *Lincoln's New Salem*, New edition, Carbondale Ill.: Southern Illinois University Press, 1987, pp. 6-9.

[5]Thomas, *Liberator*, pp. 143-146.

[6]Hertz, *Hidden*, pp. 315-316.

[7]*Niles Weekly Register*, May 7, 1831, p. 165.

[8]Pierson, George Wilson, *Tocqueville and Beaumont in America*, New York: Oxford University Press, 1938, pp. 14-35, 44-46, 49-72, 86-88, 94-108.

Chapter 26

MORE ON TOCQUEVILLE

On June 1, 1831, Tocqueville wrote up his observation on education in America and the emphasis the Americans placed upon public instruction. They smiled indulgently when told that this opinion on the need of mass education in society was not universal in Europe. Americans all agreed that education was a necessity for a free people where there is no money qualified required for voting on holding office. Europeans argued against the excessive diffusion of education, but these arguments did not apply in America as Tocqueville saw it. There was no hostility between religion and science. Also there was an outlet for moral energy and intellectual activity and no undue restlessness. Because government was limited, it was difficult in America to attack the government.

Tocqueville's impression of the Americans was that they were the happiest people in the world. Americans owed this "immense prosperity much less to its peculiar virtues, less to a form of government of itself superior to other forms, than to the particular circumstances in which it finds itself, which is peculiar to it and which make its political constitution to be perfectly in accord with its needs and its social condition." Chief among these were the immense resources found in the country and the fact that there was employment for everybody. Restlessness in Europe was racking European societies, but American restlessness cooperated toward the prosperity of the nation. Also politics in America was secondary to economics. The price of cotton took up more room in the newspapers than general questions on government. Most periodical coverage dealt with local questions.

The want of intellectual tone, Livingston told Tocqueville, was due principally to the inheritance law. He could still remember when he was young and the country was "peopled with rich proprietors who lived on their lands like English gentry, cultivated the mind, and followed certain traditions of thought and manners. High morals and distinction of mind then existed among a certain class of the nation. The law equalizing the portions has constantly worked to destroy and redistribute fortunes; those morals and those ideas became lost and are now finally disappearing. Lands change hands with unbelievable rapidity, no one has time to become attached to a place. Everyone has to resort to practical work to sustain himself in the position his father occupied. Families almost all disappear at the second and third generation."

There was nothing like the influence of landed proprietors left because each man only has as much influence as he himself is worth. The wealthy classes accept this as one of the necessities of existence because there was no way to prevent it. There was no animosity between the wealthy people and the masses. Because all classes co-operated in the revolution, the power of democracy became so invincible that none would struggle against it. The people easily elect the wealthiest and best educated without a qualm. The equality of the people of the United States was not as pronounced as it might appear by the handshakes on the street. It is merely good manners, a formality. Wealth changes hands so fast that the pretensions have no power. Generally second rank people now hold public office, because there is not enough wealth, power, and consideration to attract the more ambitious and the more able. It was different at the beginning of the Republic, but those who would be statesmen were employed in other careers.

There were no powerful neighbors and there was plenty, if cheap, land to the west. There was no great central authority. Americans gloried in their ungoverned condition. The needs of the people were met in business. The space and natural resources had turned the interests of the European settlers to farming, industry, and trade. Americans believed in progress and themselves. Frenchmen did not feel the same way. This was America's intellectual movement or a part of it at any rate. The traditional safeguards of all this was religion and education, a segment of the Puritan program.

Also in June, while working of the new city juvenile delinquency solutions of a juvenile detention home, the two Frenchmen learned from Reverend John Power, vicar of the Catholic Church in New York that church and state were separate among Catholics in America. Of Power himself, Tocqueville and Beaumont noted his lack of prejudice against republican institutions and that he regarded education to be favorable to morality and religion. They also talked to the Protestant Jonathan Mayhew Wainwright and learned of the separation of church and state there. Ministers were not involved in politics in America. He noted that "we should think that were injuring our standing if we were to concern ourselves with a political matter. A great number among us even abstain from voting at the elections; that what I myself am always careful to do," Wainwright said.

Albert Gallatin talked of the towns of the Republic. There were no villages on the European mode, because the farmers lived on their land with houses scattered through the countryside. Farm populations were composed of merchants, artisans, and lawyers. Lawyers were common in the country, where they exerted great influence, mostly conservative instead of the restless disturbance of European lawyers. The majority of legislators are lawyers. Magistrates are all taken from among the lawyers. Tocqueville soon went to see the American frontier. [1]

It was in June of 1831 that a man named Matthew Maury was waiting for a steamboat at White River Landing near the mouth of the Arkansas River. He saw there another man waiting on the shore. He had two dogs and a gun and wore an old straw hat and a coarse calico hunting shirt. He did not have the usual traveling bag, but brought with him Indian knapsacks and buffalo skins. He was clearly a man of the Indians. Someone introduced him to Maury as former governor Sam Houston of Tennessee.

It was dinnertime and the two men went to their respective tables. After the meal was consumed, Houston went over to the Maury and his friends' table and began talking. He talked of the Indians of Arkansas about whom he had knowledge and of the value of the domains of unoccupied lands in keeping the United States united. He put forth his idea that the United States should acquire the Pacific Northwest, if he could get enough capitalists to join his vision, he would establish a government on the Columbia River. Houston was obviously a man with ideas, but this one was never to get off the ground.

Maury discerned Houston's ideas of the extension of civilization, which were common enough for his time and place. Houston spoke of the American fondness for moving to new lands and that republican government was ill adapted to a densely settled country or so it seemed. Maury wondered about this and its truth or falseness. He amused himself about universal suffrage making a man. Maury thought Houston had no general knowledge and information, which he felt a governor or former governor should have. How could such a man become governor of a state?

Six months later, the travelers and observers of democracy in America, Alexis de Tocqueville and Gustave de Beaumont met Houston at the same place, again awaiting a steamboat. When Tocqueville questioned his fellow passengers about who this man was, they told him that the American was former governor of Tennessee. Tocqueville was unimpressed and wrote that Houston was the personification of the "unpleasant consequences of popular sovereignty." However, the Frenchman did note the apparent physical and moral energy of Houston and they talked of the Indians and their life and government policy toward them in America. [2]

The Frenchman wrote in his book that "the democracy is not only deficient in that soundness of judgments which is necessary to select men really deserving of its confidence, but it has neither the desire or the inclination to find them out." Houston was not the only public official whom Tocqueville thought undeserving of office. Equality he thought could never be entirely satisfied and the Americans were doomed to be ever disappointed in their pursuit of equality. Tocqueville held "it to be sufficiently demonstrated that universal suffrage is by no means a guarantee of the wisdom of the popular choice; and that whatever its advantages may be. This is not one of them." [3]

The Choctaw who emigrated found themselves in a near starving condition. The government acted to arrange the purchase of food for them and settled them, but it was no easy time for those Indians who made it that far. Not all of the tribesmen did. Back home, the Choctaw, not knowing whether they would be moved or not, did not plant crops. Instead they had nothing but still the menfolk purchased whiskey. They had little money left for food, and many of the Indians had to subsist on roots.

The government sent William S. Colquehoun of Virginia to meet with La Flore and find out how many Indians would migrate in the fall and get Le Flore views on the various aspects of the subject. It was suggested that Gaines be selected to conduct the Indians on the Red River country, which pleased the Choctaw since they had a good opinion of the man.

On May 22, 1831, the Indians wrote George Gaines that they in the Southern district wished him to do business for them. Chief Nithickachee went to Gaines' house to discuss what was to be done. The warriors who wrote expressed their desire to go west in the autumn but they needed blankets, leads, powder, and cloth for tents. They would need provisions as promised by the government and wagons and steamboats for the trip. The Indians asked Eaton to appoint Gaines to guide them and Eaton did this. Arrangements and decisions were made over the next months and it seemed certain that perhaps a third of the Choctaws would move. [4]

The Sac Indians had long since made their peace with the whites except for one chief. This recalcitrant warrior was Black Hawk. Now an old man, Black Hawk had been a warrior all of his life and never had been defeated. In the War of 1812, he had been aide-de-camp to the great Tecumseh. He had integrity and courage and had clemency for his foes when he had defeated them. A kind father and husband, he had never swerved in his loyalties with the British, and kept up his ties with Canada. He dealt well with the Indian traders but he thirsted for revenge. Black Hawk denied the validity of treaties and said they had been illegally fostered on the Indians by getting some of them drunk, and were not binding upon a nation that had not agreed to them at the time. He would not take his people for permanent residence in the country west of the Mississippi.

In the spring of 1831, he recrossed the great river with his entire tribe and some Potawatomie and Kickapoo tribe people. Returning to his old hunting grounds, he and his warriors drove the settlers away by force, destroyed their improvements and killed their stock, threatening death if they did not leave. The settlers complained to Illinois Governor John Reynolds. The governor called it an invasion and wrote General Edmund P. Gaines and to General William Clark, Indian affairs superintendent for them to peacefully expel the Indians or if necessary use force to force them back to Indian lands across the river.

Gaines brought a few companies of regular soldiers and soon discovered Black Hawk would not leave. So, he asked Reynolds for seven hundred mounted volunteers. The governor issued the call and got over twice that number. They gathered at Rockport south of the Rock River. Gaines joined them with a steamboat of provisions. Their general Joseph Duncan consulted with Gaines and they arrived at a plan for action. They all went by steamboat upriver to Vandruff's Island where they expected to fight the Sac, opposite the Indian town.

The Americans landed and were soon in a sad condition of confusion. They finally crossed the river to the town and found it deserted. Then Indian envoys came asking for peace for their band and were told to return to the west bank, which they did. Peace was thus established for that portion. The soldiers however, seeking revenge, burnt the large

Indian town to the ground. After this Black Hawk sued for peace and the settlers returned to their lands. It seemed for them that the incident was over and they rebuilt their houses and fences. [5]

Black Hawk, American Indian chief of the Sac tribe, was born in 1767 in the village of Saukenuk on the Rock River near its confluence with the Mississippi in what was to become the state of Illinois. He was a descendant of chiefs. As a young man of fifteen in the war against the Osages, he made his first kill and thereafter led in small parties and larger successful raids and battles. In one fight, he killed three Cherokee braves, but lost his father, the chief. Becoming chief, he continued in the ensuring years to lead war parties against neighboring tribes. He visited Spanish St. Louis and was there when Americans took control on March 9, 1804. When Zebulon Pike came through, Black Hawk treated him well and Pike presented him with an American flag, but the Indian was loyal to his British "father." The Sac kept their British medals.

The conflict with the whites came with the treaty of 1804 in which the Sac unknowingly gave up most of their land and with the building of a fort in the area. After a time, Black Hawk led a force of warriors against Fort Madison as it was called, in which a few men were killed and the Sac chieftain advised setting the fort on fire. Flaming arrows started fires but there were always instantly extinguished. Unable to take the fort, the Indians left. Soon the War of 1812 erupted and many Indian tribes joined the British. When made a general, Black Hawk led the allied Indians forces. At one point, he stopped a massacre of prisoners the British had taken. Toward the end of the war, Black Hawk led a party to attack some American boats with some success when one was grounded along the riverbank. There was another action below the war ended.

Time passed and ever more settlers moved into the interior and coveted the Sac village. There was a split in Sac leadership. Keokuk headed the peace party and did as the American wished. He led his followers to an Indian settlement on the Iowa River to the west. Black Hawk headed the resistance party. Whites took the Sac cornfields and the village. Soldiers forced him to go to the west also.

One trouble facing the Sac after this was a lack of food for their families so a small party of braves went over to their fields to get the corn they had planted. The whites, which now claimed the fields, discovered the warriors and fired without injury to the Indians. Settlers complained about this depredation. According to the agent, there was a provision in one of the treaties for assistance in agriculture, so Black Hawk appealed to him for a log cabin and to have a field in the Sac's new home ploughed so he could plant corn at the next planting season. The agent promised that this would be done.

Meanwhile, Ne-a-pope returned from Malden in Canada, where he had talked to a British leader. The Indians asked if the Americans could force the Sac out of their village. He replied that unless the Sac had sold their land by the voice and will of the entire nation, they could not. Ne-a-pope replied to this exchange with Black Hawk and told him that the Britisher had said they would assist the Sac in case of war. The prophet said that the Indians' British father would send them guns, ammunition, provisions, and clothing early in the spring, when Ne-a-pope visited him. Further, the other Indian tribes would join with the Sac. In this manner Black Hawk was deceived; a fatal deception. He believed what he heard and tried once again to bring over Ke-o-kuck and the Fox tribe without success.

Black Hawk planned to move on to regain his former village in a march up the Mississippi and the Rock River. His preparation was capped when the prophet joined them and promised that as long as they remained peaceable, the Americans would not interfere. This was another peace of bad advice. The chief planned to join with the British and the Indians and to have an army, which could withstand another. Underway, the Sac encountered no opposition, but when he failed to receive any help, Black Hawk realized he had been deceived, but he did not tell his people. Instead he lied, telling them he would soon meet with a chief of our British father.

The Indian chief did entertain hopes to return to Iowa, but this plan was sidetracked by two battles. When the soldiers came after them, Black Hawk sent peace delegations to them. They did not heed them, but attacked the Indians in a charge. Black Hawk's Indians fired and themselves charged. To their surprise, the soldiers retreated. The Indians routed the soldiers, pursuing them. This was the battle of Sycamore Creek of May 14, 1832. It encouraged some other Indians to join Black Hawk, who led his army and his women and children into the swamp country. The days passed and Black Hawk led them on to the west. At the Wisconsin River, he was getting the families in his tribe across, when attacked. In a fine tactical move, he met the soldiers. However, he failed to take an unoccupied hill before the Americans and had to fight from a ravine. Sac warriors once again won and headed for the Mississippi where disaster struck when whites massacred many Sac Indians, men, women, and children and the Sioux finished off those who made it across the Mississippi. Black Hawk gave himself up.

Taken into captivity, Black Hawk was put under the charge of Lieutenant Jefferson Davis, who escorted the prisoners to Jefferson Barracks with the prophet and Ne-a-pope. There they remained until the spring of 1833, when they were taken to Washington, met President Andrew Jackson and were taken on a tour of the northeast which could not fail to impress Black Hawk. All were then returned home to the Iowa. Black Hawk dictated his autobiography and lived for five years after that in retirement, bitter against Ke-o-kuck to the end. He died on October 3, 1838. [6]

---

[1]Pierson, *Tocqueville*, pp. 114-118, 121-125, 137-189.

[2]Friend, *Sam Houston*, pp. 3-4.

[3]Tocqueville, Alexis de, *Democracy in America*, Trans. Henry Reeve, 2 vols., New Rochelle, N.Y.: Arlington House, n.d., pp. 188-189. Quotes on pp. 188, 189.

[4]Foreman, *Indian Removal*, pp. 42-48.

[5]Ford, Thomas, *A History of Illinois: From Its Commencement as a State in 1818 to 1847*, Chicago: S.C. Griggs, 1854, 1995 reprint, pp. 72-77.

[6]Black Hawk, *Black Hawk: an Autobiography*, ed. Jackson, Donald, Urbana: University of Illinois Press, 1964, pp. 41, 46-83, 86-90, 95-151, 155-156.

Chapter 27

BLACK HAWK WAR

Governor John Reynolds acted promptly to protect the citizens of Illinois from the Indians. In his letter of May 26th to the superintendent, he noted that he had called out the militia. First among his actions was to send the troops to remove the Sac Indians near Rock Island to prevent the natives from harming settlers. He would send the Sac to the western side of the Mississippi. There was Reynolds who said "no disposition on the part of the people of this state to injure those unfortunate savages, if they will let us alone; but a government that does not protect its citizens, deserves not the name of a government."

In St. Louis, Superintendant William Clark quickly prepared a reply in which he charged General Edmund P. Gaines the task to protect the citizens of Illinois and not Reynolds. Reynolds wrote Gaines giving the information of the invasion of the Sac under Black Hawk. John left it up to Gaines what action the general should take. For himself, he would prepare the Illinois militia for the conflict. When this took place, Abraham Lincoln, a young man then unknown, would march with the state force. Gaines acted to send forth an army of six companies from those encamped at Jefferson Barracks and four companies from those stationed at Prairie du Chien. Although Gaines wrote Reynolds that he would not need the militia in the encounter, the governor continued to prepare for the Indian war. [1]

The first great cause, which the successful young lawyer of Gettysburg, Thaddeus Stevens, joined was Anti-Masonry. Entering politics against the secret order Masonry, he became an ardent leader and launched a political career, which later in the black cause was to lead him to the heights of the nation. Stevens' life was determined by a deformity. He was born on April 4, 1792, with a clubfoot. This shaped an early life in which friendship was impossible and left him an embittered person. As a crippled from birth, he was to engage in a life of humiliation and hardships. He never lost his bitterness despite great intellectual successes. He could not run and play with the other boys. They rejected him and made fun of him.

With a mother's interest, Sara Stevens early turned the child toward an education. His father, Joshua Stevens was an excellent boot maker who preferred to drink in bars to work. Seldom at home, he finally made such rare visits that Sara refused to take him in and he disappeared to history. The boy had everything against him that his mother could not change. She countered with a program of education. Thaddeus was to feel the clubfoot to be a stigma and disgrace. He believed that God had unjustly punished him. Always lonely, he developed an affection for education and was a strong supporter of schools for the masses in his adulthood. Like Lincoln, he would travel miles for a book.

Opportunities were rare in the rural community. When the two towns of Danville and Peacham had to decide which would have the courthouse and which would have the academy, Peacham decided for the school. A careful observer of the debates and decisions, Mrs. Stevens moved with her children to that town. Thaddeus was five when the building was built. The boy went to school in an upstairs room with its hand-hewn benches and a very scant collection of books. There was only one instructor who used the few standard classics they had a few copies of texts, and a globe to teach the children. Made fun of in the playfield, he was the best student in the classroom. Little is known about his later childhood, but in 1811, he entered Dartmouth College and then the University of Vermont. Back at Dartmouth, he graduated in August of 1814. Once finished with his formal education, he moved to York, Pennsylvania, to teach and study law in his spare time.

He earned enemies who blocked his admission to the bar in York, so Stevens went to Bel Air, Maryland, where he successfully passed a brief examination, supplying the judge with the customary Madeira. Lancaster was too aristocratic for the young man and York was inhospitable, so he went to the little town of Gettysburg to practice law. He got to know the fields of grain in what was in the future was to be the battlefield. The times he lived in had just seen a war, but there was little likelihood of another in the foreseeable future except against the Indians on the frontier. It was a time of peace.

The early months were difficult. His defense of an unhinged murderer who the people of the town and countryside did not feel deserved defense, made him hated. Although he was despised and disliked, he became more and more of a successful lawyer, taking the cases that his colleagues turned down. To augment his condition, he began buying real estate. Nine years later, he was the largest individual landowner in Gettysburg. By this time, he had earned friends and position.

In 1825, there were anti-Mason rumblings and a democratic Stevens was interested. He shortly adopted the idea and when a party developed around the Morgan episode, he joined the movement. After a time, that party began go dissolve and other anti-Masons joined the Whig party. Stevens did not follow them because many of the Whig leaders were Free Masons. Meanwhile, he was influential in making Anti-Masonry popular in his county and in the surrounding countryside. He made both friends and enemies in his campaign.

Stevens made his most noted attack on Masons in a speech of June fourth in 1831 in Hagerstown, Maryland. For this, the global Gettysburg editor Charles Lafever attacked him in his newspaper, Stevens successfully sued. In a criminal suit, Lefever was convicted and sentenced. The editor spent a few days in jail before Mason George Wolfe pardoned him as governor of Pennsylvania. His civil suit dragged on for years, but finally the court awarded the lawyer $1,800 damages when it was concluded. Stevens allowed Lefever and his wife to keep their small property, forgoing the award. It was a matter of principle for him. [2]

With John M. Berrien leaving the administration, there was a vacancy in the attorney generalship and Dr. William Jones of Washington suggested Roger Brooke Taney's name for his replacement. Taney's brother-in-law was active in promoting Taney. Francis Scott Key, whose sister Roger married, told the president that Taney should be appointed. Taney was modest and wished Berrien to continue in office for the good of the Democratic party. After being told this, the retiring attorney general asked who was talked about as his successor. Key thought James Buchanan was more likely to be named. Although he was mentioned, Taney did not think he would be named, but that he might possibly accept if appointed. After his meeting with Berrien, Key saw Edward Livingston, who told him that Taney was being talked about for the position.

Key returned home to his house in Geogetown where a letter from Andrew Jackson awaited him. He opened it and read that Jackson wished him to call at the White House. Despite its being almost nine o'clock in the evening, the president met with Key that night. He told the author of the "Star-Spangled Banner," that he wished to offer Taney the position and asked Key to find out before he offered the place, if Taney would accept the post. To cover all bases, Key said that he knew that Taney would prefer that Jackson continue Berrien in that office, but Jackson said with emphasis that this was entirely out of the question. Key said he would write Taney and sound him out. Because Taney would feel the acceptance would be duty, he was sure to accept.

In his letter, Key wrote Taney about Jackson's wish, that "it would give pleasure to his heart to understand that he would--that he would be gratified to have you in his counsels, that your doctrines upon the leading constitutional questions he knew to be sound and your standing in the Supreme Court he well knew." Key asked Taney to reply promptly with an acceptance. Key continued that he believed that "is one of those instances, in which the general has acted from his own impulses and that you will find yourself, both as to him and his Cabinet, acting with men who know and value you and with whom you will have the influence you ought to have and which you can do something efficient with. As to your business, you can be as much in Baltimore as you were to come over, whenever wanted. This would only be, when you were wanted at a meeting of the Cabinet or anything important; one ordinary occasions and applications for opinion from the Departments, they could send you the papers at Baltimore and you could reply from there. As to the Supreme Court, it would, of course, suit you entirely and the increase in your business there would make up well for lesser matters."

Taney said he would accept and Jackson named him attorney general on June 21, 1831. He got his Baltimore affairs in order and Berrien arranged his Washington affairs and Taney took the oath. During the next month or so, Taney carried the portfolio of the

War Department until Lewis Cass could arrive in the national capital. General McComb handled most military matters under Taney in Washington DC. Taney became one of the most influential officials in the capital and was soon one of the kitchen cabinet members. [3]

In the face of nullification, John Quincy Adams spoke out in Quincy, Massachusetts, in the fourth of July speech he was making on that day of glory. There might be war. The ex-president feared its results. In the event of a conflict of arms between the national government and one of its states would be calamity to all states. He referred to history in his litany of terrible results arising from the break up of confederations. Concerning these examples in Israel of ancient times, Adams stated that such would come to America. Their was a heavy price to the breaking up of confederations in history. It might result in the extermination of one member or the struggle of two rivals leading to foreign domination or the yoke of a tyrant at home. In America the issue at stake was the destinies of America and the world. [4]

It was in mid-summer of 1831 that Jackson learned of an attack on an American merchant man on the opposite side of the world. After some investigation, the administration found out all that had happened and Jackson gave orders to attack. It had all started when the American ship *Friendship* was loading pepper at the west Sumatran port of Quallah Battoo. The captain, two of his officers, and four crewmen were ashore to supervise the weighting of freight and crewmen were busy abroad.

That afternoon, the native Malays suddenly attacked first officer Charles Knight and shipmates. Knight and two seamen died by the knife while three others were wounded. Four men dived overboard and swam to safety in the bushes some two miles away. Captain Endicott saw what was happening on board his ship and headed for it until chased by three Malay boats of some 150 men. It was clearly too late to do any good so the American captain headed for the nearby port of Muckie. He made the port safely and got the aid of three American ship to chase the pirate with their haul of gold and silver then worth $12,000, $8,000 in opium, and easily carried instruments and provisions. The pirate abandoned the ship and Endicott sailed it back to an American port.

American captains in Sumatra protested the robbery to the Sultan Mahomed Shab who would not take responsibility except for a bribe to ensure safety. A better complaint was soon made back in Washington. American merchants received word of the incident and worked to gain intervention from their congressmen. They met their best reception in the secretary of the navy, married into a Maine merchant family. He was Levi Woodbury and his boss was Jackson. An investigation was made and when the facts sustained the complaints, Jackson decided upon sending the *Potomac* to punish the natives of Quallah.

Captain John Downes was in command of the frigate *Potomac* that had been designed to escort Van Buren to London. The plan was changed. Downes headed his ship for Sumatra. It was at Rio De Janeiro in early November in 1831 and reached its objective in February of 1832.

The ship sailed into the port under Danish flag. The Malays were fooled into believing that the ship was a merchant marine ship out of Denmark. Plans were made for an attack. In the dark before dawn on February 6, 1832, the marines landed and launched an attack on the town's three forts. After a bloody attack, the forts were taken and next the marines searched for the booty of the previous encounter and finding nothing, plundered and set ablaze the forts. There was a loss of two men on the American side and over one hundred killed among the Malays. The Malays punished, the naval ship returned to the United States. [5]

In July of 1831, the treaty of indemnity against France for losses to American vessels during the Napoleonic wars was signed. For their part the Americans cut duties on French wines. Jackson kept his agreements but the French legislature stalled payments of five millions in six annual installments. Jackson then set about to obtain the indemnity, using the services of Edward Livingston and John Forsyth, both urbane and diplomatic.

Livingston was a good debater as well as Forsyth. The former had written an able code on reform and prison discipline, which was acceptable by the government of Guatemala without the change of a word. His ability was lauded in Europe. Forsyth was "generally respected and admired for ability and elegance of manner." Livingston was minister at Paris and Forsyth secretary of state at Washington.

Livingston was well accepted in the French king's court. There he awaited French action. At home, Jackson wrote his latest message including demands for the payment of the indemnity. The danger seemed great in Paris and Clay and other congressmen in Washington supported French failure to pay as a means of getting at Jackson. This did not win friends for Clay at home and probably lost him votes in 1832 of those who stood to gain from the payment, voters who would normally vote for him. Jackson was all the more popular for standing up to France and he knew how to turn that popularity into 1832 votes. [6]

Now Calhoun took his next step toward 1832 and beyond. He decided with other Southerners that policy of states' rights which was to remain with him the rest of his life. The Constitution he was to preach was a compact of independent states. Every state had the right to judge for itself what power he had delegated to the Union. The government rested in the state sovereignty and not majority rule. Majority rule was the fundamental principle of the American system. For Calhoun ultimate authority was in the hands of the individual states, which had called the government into being in 1787. Had Calhoun and then Davis won, this would have crippled the United States in the Twentieth Century. The possibilities were dangerous for the world. [7]

Stevens had gone whole-heartedly into politics and worked to expand his influence outside the state of Pennsylvania. His address to the citizens of Hagerstown, Maryland, was the first step in that on June 4th. He said that Anti-Masonry was consistent with pure morals, true religion, and true liberty. To suppress what he thought was an evil, it was necessary to opposed it politically. He then began a sharp attack on the Masons for their ritual and its religious symbolism. For him it was a travesty upon the Christian faith. He thought it to be a revolting atrocity and compared it to Cataline. Charging that their order bound them to protect Masons who committed crimes, he noted its secret nature and stated that it was a blow at liberty. They promoted each other's political preferment. He called upon the people of Hagerstown to unit in a crusade to fight the Masons. The political leaders of the nation in both parties were Masons as he averred, and this doubtless led to their successes, but they would have risen anyway without Masonry. He. did not think so and was unrelenting in his attack. For this Editor Lefever attacked Stevens in the *Gettysburg Compiler* on the 21st. Steven sued him. Lafever was a Mason protecting Masons and Wolfe was too, so they gave a basis to the Stevens attack.

In 1830, the Anti-Masonic party had some election successes but it was and remained a minority party. In the first presidential convention in September of 1831, the party nominated William Wirt as president and Amos Ellmaker as vice-president. Ellmaker was a close friend of Stevens'. Men from ten states were present. By having a convention, the party gave this idea to the other parties. It was to be their major contribution to political life in the United States. Fall 1831 elections resulted in only two state senators and twenty assemblymen elected. Stevens was unable even to carry his county. Anti-masons organized their party after that and established newspapers, most of which appealed to German-Americans. Second effect was to induce the dissolution of many Masonic lodges in the interest of public welfare and to avoid strife. Large numbers of Mason lodges notably in Pennsylvania and New York State folded up, stating that it was not due to the charges. However, Stevens and his fellows with their attacks were the cause of the fall of Mason strength in the two states. [8]

---

[1]*Niles Weekly Register*, July 9, 1831, p. 335.

[2]Woodley, Thomas Frederick, *Great Leveler: The Life of Thaddeus Stevens*, 1937, Rep. Freeport NY: Books for Libraries Press, 1969, pp. 8-11, 15-44.

[3]Steiner, Bernard Christian, *Life of Roger Brooke Taney: Chief Justice of the United States Supreme Court*, Baltimore: Williams & Wilkins, 1922, Rep. Westport Ct: Greenwood Press, 1970, pp. 100-102ff.

[4]Seward, William H., *Life and Public Services of John Quincy Adams*, 1849, pp. 250-251.

[5]Belohlavek, John M., "Andrew Jackson and the Malaysian Pirates," *Tennessee Historical Quarterly*, Spring 1977, pp. 19ff.

[6]Bowers, *Party*, pp. 133-136, 386-390ff. Quote on p. 386.

[7]Coit, *Calhoun*, pp. 231-233.

[8]Woodley, *Great Leveller*, pp. 40-46.

Chapter 28

CALHOUN FOR PRESIDENT

Calhoun's quest for the presidency began to bear fruit in the North. In New York City, overwhelming crowds greeted him in Broadway House on August 9, 1831. The crowds braved heavy rains and probably many of the men there thought Calhoun, popular as he was with them, had a good chance for the presidency. Calhoun himself, realizing the unpopularity of his constitutional stand, expected to do poorly in the South and see the west and north divided between Clay and Jackson. If it were divided right, the election the following year might end up in the House where his followers might have the balance of power. This was his great hope since he knew he could not gain the presidency by popular means. He knew that he was not strong enough to win outright.

Unknown to him, he had no chance of being president. Life had passed him by because of his opposition to Jackson. His star had set since he could not gain enough popularity in the South, which would have been his logical base. Jackson was popular there with the exception of South Carolina. Calhoun was never able to gain popularity although many followed his views closely. This was to increase but not enough for a successful try at the president's office. Once he had been powerful in the land and was the logical successor to Jackson, but not now. [1]

On August 17, 1831, Horace Greeley entered New York City for the first time, without any prospects for success in that hard metropolis. He had only $7.50 in his pockets and no job lined up, but he was sure from the start that the exciting city was the place to be. Finding poorly suitable work at a print shop, he set type for a pocket-sized New Testament with its small type, a demanding and slow work at piecework set for easier and faster work. He managed to take home as much as six dollars a week by working up to fourteen hours a day. When the job was finished, he was out of work and for awhile found odd jobs from time to time before he found regular employment for a new sporting and betting weekly. Unfortunately, it failed after a few months. Greeley proved to be able to outwork his fellow typesetters even while chattering all day long. After work, he enjoyed the theater. [2]

The slave Nat Turner, who was soon to cause so much fear in the South, had had two heavenly visions and was a preacher among his fellow African Americans in Southampton County, Virginia, along the South Carolina State line to the south. About 1825, he had baptized a white man and been highly considered as a religious man among his own people. Nat had been born the slave of Benjamin Turner on October 2, 1800. Upon his majority, he had run away from home, returning voluntarily after a month away. One year later, after the death of Samuel Turner, he was sold to Thomas Moore. About January of 1830, the widow Moore took him with her when she married Joseph Travis.

Keeping his plans to himself, Turner bided his time, but he soon felt his opportunities for a slave revolt were coming. The appearance of a day-long atmospheric phenomenon that made the sun bluish-green on August 13, 1831, was considered by him to be a sign. One week later, Nat told his lieutenants to meet him the next day to plan a revolt. That day, August 21st, a Sunday, Hark, Henry, Nelson, Sam, Jack, and Will came to Cabin Pond and cooked a pig. They had brandy to drink. In mid-afternoon, Nat joined them and they began to plan. They were to attack before dawn on the next day.

They began with the Travis plantation, brutally killing Travis, his wife, and child, and two apprentices of whom one of them, Putnam Moore was Nat's legal owner. Turner delivered the first blow. Heading for the house of Salathiel Francis, they killed him. Bypassing two homes, they murdered those at the home of Mrs. Piety Reese. Once there, the farm managers escaped death although severely wounded. Shortly before sunrise the murderers were driven back from the home of Wiley Francis.

A sunrise attack was made on the home of Mrs. Elizabeth Turner. With the early hours of dawn passed, the force divided into two groups and several more plantations were hit. More whites were killed. The Porters had fled, but others nearby were less fortunate. The blacks killed more people. Some fifty-seven whites were eventually to lose their lives. More and more the blacks were to find deserted houses, the alarm had been sounded.

Various blacks joined the killers until there were fifty or sixty of them all mounted with stolen animals. Nat Turner led them now in the direction of Jerusalem, Virginia. It was noon on the 22d by this time. That afternoon, mounted militia met the blacks. Both sides fired shots. No one on either side was hit. The white force had one victory: the inconclusive fight led to disorganization on the part of the group they met. By nighttime, the blacks were increasingly meeting resistance and having their force vanish from fear on the part of the killers. On the next day, the Turner force was repulsed at the home of Dr. Simon Blunt.

Turner was now alone and went into hiding. The killers were rounded up and then on October 31, 1831, having been captured, were tried, convicted, sentenced and hung. This uprising was finished, but executions continued for awhile in North Carolina where justice was sometimes not to be had. Some slaves were convicted and executed who were not involved in the Turner uprising; however, some free African Americans were acquitted and freed. This was the basic story of the uprising of the slaves, now for the white reaction.

The *Constitutional Whig*, a newspaper in Richmond, Virginia, had the earliest scoop of the newspapers about the revolt. What were called disagreeable rumors beset the state capital's citizens. There were reports of a slave insurrection in Southampton County, that African Americans had killed off several families in the area of the revolt. Governor Floyd took prompt measures to send the militia to put down the revolt and establish an alert in southern Virginia's case of future acts of violence. This newspaper warned its public against ungrounded rumors that the revolt was spreading. The troubles were confined to that county. News reports in the *Whig* came out on the same day during which the mob was defeated and Nat Turner fled for his hiding places.

More detailed reports flowed in from Southampton. Colonel Trezevant sent a hurried letter. It was received in Petersburg and starred a movement among Petersburg Volunteers to march for the scene of the insurrection. Meanwhile, other militia troops headed for the scene of the trouble from surrounding counties in southern Virginia. The people of Petersburg were excited. All sorts of rumor were perpetuated about the uprising. Numbers were exaggerated. The trouble of the days were said to have become passed, black insurrectionists were reported being surrounded by militia and volunteers and having fled to the swamps for protection from southern revenge. A white from Belfield in Greenville County wrote that the African Americans were headed for the Dismal Swamp but due to being surrounded it would be made impossible for them to arrive there.

Richmond troops made a fatiguing ride from the capital in a rapid and hot movement. Along their way, they learned a multitude of false reports, each different from the other. Passing through Petersburg, they reached a deserted land where every man was armed and farms were abandoned for the time being, left in the possessions of slaves. It was mass hysteria. Ladies left the countryside seeking protection from the murderous attacks. Nearing the troubled area, they learned that the blacks did not number a thousand men as one report had it. Only one county was involved and atrocities were exaggerated in early reports. The excitement and hysteria began to subside and the people soon returned to their plantations, having showed the slaves how much they feared them. [3]

There was a different hysteria in Washington DC involving Mrs. Eaton. Mrs. Smith went greatly overboard when she wrote on August 19, 1831, that Jackson was "completely under the government of Mrs. Eaton, one of the most ambitious, violent, malignant, yet silly women you ever heard of. You will soon see the recall of the Dutch minister announced. Madame Huygen's spirited conduct in refusing to visit Mrs. Eaton is undoubtedly the cause. The new cabinet if they do not yield to the president's will on the point, will, it is supposed, soon be dismissed. Several of them in order to avoid this dilemma, are to determined not to keep house or bring on their families. Therefore, not keeping house, they will not give parties and may thus avoid the disgrace of entertaining the favorite. It was hoped, on her husband's going out of office, she would have left the city, *but she will not*. She hopes for a complete triumph and is not satisfied with having the cabinet broken up and a virtuous and intelligent minister recalled, and many of our best citizens frowned upon by the president. Our society is in a sad state. Intrigues and parasites in favor, divisions and animosity existing."[4]

There was a meeting of opponents to Jackson in Richmond. Delegates were elected to the next convention on September 7, 1831, "was denounced for his ignorance of the Constitution and the laws, for his arbitrary temper, for his appointment of numerous members of Congress to official positions, and for his inconsistent position on the tariff and internal improvements." [5]

Having been educated at Transylvania in Lexington, Kentucky, Cassius Marcellus Clay went east. He had letters of introduction to Jackson and other politicians so when he was in Washington, he visited them to discover why they were successful. Clay met John Quincy Adams and Daniel Webster and the lesser lights. He talked with poet John Greenleaf Whittier, song writer Julia Ward Howe, and lawyer John Andrew. Proceeding northeast, Cassius enrolled in the junior class of Yale University where he fitted easily into the academic community. He debated and gave speeches and joined a Yale literary society. In the examination of September of 1831, he ranked third in a class. He engaged in pranks. However, he soon tired of school and was eager for a political life.

Then he met Garrison and heard him denounce slavery. Back home he had joined an emancipation society, but he had felt nothing could be done about the problem. However, with this encounter, he decided he would do something about slavery. While in New England, he compared progressive and prosperous Yankees who had done well on a poor soil, and belated backward Kentucky with its fine soil. Clay blamed the institution of slavery for this. He wrote his brother Brutus Clay that the slave question was assuming an importance in enlightened and humane thought, which could be not withstood. He predicted the dissolution of the Union within fifty years and the freeing of the slaves. [6]

In Boston on September 12, 1831, Tocqueville and Beaumont march in a parade to celebrate the consecration of two flags to the sent the revolting Poles, striving for the national freedom the Americans had already obtained. In the parade, the militia and the regular troops marched with officialdom and the learned bodies and other Bostonians to Faneuil Hall, where the people gathered for the occasion. The women were in the gallery and the men were on the floor. A Congregational minister, Lyman Beecher, blasted despotism and oppression with great power and a pompous eulogy of insurrection and liberty. Next the two flags were unfurled with their inscriptions such as the last words of Poniatowksi that "it is better to die with glory than to surrender."

The crowd applauded this and the announcement that the flags could go to Lafayette, to whom they were sending the flags for him to see that they reached their destination. They sung hymns and odes and closed the meeting. The names of Skrzynecki and Kosciusco were prominently displayed. Jan Skrzynecki was the commander-in-chief of the Polish army in rebellion against Russia and Thaddeus Kosciusco, a Polish volunteer in the army of the Americans in the Revolutionary War, who became a general and later dictator of Poland.

Gustave Beaumont wrote at the time that "a great number of the participants found this patriotic folderol ridiculous. What use will these Boston flags to the Poles? This manifestation of enthusiasm for the cause of the brave Poles would mean something only if, with their phrases, some money were sent at the same time. Now, they scarcely had enough to cover the expense of the ceremony. I have seen a crowd of sensible people who regretted this foolishness; but it was organized by some young men, who got everything started without there being anyway to stop them." The meeting cost $800 and $650 had already been subscribed. In Poland the rebellion was being snuffed out and there was after all nothing the Americans could do to change history. There was no way to successfully come to the aid of the Poles.

The demonstration expressed American sympathies and helped the French commissioners in prison reform become known to college president Josiah Quincy, Jr., and the retiring mayor of Boston, Harrison Gray Otis, and his hospitality. Quincy was able to provide them with documents and information of value and Otis's acceptance of the young aristocrats gained their entry to the circle around his daughter-in-law. They gained the friendship of Professor George Ticknor of Harvard who taught foreign language. When the French visited the new penitentiary at Charleston, they meet Boston philanthropists and social workers including the prison specialist Samuel Atkins Eliot and prison inspector Francis Calley Gray. Reverend Louis Dwight, secretary of the Boston Prison Discipline Society guided them and provided them with information. Beaumont quickly grew to respect the philanthropist and reforming Tappan brothers.

They dined at multi-millionaire David Sear's, where he lived in great luxury and the Frenchmen ate sumptuous dinners and chatted with his pretty niece. Next, they attended several dances. Society in Boston resembled the society of Europe and the upper class could speak French, were interested in intellectual matters, and there was refinement. Also, Boston had men and women who were able to delve into the literary arts. Religious matters were uppermost unlike the commercialism of New York City.

Joseph Coolidge Jr. introduced them to the Reverend Jared Sparks, the famous editor and historian. Coolidge was a shipping merchant engaged in the China trade who was a man of wide interests and who took a desire to help Tocqueville and Beaumont to the extent of an interesting introduction. The Frenchmen were amazed at the possession of Washingtonian letters in the hands of Sparks, who took great care and detail in handling the manuscript collections. Sparks had already published the correspondence of ambassadors and men of mark at the time of the American Revolution and was engaged upon a life of George Washington.

Sparks had decided views on Jackson as president. Most enlightened men now recognized that Jackson lacked experience and was too old for civil government. He would nevertheless be re-elected, because public opinion favored him. Public opinion was created slowly in America and the people are not surprised, although subject to error. The president's supporters worked hard to get it accepted that General Jackson was a great man and honored America. There was not time to get that opinion reversed. [7]

In Texas, a group of Cherokees applied to the Spanish government for a grant of land on the headwaters of the Trinity River and the banks of the Sabine River. The Governor of Coahuila and Texas wrote the political chief at San Antonio, Ramon Musquiz that he take the necessary measures for the Indians to have an attorney at the hearing on the grant of land. Musquiz replied that because the Indians were poor they would not be able to hire an attorney. Also they would be unable to pay the necessary fees. His solution was to have the Cherokees admitted as colonialists. The Cherokees were subsequently settled on vacant lands to be a barrier against the barbaric tribes. [8]

[1] Wiltse, *Calhoun*, pp. 121ff.

[2] Hale, W.H., 1950, pp. 15-19, Greeley, Horace, *Recollections*, 1868, pp. 83-88.

[3] Tragle, Henry Irving, *The Southampton Slave Revolt of 1831: A Compilation of Source Material*, 1971, *passim*.

[4] Smith, *Forty*, pp. 318-319. Quotes on pp. 318-319.

[5] Simms, H., 1929, p. 40. Quote on p. 40.

[6] Smiley, David L., *Lion of White Hall: The Life of Cassius M. Clay*, Madison: University of Wisconsin Press, 1962, pp. 19-23.

[7] Pierson, *Tocqueville*, pp. 357-368. Quote on pp. 360-361.

[8] Winfrey, *Texas Indian Papers*, pp. 1-6.

Chapter 29

Anti-Masons

At its 1831 national convention, Anti-Masonry partisans made an address of their position. The author or authors of the platform noted that the party's delegates had been selected by groups of enlightened and honest freemen and could not fail to affect the essential rights of the public. Writing of the spectacle of the movement, he noted the importance of qualifications and principles of candidates of Anti-Masonry. They felt that the great use of a government is to secure rights and those who had united to form the government. People must be allowed liberty and the pursuit of happiness through orders to arbitrate internal differences and to protect from foreign aggression. The object of this government was "to bring the public wisdom to the direction of the public will, for the public good."

People must understand their rights, duties, and interests. The leader of such a people must be industrious, intelligent and wise, honest and prudent, independence and vigilant, and disinterested and patriotic. His administration would harmonize order and right to provide justice. In foreign affairs it would maintain "peace, commerce and honest friendship with all nations, entangling alliances with none." Anti-Masons supported economy but would encourage agriculture, commerce, and manufactures, and promote lower education and scientific education. They believed in frequent rotation in office.

The platform next dealt with crime whether in secret or in public, a reference to the murder of William Morgan by Masons. Because of this organization, correct principles were endangered. The party's foe was freemasonry. Honorable men in estimation of the party have joined it and learned to hate freemasonry. Early in its history according to the Anti-Masons it was innocent, laudable, and not secret. From being benefactors, it introduced distinctions and abuses were introduced. In the Masonic order, as then constituted, were developed degrading ceremonies, titles, lodges, badges, secrecy, oaths, penalties, allegiances, degrees, and means of private recognition. It had become dangerous. Concealment of crimes became a duty when a fellow Mason was involved as perpetrator. [1]

There was a riot in Providence, Rhode Island, at this time. Some white sailors attacked some houses inhabited by African Americans, allegedly of some dissolute nature. The African Americans fired upon their attackers, killing one sailor and wounded others. In the ensuing days and nights, crowds of white citizens set forth to obtain their vengeance upon African Americans in the city. They pulled down about 15 houses involved in the matter. Authorities sent in sailors who refused to fire upon the mobs although pelted by staves and other missiles, giving way instead. The riots continued and on the next night soldiers were sent into enforce order. This time, the soldiers fired back. Two rioters were killed and four were wounded. The mob dispersed and law and order was re-established. [2]

A free African American from Savannah wrote the American Colonization Society at this time of his willingness to go to Africa to live. He noted that he had "always viewed the principle on which the Society was grounded, as one of much policy, through I saw it was aided by a great deal of benevolence." He viewed his situation with others of his situation among blacks. The freeman noted that he had "often almost come to the conclusion that I would make the sacrifice, and have only been prevented by the unfavorable accounts of the climate. I have always therefore, viewed it as a matter of temporal interest, but now I view it spiritually."

He could provide the necessary aid as a wheelwright, blacksmith, and carpenter. He had a knowledge of manufacturing to some degree. In addition, he expected that he would help in the promotion of Christianity in dark Africa. Able to pay his way, he needed to be allowed to take more baggage than usually allowed, at his expense of course. This fellow could make a fine contribution to the black colony of Liberia. He and others expected to escape prejudice and bad treatment from the whites with their own homeland in western Africa. [3]

In the autumn of 1831 were held fairs to display American goods. Also there were conventions of various sizes for the discussion of economic policy. The American Institute held its fair in New York City at which 390 exhibitors showed their goods to a large crowd of seven thousand in one day alone. Fair goers saw hemp and wool of high quality, glass displayed by a young lady of Connecticut, and plenty of iron goods and wares. Other goods were of broad cloths, carpeting, and silk. At the finish of the New York display, the great speech giver Edward Everett made his oration.

The Franklin Institute of Philadelphia presented its fair at which many delegates to a free trade convention saw various all-American products. One of these, two splendid pieces of woolen broad cloth made of American wool and priced at $10 a yard were shown. American merchants displayed leather goods made in this country, of high quality, worth more than cotton and protected by a tariff of thirty percent.

Of the various meetings was one that editor Hezekiah Niles of Baltimore attended as one of the delegates from Baltimore. Free trade meetings were small, at most thirty one attendees, while delegates attending protective tariff conferences were attended by as many as three thousand. A multitude of people readily supported the American System despite the departure of protectionists from many of the offices of power including the

American presidency. Chief among the supporters of tariffs was Henry Clay who was soon to lose the presidency one year hence. [4]

A self-effacing power in the Abolitionist movement, a harsh looking but soul shining Theodore Weld was a Puritan of hard work and strong morals, brought up on stern dogmatic theology from childhood. When fourteen, he worked at a farm to earn money for an education at Phillips Academy. He made a speaking tour on memory and attended Hamilton College. Some weeks later, the campus was excited by the sermons of the spellbinder Charles Grandison Finney. Weld would not attend the sermon and claimed that Finney was no true minister of God. He preferred a grave and courteous preacher like his father.

Later, his aunt tricked him into going to a Finney sermon. This did not change his mind and on the following day, he denounced Finney to some loungers at a store in Utica. Finney was brought in but Weld abused him. Overcome with remorse, Weld went to Finney's dwelling and Weld was converted. From denouncement, he went to praise. Next, in an interesting succession, Charles Stuart converted Weld to the cause of anti-slavery. Stuart induced Weld to go to Oneida Institute to become a preacher. An ardent Weld delivered temperance lectures and then went on a tour to raise money for Oneida. He proved a born reformer. In the autumn of 1831, the Tappans recruited Weld to promote schools using manual labor as a part of their program of education. [5]

Meanwhile in Boston, Garrison was hard pressed financially to keep his antislavery newspaper going. By organizing free blacks in Boston and lecturing in Providence, New York, and Philadelphia, the editor brought in some money. However, it was insufficient. Organization was the key and he called for an anti-slavery society in Boston. The Sunday afternoon of November 13, 1831, fifteen men met to hear Garrison to speak on the subject. In a long and earnest speech, he talked about the merits of the British model for a society and the virtues of immediate emancipation. After, he finished, they voted. Nine agreed with Garrison, but six disagreed, fearing the reaction of the Boston upper class to such radicalism.

One month passed. Then another meeting was held and Garrison and a committee drew up a constitution, which was adopted on New Years day of 1832. They formed the New England Anti-Slavery Society with Quaker hatter Arnold Buffum as president. The self-educated Buffum was an amateur inventor, educational reformer, and abolitionist. He proved an able worker for the cause, organizing local societies and speaking for Garrison and abolition throughout southern New England. Oliver Johnson worked alongside Buffum in the town for a moral rebirth in the interests of freedom for the slave. [6]

Jackson was losing some of his popularity by the fall of 1831. To be Jacksonian was not to be favored among many of the people in the nation. In Massachusetts, the Jacksonian candidate for governor finished third in a race of three. Of course the state was Adams territory, but other states which were not, saw Jackson losing support. In Adams' state, for governor, the National Republican Levi Lincoln Jr. won a majority with 22,622 votes, while the Anti-Masonic Lathrop won 10,585 and the Jacksonian

Morton with 9,038 or less than twenty-two percent of the vote. Levi Lincoln Jr. had been governor since 1825 and was gratified to be re-elected. He served in this office until 1834. His father was a prominent man and himself was governor of the state with the aid of friends years before. The father had been an apprenticed blacksmith when friends secured his admission to Harvard.

The president did better in New York State where there was a choice between that state's Jacksonians and Anti-Masons only. There was a small drop in Jacksonian legislators from 95 to 93, with an opposition of 35 members. In Kentucky, Henry Clay won a senatorial seat with a vote of 73 to 65. Jacksonians as represented by the *Washington Globe* had harsh things to say about Clay. They believed that Clay would but consummate his ruin in the national senate. The senator would not represent the people, the editors said. To the west in Missouri, Clay supporters won against the Jacksonians by a decided majority when General Ashley ran and won as an independent for governor. [7]

General Samuel Smith wrote Nicholas Biddle on December 7, 1831, that all the cabinet except Taney were favorable to the Bank. Taney was the strongman for a veto of a Bank bill, because even Jackson was wavering. Two months later, Charles J. Ingersoll wrote Biddle the same thing. They were lying to mislead Biddle. On June 17, 1832, Taney wrote a very long letter to state his case for a veto of a bank recharter bill. Jackson was to agree and used Taney's aid in drawing up the veto message. [8]

Sent to Washington by Biddle, Thomas Cadwalader arrived on December 20, 1831, and sought out officials in order to make a survey for the banker. Biddle wanted to know whether to submit an application for rechartering his Bank of the United States to Congress. Cadwalader wrote him that Jackson would positively reject any bill to this effect. It would be hostile of Biddle to submit the matter this session before the election. The president considered that it would put him on the spot. Jackson, according to McLane, would veto passage even if it meant he would be defeated in 1832. McLane felt that party considerations would influence many pro-Bank congressmen to vote against recharter. For instance Senator Mangum of North Carolina, friend of the Bank, would vote with the Democratic Party. McLane told Cadwalalder that "if you apply now, you assuredly will fail--if you wait, you will as certainly succeed."

McDuffie disagreed, Cadwalader reported, and thought application should be made now. Biddle had the highest confidence in McDuffie's opinion and decided eventually in favor of immediate application largely upon McDuffie's estimate of the situation. The chief reason, however, was a matter of time. Biddle thought that it was time now, to wait would put them closer to the deadline of March 1836. He felt it would be too close. He could not stand the uncertainty. Writing that it would unsettle the markets and lead to doubt in the economy, he did not want the unsettling effect on economic events. There should be no anxiety about the whole mony system. He wanted to avoid any sudden and dangerous shocks. As time was to prove, he could not prevent them. The sooner the country knew the fate of the Bank the better. He could not wait. Biddle soon afterwards submitted his application to Congress. The measure passed both houses, but Jackson vetoed it. Congress could not muster enough votes to override the veto. The Bank was doomed after March of 1836. Biddle got his decision. As long as there was a Jackson in the White House the bank could not exist. [9]

In his veto message of the Bank charter, Jackson labeled the Bank of the United States, a monopoly. It was an erroneous appellation since the Bank was not a monopoly however dominant it was in exchange actions. Jackson stated that the Bank was one, but there were other banks. The federal government actually chartered some banks in Washington, DC and there were many state chartered banks in the country. What Jackson was doing was to promote the interests of the state-chartered banks and fight the powerful economic interests of the eastern region, destroying Biddle and his associates. It was a vindictive war.

Jackson was hostile to all banks, stating in his message that their interests were opposed to that of the people. The president was highly unsophisticated and did not see clearly the economic benefits to the economy of the banks. He did not want to see them. Jackson was very set in his ways, always espousing the views of those supporters he favored for personal and political reasons. Clearly he was not able to get along without banks for the governmental work and the people would not have long stood for the demolishing of all banks. He was to have to turn to the state banks after harming the big bank of the nation.

Raising the specter of sectionalism, the president stated that the debt of westerners to the Bank of the United States "is principally a debt to the eastern and foreign stockholders; that the interest they pay upon it is carried into the eastern states and into Europe, and that it is burden upon their industry and a drain of their currency, which no country can bear without inconvenience and occasional distress." In his discussion of the veto message, Peter denied that this was true. The Bank was a benefit to the west since it was a means for westerners to obtain loans vital for their economy. Jackson was not interested in this. He simply did not believe in the processes of capital and debt. He had been burned and lashed out at the system the rest of his life. Now he was able to destroy the best bank in the nation. Hate blinds people and Jackson was blind. [10]

Democrats in the urban areas in and around Philadelphia wanted the Bank of the United States to be eventually rechartered, but they wanted the issue delayed so that they would not have to choose between the Bank and Jackson. The rural areas nearby were stolidly behind Jackson and would follow his wishes in any matter. When Jackson did veto the recharter, they largely supported Jackson. Local Democrats expressed themselves in Benjamin Mifflin's *Pennsylvanian*, supporting Jackson and the veto. Minority Democrats in Philadelphia left. Their newspapers raged against the veto and stressed the benefits of the Bank to the national currency, economy, and Philadelphia business and labor groups.

On July 16, 1832, a mass rally was held in Independence Square, Philadelphia, where former Jacksonians and others denounced Jackson's veto to a large crowd. Loyal Jacksonians held an even bigger rally there a week later. They had bands for marching Democrats. Congressmen Henry Horn explained away his early vote for recharter as a response for his constituents and aligned himself now with Jackson in agreement with his conscience. He said this, but it might have been that he now wanted to be on the winning side. Senator Dallas praised Jackson and his first term without mentioning the bank issue. Charles J. Ingersoll who had worked for a compromise recharter bill five months earlier, now spoke for General Jackson without speaking against the Bank. The resolutions of the pro-Jackson rally praised their leader for his defense of the people against what they called odious and dangerous monopolies.

There was a continued controversy between pro-Jackson Democrats and Philadelphia supporters of the Bank. In the next elections the Jacksonian Democrats received a reduced number of votes and Democrat Governor George Wolf came close to losing because of the vote in Philadelphia which went to Joseph Ritner. The Democrats had a hard time in local elections with the anti-Jacksonians being ahead in most contests. The only congressman from Pennsylvania to vote against the Bank was roundly defeated. Later, Jackson won Pennsylvania in the presidential elections by a reduced majority, receiving 57.6% of the state vote compared to 66.6% four years earlier and 45.7% of the city-county vote versus 66.5% in 1828. [11]

The National Republicans, soon to become the Whigs, held their convention in Baltimore in early December of 1831 planning for the next election year, 1832. Bad weather delayed the arrival of many delegates. There were 155 delegates there. Delegates from Tennessee could not arrive in time, but there were enough present for a convention to nominate their presidential candidate. All were in favor of Clay and they voted for him unanimously.

A delegation was prepared to notify Clay of his nomination. There was one from each state. This committee named a sub-committee of seven to do the actual announcing to Clay who was in Washington DC attending Congress. Clay handled them a letter dated December 13, 1831, and they returned with it without delay. The nominee was grateful. He showed humility in his letter: "although I should have been glad if the convention had designated some citizen of the United States more competent than myself to be the instrument of accomplishing the patriotic objects which they have in view, I do not feel at liberty to decline their nomination." He then accepted their nomination.

Delegates then unanimously selected John Sergeant for nomination as vice-president nominee. John had been born on December 5, 1779, and had become a most able lawyer in Philadelphia. Having served as a legislator, he was elected to the House in Congress. There he supported the American system of Clay and others. This made him a supporter of Clay, which led to Sergeant's nomination for vice-president. His service in Congress ran from 1815 to 1823, from 1827 to 1829, and afterwards from 1837 to 1841. [12]

A sailor named Ambrose Fulton was in Benton, Mississippi, during the year 1831. Entering the town, he "learned that the renowned and natural orator, Colonel Davy Crockett, a Whig and a member of Congress from Tennessee, was to address the people. The hour arrived; an old cart was run into the arena to be used as a rostrum." Crockett stood up and began a speech, a Cicero could not surpass Fulton felt in eloquence and technical precision. Crockett spoke of the greats, but "said that worth and greatness were also embodied in the man that cleared the thicket, drained the marsh, built ships, erected mansions and factories to give employment and bread to his fellowmen.

Crockett then attacked Jackson, of whom he said he lacked executive ability. Jackson "has spread desolation and distress throughout a once prosperous and happy land, where perfect felicity had long dwelt, and that he had wrecked the ship of state, leaving a small salvage for the people." The Whig orator then blasted the Jackson cabinet. The orator was convincing and commanding, and it was to Fulton's regret to see him end his address. Fulton ended his own account with the words that he "admired his flow of soul and flight of mind, although I had very soon to come down to the hard-pan of fate's reality." [13]

[1]Schlesinger, *History*, I, 523-532. Quote on pp. 524, 527.

[2]*Niles Weekly Register*, October 1, 1831, p. 74.

[3]Woodson, Carter, Mind, *pp. 4-8.*

[4]*Niles Weekly Register*, October 22, 1831, pp. 145, 147.

[5]Thomas, Benjamin P., *Theodore Weld: Crusader for Freedom*, New Brunswick: Rutgers College, 1950, Rep. New York: Octagon Books, 1973, pp. 3-26, 31.

[6]Thomas, J.L., *Liberator*, pp. 139-142. See Anonymous, *Right and Wrong in Massachusetts*, Boston: Dow & Jackson Anti-Slavery Press, 1839, Rep. New York: Negro Universities Press, 1969, *passim*.

[7]*Niles Weekly Register*, November 26, 1831, pp. 237-238; *Encyclopedia Americana*, 1975, XVII, 507, XVIII, 401.

[8]Steiner, *Taney*, p. 107.

[9]Biddle, pp. 146-154, 161-165. Quote on p. 150.

[10]Temin, Peter, *The Jacksonian Economy*, New York: W.W. Norton, 1969, pp. 28-37; Wiltse, *Calhoun, passim*.

[11]Ambacher, Bruce I., "Urban Response to Jacksonian Democracy: Philadelphia Democrats and Bank War, 1832-1834," *Essays on Urban America*, Austin: University of Texas Press, 1975, pp. 57-62.

[12]*Niles Weekly Register*, December 17, 1831, pp. 281-282; *Dictionary of American Biography*, VIII (2), 588-589.

[13]Fulton, Ambrose Cowperthwaite, *A Life's Voyage: A Diary of a Sailor on Sea and Land, Jotted Down during a Seventy-Years' Voyage*, New York: Author, 1898, pp. 7-8. Quotes on pp. 7, 8.

Chapter 30

MARCH OUT OF MEMPHIS

A contingent of Mushulatubbe followers, numbering 406 men, women and children marched out to Memphis. There they found the roads so mud deep that they could not be traveled. So government agent for this removal John T. Fulton secured a steamboat and embarked the contingent down the Mississippi River to the White River and then up to Arkansas Post, where the Indians got off. They had to wait there for about six weeks until the river rose enough to be able to navigate to Fort Smith. Finally, they steamed up the river until stopped by low water for a time. They had to endure during their stay a very cold winter weather. When they reached Fort Smith, they had some farm implements and plows for farming.

At the same time, another party of 594 Indians made their way to Arkansas Post, arriving before the other party. They were bumped on steamboat by one hundred troops headed for Fort Gibson. However, they soon joined other groups and made their way for their new lands. All these Indians engulfed the preparations made for them. Most of them were not clad for the cold winter and had little shelter. Captain Jacob Brown observed them and wrote of their suffering. Colonel Gaines also wrote of their problems. In addition, they had difficulty in driving the cattle, many of which were on the wild side. Another observer noted that the Indians who had just received their annuity were in a confusion and uproar since there was much swearing and drinking. The Indians were in a hurry to spend their money with little concern for the future, which had seemed so bleak in the winter weather. The whites quarreled over who would have the opportunity to cheat the Indians.

George W. Hawkins wrote that "we sent our horses and oxen by land, and about 250 head of horses have died on the road. We have had very bad weather. Since we landed at this place about twenty of Nail's party had died, and still they were continuing to die." Because they had so many sick people in their party, their way was slow.

There were smaller parties, which made their way by land, not trusting the steamboat. Because of the weather, these often suffered great hardships. Some had to make their way through swamps having no guides and almost lost the will to live. Then they were rescued. Finally, they got food after six days of hunger and death among the group members. Compassionate local people helped the Indians, totally unlike those traders who had cheated them. The Indians subsisted and made their way slowly through more vicissitudes. The weather was unusually cold and they had to resort to eating pumpkins raw. There was not enough money to go around for the caring for the emigrants. Things were made worst when whites charged exorbitant prices for their produce and supplies. [1]

One of the strongest advocates of internal improvements in the west was Indiana senator William Hendricks, chairman of the Standing Committee on Roads and Canals. He promoted internal development in general and for his state in particular. Hendricks had been a representative from 1816 to 1822 and a senator from 1825. For a period of eight years, he was on the Committee on Militia, for two years he was on the Committee on Manufactures, and for two years he was on the Committee on Private Land Claims. Never missing a session, he was almost always present on roll calls and usually voted with the majority. No maverick, he fitted into the system and served the state of Indiana well. He knew what the people wanted and what they needed in his state. Of course, he was at times unable to get what he wanted passed.

Hendricks did not tie his star to any politician or president. It was unusual when he supported Van Buren in 1836; he was not used to favoring any party candidate. During all of his years in Congress, no matter who was in power, he was consistent. His policy was for internal developments such as roads and canals in the west, all paid for by the government. He wanted to see the Indians removed from their lands so whites could have their land and there would be no friction. A liberal land policy and a stable monetary system were keys to his program. Unlike many westerners, he wanted a strong national bank and a protective tariff. He supported a strong central government and the end of slavery expansion in the southwest. Land laws should be changed, according to Hendricks, to allow for cheaper more accessible land, with cessation of unsold lands to the states. [2]

The Massachusetts legislature took measures to implement some reform in debt imprisonment by prohibiting the imprisonment of men for debts under ten dollars. Five dollars had been the previous limit. Debtors imprisonment continued in Massachusetts for over a quarter of a century. In neighboring New Hampshire in the same year, the government had abolished the imprisonment of women for debts and enlarged jail-yard limits to county boundaries. The debtor had one year in which to repay or take an oath as being in poverty. In 1833, a defaulter could be released on bond the very day of his arrest. In 1840, the government abolished imprisonment for debt on future loans and contracts.

There was a need for debtors' reform in the states. A few years earlier in Rhode Island, a creditor had kept Freeborn Hazard, who was old and had been a laborer, in prison four months after he had taken the poor debtor's oath which should have allowed him his release. Next year in 1828, he was put in prison again because of a debt of one dollar and costs of $3.22. Two years later, a Providence widow was jailed because she owed sixty-eight cents to a man whose property the widow's dead husband had been trying to save when he was killed. In 1834, thir0teen debtors were confined to a small Providence cell. Affairs in Rhode Island were particularly harsh, and the general course of events was not so bad in most cases and in most states. [3]

There had long been an interest in bringing silk culture to the United States since there were great prospects for profit, but some congressmen were uncertain about its value in early 1831. They asked J.D 'Homergues for information and he replied with the statement of what could be done. He gave the basic economical and planting information and noted that in 1829, France and England had imported raw silk, paying $340 million for the product. There was a great market for silk.

Already established was sugar cane cultivation and Congress was greatly interested in the promotion and development of this agricultural resource. The House requested a manual of sugar cane production a year earlier and received the report in full from Secretary Ingham. It was reported that there were five kinds of sugar cane cultivated in Louisiana of varying utility. The most exhaustive was Creole cane. Land on which it was grown was worn out within a few years, but since the sugar derived from Creole land had more strength and body, it was preferred for exportation. The report of the Agricultural Society of Baton Rouge stressed the difficulties of the planter. In the first place, production per acre was a fifth of the West Indies. Soil conditions varied with bad results and frost often injured the crop with a decline in price. It then gave a litany of planters problems from bad weather to the high cost of slaves. One was the cost of ten percent from banks. In addition, the planters were spendthrifts and would always be in debt.

Chief among the fears of the planters was that the three-percent protectionist duty on foreign sugar would be abolished and cheap foreign sugar would ruin the Louisiana planters. Sugar cane production, they averred was the product best suited for Louisiana soil. Havana merchants would gain a monopoly of the American market. The disadvantage which Louisiana faced in competition with the Caribbean countries would make it hard to make a profit in Louisiana during bad years. A return on capital of ten percent would be reduced to three percent. The planter's time and labor would be wasted. [4]

Robert E. Lee watched the progress of the black rebellion and the resulting state convention with interest from Fort Monroe. The emancipationists were a strong minority and it was their solution that Lee favored. They wished to transport the African American slaves back to Africa to settle. The future general hoped that a bill would pass the Virginia legislature provided that this would take place. He and the others wanted to purge the nation of its black population. The planters would not part with their slaves and were glad to see the emancipationist associated in the public mind with the abolitionists and the latter's incitement of slave rebellion. At this time, Lee blamed the abolitionists for emanicipationistic decline in Virginia and opposed the two extremes of pro-slavery and abolitionism. [5]

Southerners had experienced two severe jolts in 1831. In January, Garrison had published his anti-slavery newspaper and in August, Nat Turner had made a bloody uprising. Southerners felt threatened and were exceedingly fearsome. They were to some criticism before but that was a matter of gradual emancipation in some vague future. It was not imminent. How the idea of Garrison was for immediate emancipation and it was strident in tone and degree. When the Turner episode broke forth, it was felt that Garrison was somehow responsible and that such talk against slavery would lead to more violence. They envisioned massive uprisings in the near future and a danger to their persons as well as their system.

However much as some felt that slavery was an evil for whites--the evil for African Americans did not matter--they knew that they had to rely upon slavery as a basis for easy living and all the pleasures and needs of the planters and thus of society as a whole. It was a strong reaction and one Southerners were not to forget until slavery itself ended and the threat became different and more subdued. They had suffered recent economic hardships and they were not eager for more of that. They felt themselves a minority that needed protection from the Northerners. There was a clash of systems. It became necessary to close the ranks.

And then the myths arose. Someone came up with the idea that their forebears were the aristocracy of England, directly descended from the Norman aristocracy of that mother country and had always been aristocrats since 1066. They felt that they had the natural views of the upper class landed people. They believed themselves the last survivors of a pure and noble past, not being versed in the actual history of England and ignorant of their founding in the early seventeenth century. This pure society, as they envisioned it, was not threatened by a rising tide of a materialism that came from the North, seeing themselves as consumers of those very same goods that they depreciated. They were subject to abolitionism and other evils of the North such as the idea of the right of the people to rule and not of the aristocracy to rule. [6]

---

[1]Foreman, *Indian Removal*, pp. 49-70. Quote on p. 59.

[2]Hill, Frederick D., "William Hendricks' Political Circulars to his Constituents: Second Senatorial Term, 1831-1837," *Indiana Magazine of History*, LXXI (December 1975), 319-329.

[3]Coleman, P.J., *Debtors*, 1974, *passim*.

[4]*The New American State Papers, Agriculture*, Wilmington, Del: Scholarly Resources, 1972, I, 271.

[5]Dowdey, C. *Lee*, 1965, pp. 56-58.

[6]McMurry, Richard M., *John Bell Hood and the War for Southern Independence*, Lexington Ky: University Press of Kentucky, 1982, pp. 3-5.

Chapter 31

STEWART

African American domestic Maria Stewart felt that she had received the call of God to promote the cause of abolition and equal rights for her people. Although poorly educated, Maria began to write and lecture for the good of the cause. She became the first American-born woman to lecture before a mixed man-woman audience. There was not an example before her of any race or creed. Stewart had been born in 1803 in Hartford, Connecticut of free parents. Orphaned at age five, she was sent to work as a maid for a minister's family. She started young indeed with light tasks but soon was to keep house, cook and serve meals.

Somewhere, perhaps from her employers, she got the idea of self-help and desired to improve her position in life. She picked up the rudiments of education. In a brief period on the Boston lecture circuit, she spoke about colonization, abolition, and rights for free blacks, racial unity, and the necessities of education and opportunity for her race. Steward taught racial pride and determination. After lecturing, she taught in schools and established two schools for African American children who were from free families in the national capital. She was foremost a leader in the future of the African American people. Before her tour speaking, forty male African American delegates had met in a convention to talk of the problems of the people of their origin, and in the same year that the newspaper *The Liberator* was born. [1]

Meanwhile, the legislators of Ohio established a series of laws called the "Black Code,". which limited the freedoms of free African Americans and made it almost impossible for them to come into the state. The African Americans there did not have any basic rights that the whites took for granted. They could be denied an education if there were too few for a separate school and their educational funds were kept separate so that the whites would not have to share their tax money with African American education. Because they were poorer, their taxes and hence, the money spent on education for their children were less. They could not belong to the militia or serve on juries. They could not bear witness against any white. They had to have certificates of freedom with them to work.

It was clear that the whites of Ohio did not want the African Americans to be among themselves. The African Americans were the despised race; they had hard living condition and were poor. They were wretched and treated with contempt and loathing. The Ohio whites treated them like they were sub-human. This prejudice closed off opportunity for the free African Americans. There would have been nothing much they could do to be accepted in Ohio. Judges and other whites considered the anti-black laws to be justifiable and commendable.

A committee reported that Ohio "must exclude a people whose residence among us is degrading to themselves, and fraught with so much evil to the community. The Negroes form a distinct and degraded caste and are forever excluded by the fiat of society and the laws of the land from all hopes of equality in social intercourse and political privileges." What they did hold against this minority? First, the African Americans lived in the cities. Second, the whites did not want black-type employment or to work along beside them. Third, association with the despised ones was degrading to whites. Fourth, it was claimed that they stole and lied. Fifthly, these degraded people had a bad effect upon the lives of the youth of Ohio. [2]

African Americans began visiting England for education and to raise funds for black benevolence and abolition. Black James McCune Smith was denied admission to an American university and soon headed for Britain. Once there, in 1831, Smith attended the University of Glasgow, where he was successful as a student. He soon came to praise the British system where families were safe. When he returned to New York City and discrimination; he praised the British even more to the discomfort of Americans. He devoted the rest of his life to the fight against slavery and discrimination. However, everything was not perfect and there were beggars in the streets of the British cities, a situation which did not exist in America.

There were soon others in Britain. Soon after the arrival of Smith, African American minister Nathaniel Paul reached the Isles to raise funds for the settlement of freedmen in Canada. He stayed to fight colonization in Liberia. Paul enjoyed being treated like a white and observed that some of his happiest days were spent in Ireland. He was a Baptist. The tall giant Moses Roper came to escape a return to slavery and stayed to lecture against slavery. He told of the beatings that he had received. Roper did not complete his education and go forth as a missionary as planned. These were the first three known men who became leaders in America and Britain. [3]

During the year of 1831, a journalist just starting out made a professional trip to a slave state. What he saw there made him a greater adherent to anti-slavery than he had been before. His views on the issue of slavery were mild. Gameliel Bailey Jr., was a man of great curiosity and fervent religious views. His ideas of building blocks for America and its civilization included westward expansion, the steam engine, white manhood suffrage, religious revivalism, and social reform. He was patriotic and ambitious for himself and his country. People found this young man pleasant and conventional.

His father's forebears were mariners and his mother's ancestors were physicians. Gamaliel Bailey, Sr., was a Methodist Episcopal, a revivalist convert from Calvinism. He became a preacher for spreading the Word on the road. Marrying Sarah Page, he and she had six children. Her sixth was named Gamaliel Jr. He was born on December 3, 1807. When he was not preaching, senior was a silversmith. The parents included the son in adult conversation so he learned a lot before his formal education began. Sarah had him learn to read at an early year but there were visits to Sarah's brother's home on the coast for recreation. Dr. Thomas Page introduced him to swimming and playing in the surf and to sailing. In 1816, they moved to Philadelphia. Gameliel preferred the small towns and was never to care for urban areas of any size. But, he did receive an excellent education and read the books of the Library Company of Philadelphia. Later, he and several men formed a literary society.

There were other children, numbers of whom died, so the young boy was introduced to mortality. He decided to become a doctor and received the usual limited education available, where he learned commonsense medicine. Afterwards, Bailey took a sea voyage to China. It turned out to be a bore, except of the stop in China, where he had to attend to his shipmates caught by the cholera epidemic there. Since he did not want to practice medicine, he jumped at the chance to become the editor of the *Methodist Protestant*, a periodical for his father's church, an offshoot which did not have bishops. It was a religious paper, so he stuck to those topics, but he was able to include articles on history written by himself. In the paper, he was for temperance, goodness, revivals, conventional religion, Christian unity, liberty, and benevolence, the spreading of the Gospel, education, anti-slavery, and religious betterment in general. [4]

Thomas Carmichael Hindman, Sr., was a businessman in Tennessee who gained contact with the Cherokees of the area for trading and friendship. He was licensed to trade with the Indians along the state boundary lines of Tennessee. His business transactions brought him into contact with Lewis Ross, who was the brother of John Ross, elected chief in 1828. He made frequent business trips to Alabama and while there bought town lots in Jacksonville, a new settlement in what had been Cherokee lands. he next moved his family down to Jacksonville. He and his children enjoyed the trip. They liked the river route and enjoyed the nights out in the open over the days. They went down the Tennessee River by flatboat and then overland by wagon. With them were supplies of food and goods to sell in their new hometown. He was prosperous and indulged his family, until his wife had to upbraid him for his extravagances. He told her that he had the money and wished his family to live well.

He was known for his honest dealings with the Cherokee unlike so many others. He was popular with the Indians which lead the Rosses to petition President Andrew Jackson to make him the agent for the Cherokees. He had already been appointed sub-agent by James Monroe years before. Hindman testified against those who would defraud widows ands harm individuals. The Cherokees appreciated this. When the Cherokees moved west on the trail of tears, he was the quartermaster and inspector and finder of campsites which made the trip one of less pain than it would have been. He later spoke for the Cherokee in Washington and although a claimed friend of the Cherokee, he acted for the whites in many matters. In 1841, he tried to persuade the mountainous tribe of North Carolina Cherokees to emigrate west, but they refused and are still in the mountains of North Carolina on the border with Tennessee. [5]

Missionary priests had early taught the Iroquois Indians of Canada and when some of these lived among the Flatheads in the west, they told them of the Jesuit black robes and the book called the "White Man's Book of God." The Flatheads wanted the teaching of these black robes and set out for St. Louis to obtain this from the white man's city. St. Louis was picked because they knew William Clark, Indian Commissioner for the western lands. In 1831, they sent four warriors down the trail to seek Clark and ask him for the black robes. They were careful on their trail to avoid hostile Sioux and Blackfeet.

When they arrived at St. Louis, the Indian envoys were treated with respect, feasted, and entertained. They spoke with William Clark, but he could not grant their wish. There were no Jesuit friars in St. Louis. While they were in the white man's city, two of the Indians died and were buried. Two set out for home; one dying along the way. Only one of the four reached home with the negative news.

The Indian search received wide publicity in the United States, especially when the story appeared in the widely read New York *Christian Advocate*. Several missionaries were encouraged to travel to the western plains and mountains when they read the story. Two of them were Jason and Daniel Lee. The uncle and nephew were young Methodist Episcopal ministers and were called upon to set out for the Flathead mission. They were accompanied by three lay assistants and reached Oregon where they set up a town. The Flatheads, expecting black robe teachers, rejected the Lee mission and uncle and nephew began to talk and preach to other Indian tribes.

The Flathead were persistent. Three more times, they sent their young men to St. Louis. Twice they met no favorable response, but the third time as they were passing by a point in Iowa (near present day Council Bluffs) they met Father Pierre De Smet, who was preaching to the Pottawattomie Indians and he agreed to make a trip to their settlements the next year. With the passing of the snows the next year Father De Smet prepared himself and was able to join a fur brigade headed westward in that year of 1840. The journey was a long one to the rendezvous on the Green River, but long strides got the party there. It was at this point that De Smet left the party and journeyed to Pierre's Hole where the Flatheads met him. Escorted into the Gallatin Valley, he began preaching and introduced them to the mass.

Before winter set in, Father De Smet left the village to go back to St. Louis where, as he had promised, and gathered up two priests and a blacksmith, a carpenter, and a tinner to assist in the mission. Another laymen joined the party and in the spring of 1841, they made the journey back to the Flatheads building the church in Montana. [6]

When Lincoln arrived in New Salem, he made an unkempt appearance and seemed a rough frontier type, a country bumpkin. He drifted in as a flatboat man and hog driver. But when he talked, they found him to be "strikingly articulate, exhibiting book learning and political acuity, and animated by a lively intelligence." Lincoln had been an ardent reader before and after coming to New Salem. He also had an excellent memory. Still his learning was limited. Because he spent so much time reading, he was called lazy. He did however prefer reading to physical work. He was a good worker and lived up to his duty. He read all of the newspapers he could get, including the *Congressional Globe*. He also studied grammar. Joining the literary clubs available, he presented his contributions and was a good storyteller. Poetry particularly suited him, especially Robert Burns, the Scottish poet. He could quote long passages of Shakespeare while fishing with Jack Kelso. Soon he was reading law books and was able to try his first case in simple frontier justice.

Young Abraham was no sooner settled in Illinois than he was faced with a challenge. Wrestling matches were common place on the frontier and Lincoln was especially adapt at this form of athletics and manhood of the time. It was also common that a newcomer was tested by men of his own age when he arrived in the community. He won his matches and was noted when he got in a bout with Jack Armstrong as we have seen. Here was a man, they thought, and Lincoln was accepted and began to get a good name for himself in the community, which led to his later success there, along with his work in self-education. He was to become a leader in the settlements and well thought of by all classes. [7]

[1]Stevenson, Brenda E., "Abolition Movement," *Black Women in America: An Historical Encyclopedia*, ed. Hine, Darlene Clark etal, 2 vols., Bloomington: Indiana University Press, 1993, I, 3.

[2]Quillin, Frank U., *The Color Line in Ohio*, Ann Arbor: George Wahr, 1913, pp. 23-30. Quote on p. 30.

[3]Blackett, R.J.M., *Building an Antislavery Wall: Black Americans in the Atlantic Abolitionist Movement, 1830-1860*, Baton Rouge: Louisiana State University Press, 1983, pp. 4, 8, 15-18, 23, 28, 40, 45-46, 157, 196-198, 204-207.

[4]Harrold, Stanley, *Gamaliel Bailey and Antislavery Union*, Kent, Ohio: Kent State University Press, 1986, pp. 1-11.

[5]Neal, Diane and Kremm, Thomas W., *Lions of the South; General Thomas C. Hindman*, Macon, Ga: Mercer University Press, 1993, pp. 2-3.

[6]Abbott, *Montana*.

[7]Wilson, Douglas L., *Honor's Voice: The Transformation of Abraham Lincoln*, New York: Alfred A. Knopf, 1998, pp. 19-85, 100-104. Quote on p. 35.

Chapter 32

TEXAS IN 1831

It cost twenty dollars to travel by sailing vessel from New Orleans to Brazoria on the Brazos, a Texas river flowing from the upper plains to the Gulf of Mexico. The weather was good and the passengers were mostly emigrants bound for the colony with all good hope of a better life and greater opportunities. One of the passengers was a young Brazorian merchant. The cargo consisted of flour, provisions and clothes mostly belonging to him. Except for the merchant, the passengers knew nothing of Texas except for the good reports of the land they had heard from friends. They were Southerners; one had two slaves with him.

The slave owner had heard that slavery was illegal in Mexico, to which Texas belonged, but he was sure he could evade the law. Indeed, there were many settlers with slaves in Texas and authorities in the possession of their human property did not trouble them. By having them sign ninety nine-year indentures, he hoped to prevent confiscation and advised another man with several slaves to do the same, giving them minute instructions in the matter. Captain Sears told passengers that he had once sailed with the notorious pirate Gibbs, who was then under arrest in New York City.

When they arrived past Galveston Island, they saw a coastal plain. Navigation up the river was difficult because of the shallow soundings. Many were impassable except for a short distance. There were few inhabitants in 1831. Mexican laws forbade Americans from living within twenty leagues of the coast if they exceeded the Mexicans there by fifty percent. At the mouth of the Brazos, there was an inn run by Captain Cotton and Mexican soldiers were there to enforce tariff duties. The Brazos was crooked and on both sides of the river were two cotton plantations. Vegetables thrive and cattle were left to room on richly grassed prairies of Texas. There were other rivers in Texas all flowing in well-drained country, to the Gulf. Along the coast, there was little timber, but inland woods could be found. [1]

William Austin, son of organizer Moses Austin had a house at Brazoria in which visitor could stay, constructed of logs with a breezeway between the two parts. The breezeway was covered by a roof and served as a porch. There was no glass in the windows in the house, which served as a hotel, small as it was. It could house thirty boarders in a crowded condition common to hotels in frontier areas of North America. The village, inhabited by settlers, had several shops. Mrs. William Austin came from New York and the wife of a nearby plantation owner had been educated in the North.

An unnamed traveler noticed a great difference in the land's vast extent. A plantation might cover a large tract and since the cattle ran wild, there was no need for any labor. Planter McNeil had a man for the sole purpose of killing game for them to eat. There was a lumber mill at Harrisburg, inland from Galveston Island and twenty houses, mostly built of logs. There were vessels there to buy the lumber for export. At nearby San Jacinto River, a Mr. Lynch lived on Buffalo Bayou in low and marshy terrain. He had a store and inn and was working on a salt works. David Burnet from New Jersey was making plans to establish a steam sawmill there to take advantage of forests he found there. There were pine, oak, and cedar.

Anahuac near the coast had been founded as a military post by Mexican General Teran's order. His second in command, Colonel Bradburn had supervised its construction with one hundred or so soldiers. Previously it had was named Perry's Point by the Americans. It was at the northeastern corner of Galveston Bay with a steep bank. The seven mouths of the Trinity River were nearby. In 1831, there were fifteen or twenty houses and seven shops and a military barracks. The soil was poor but Indian corn could be easy grown and was planted. Except for the soldiers most of the people there were American immigrants. Sugar cane was grown in the area, planted every three years. There were birds of all kinds including turkeys and numerous deer. There were other wild animals but few wild cats and panthers. Wild boars were aggressive, attacking even when unprovoked. There were many kinds of fish and alligators. Not far away Colonel Edwards had a fine plantation. [2]

In 1831, Jefferson Davis supervised a sawmill on the Yellow River near Fort Winnebago. When the weather became inclement, he was caught out in it and developed a serious case of pneumonia. It was a severe case and only the nursing of James Pemberton, his slave, brought the young officer through. Still he lost a lot of weight and was weak. James could pick him up in his arms like Davis was a child. There were complications and Davis had a long recovery. He got well enough to serve in the Black Hawk War. In another severe illness after the war, he suffered from a chronic affliction of the lungs at Camp Jackson in 1833. [3]

Also in that year, Daniel Appleton and his son William Appleton founded a publishing company. Daniel was born on December 10, 1785, in Haverhill, Massachusetts, and William Henry was born there on January 27, 1814. William's mother was Hannah Adams Appleton and she bore eight children. After a time, Daniel moved his general store to Boston. In addition to his usual merchandise, he included English goods and books. In 1826, they moved to New York City and Daniel encouraged his son William to build up the book department so it was natural for them to go into publishing. Many of the early books were religious. In 1835, Daniel sent William to

London and D. Appleton & Company became one of the leading publishers in America from that book center in New York City. [4]

Hetty Jefferson was the daughter of actor Joseph Jefferson. The famous nineteenth century thespian did not educated his daughter to go on the stage, but gave her the liberal education of the day. He sent her to one of the best boarding schools in Philadelphia. Hetty met and married a young bookseller in Pottsville, Pennsylvania, in 1829. His name was Alexander Mackenzie. Joseph Jefferson wanted the welfare of the pair and persuaded Mackenzie to join him in the lease of theaters in Lancaster, Harrisburg, and Washington DC. When this was done, it came about that Hetty Mackenzie took a role in the "Mountaineers." She was a success. She specialized in old women. With make-up, she did quite well in Washington and Baltimore.

Hetty played a number of characters including Mrs. Malaprop, Lady Priory, and Lady Brumbach. Cooperative and a student of acting, she applied herself and became popular as an actress. In 1837, she was to play Helen in the "Hunchback" in Chicago, a then young town. It was the first theatrical performance the town had had. By this time, her husband was a theatrical manager. She played in the South and then had to give up the theater on account of bad health in 1844. She was soon to die of cancer. Virtuous, amiable, and graceful in mind, Hetty won many friends. [5]

---

[1]*Visit To Texas: Being the Journal of a Traveler through Those Parts Most Interesting to American Settlers, with Descriptions of Scenery, Habits, etc.*, New York: Goodrich & Wiley, 1932, pp. 1-29.

[2]*Ibid.*, pp. 30-51, 77-78, 90-93, 112.

[3]Riley, Harris D., Jr., "Jefferson Davis and His Health, Part I: June, 1808," *The Journal of Mississippi History*, XLIX No. 3 (August 1987), 184-185.

[4]"Appleton, Daniel" and "Appleton, William Henry," *Encyclopedia Americana*, II, 89, 90.

[5]Brown, *History*, p. 228.